Social Democracy in Transition

Northern, Southern and Eastern Europe

Edited by

LAURI KARVONEN

and

JAN SUNDBERG

Dartmouth

Aldershot · Brookfield USA · Hong Kong · Singapore · Sydney

Published by
Dartmouth Publishing Company Limited
Gower House
Croft Road
Aldershot
Hants GU11 3HR
England

Dartmouth Publishing Company
Old Post Road
Brookfield
Vermont 05036
USA

Dartmouth Publishing Company Limited
Distributed in the United States by
Ashgate Publishing Company
Old Post Road
Brookfield
Vermont 05036
U.S.A.

Reprinted 1996

11211636

A CIP catalogue record for this book is available from the British Library and the US Library of Congress.

ISBN 1 85521 111 4

Printed and bound in Great Britain by Biddles Limited, Guildford and King's Lynn

Contents

PART II: CURRENT PREDICAMENTS

PART III: BEYOND SCANDINAVIA

Preface

This book stems from a Nordic research project which was originally suggested by Ulf Lindström. Its initial phase was financed through a grant from the Nordic Cultural Fund; it enabled us to meet in Visby in 1988 for a necessary planning session. A meeting in Helsinki a year later represented the critical take-off stage of the project; without the financial support of the Joint Nordic Committee of the Nordic Social Science Research Councils (NOS-S), this meeting would not have been possible. A workshop on comparative social democracy in connection with the IX Nordic Political Science Convention in Reykjavik in August 1990 provided a valuable forum for the final review of the manuscripts. Special thanks are due to the Norwegian Research Centre in Organization and Management (LOS) in Bergen for the generous support we received in connection with the final editorial work. This institution furnished us with secretarial assistance and we address our thanks to Maila Solheim for her valuabale contribution in the last phase of the book project while Jan Sundberg had the opportunity to be part of the inspiring LOS milieu as a visiting scholar. Moreover, LOS financed the linguistic correction of the manuscript.

While these institutions and individuals decisively helped our work to reach a satisfactory state of completion, they bear no responsibility for the views presented in the book or any errors that may remain.

Åbo and Bergen, February 1991

Lauri Karvonen & Jan Sundberg

Introduction:
Social Democracy Old and New

Lauri Karvonen & Jan Sundberg

The aim and scope of the book

This book looks at European social democracy in relation to three geographically and temporally distinct waves of political mobilization: the process which led to the strong position of social democracy in Scandinavia, the rise to prominence of democratic socialism in southern Europe from the mid-1970s on, and what today seems to be a flat rejection of social democracy in central Europe after the revolution of 1989. It seeks to understand whether these differences simply reflect the epochal nature of history; some periods witness the ascendance of certain political movements, while others entail a rejection of those same forces. Or do they, rather, represent political opportunities seized or wasted? In this view a party has the success it deserves; political *savoir-faire*, rather than inexorable historical and structural circumstances, determines the fate of a movement. Moreover, what is the significance of learning from previous experiences in other national contexts? Has the Scandinavian record had differential impacts on democratic socialism in southern and eastern Europe?

Through this focus the book aims at highlighting the role of social democracy both in a comparative perspective and in each separate historical and cultural context. The historical and structural determinants of social democracy form an important part of the analysis, but it is equally necessary to examine critically the self-perception of the various movements in order to understand their behaviour at given historical junctures. Moreover, the scope of this book also

1

accommodates insights into the 'history of losers' while maintaining an emphasis on the more prominent representatives of social democracy.

Scandinavia is undoubtedly the region which is most commonly associated with social democracy. The Nordic welfare state is, to the delight of Scandinavian social democrats and to the equal annoyance of their political opponents, generally regarded as a social democratic product. The bulk of this book examines characteristic features of Scandinavian social democracy.

It would, of course, be highly exaggerated to see the specific Scandinavian features solely as a result of social democratic influence. The four countries share a wide variety of historical and structural characteristics that cannot be overlooked when explaining their political development. For one thing, they are culturally highly homogeneous, meaning that there has been a limited number of politically relevant cleavages in their societies. Moreover, a central role has often been attributed to the traditionally egalitarian social structures in the formation of the 'Scandinavian model'. It has also been pointed out that economic and political development go hand in hand. In the case of Scandinavia the formation of the welfare state has rested on productive structures well suited to meet the needs of an industrial Europe; the growth necessary to produce social reforms has been created through an export-oriented economy.

On the other hand, historical and structural explanations are often overly deterministic; they tend to do away with concrete *actors*, their aspirations and strategies. In this book several critical junctures in the history of prewar social democracy are examined in order to understand the choices that made for social democratic influence in the four countries. It is argued that Scandinavian social democracy managed at an early stage to reconcile itself to the central political institutions and to a basic mood of nationalism prevailing in these countries. Moreover, the ability of the four parties to form coalitions with other parties at critical historical moments offers an explanation of their influence upon the political and social development of the four countries. In a comparative perspective, it seems to be a central question whether these Scandinavian experiences have been or can be repeated in connection with the more recent waves of democratization in Europe. Is the rise of democratic socialism in southern Europe a product of similar reorientations vis-à-vis state, nation and political compromise as in interwar Scandinavia? By the same token, is the recent failure of social democracy in central Europe explicable in terms of an absence of these factors in social democratic strategy?

On the other hand, this comparative perspective not only invites analyses which examine the functioning of social and political mechanisms from period to period. It is equally important to ask what the possible effects of the images of 'really existing social democracy' may be in those countries where democratic socialism is a more recent phenomenon. The second part of the book discusses problems of contemporary Scandinavian social democracy; these have to do with ideology, organization as well as electoral support. In a comparative perspective, it is quite imaginable that the recent problems of Scandinavian social democracy have reduced the general international appeal of social democratic policies. Moreover, they may have led social democratic parties elsewhere in Europe to adopt strategies and policies that stand in some contrast to the 'Scandisclerosis' often attributed to the Nordic welfare states.

The formative years

In the bird's-eye view of most cross-cultural analysis, Scandinavia stands out as a highly homogeneous area with little significant intra-regional variation. One might be led to believe that this general similarity applies to the history of the social democratic parties as well. A survey of their past reveals, however, something of a pendular movement. Several times during the course of the past century, *Socialdemokratiet* in Denmark, the SDP in Finland, the DNA in Norway and the SAP in Sweden have seemingly been moving away from each other in terms of ideology, strategy and position in national politics. Each time, however, the dispersion has been reversed, and the result has been highly similar in all four countries.

Studies which wish to emphasize the *similarity* of the Scandinavian countries tend to look for explanatory factors related to the basic structural characteristics of these societies. In such analyses, a central role is often attributed to the peasantry. The predominance of

3

independent small farming and the limited role of manorial farms is seen as a crucial prerequisite of popular involvement in the democratic institutions at an early stage. The massive support which the peasantry could mobilize for parliamentary democracy safeguarded the democratic system against attacks from the right as well as from the left. Moreover, it served to lessen the political polarization around the parliamentary system as such, thus making for a more conciliatory political climate in general.

In close connection with this factor, the basic political cleavage structure is often mentioned as a major source of social democratic strength in Scandinavia. The political organization of the peasantry weakened the role of the bourgeoisie, who could never count on a numerous and reliable rural ally. During the crucial interwar years, none of the four countries ever saw a united bourgeois front rallying the moneyed bourgeoisie, the peasantry, the military, the church and the civil servants under the same hat. Rather, the political parties representing these groups - the conservatives, the liberals and the agrarians - at all times remained wary and suspicious of each other's intentions. This split of the bourgeois forces enabled the social democrats to exert considerable political influence even from a minority position. Moreover, it increased the need for the bourgeois parties to look for alternative coalition partners in order to create necessary parliamentary majorities.

These structural and historical factors seem to offer a feasible background to the major choices guiding Scandinavian social democracy towards increased ideological moderation and predominance in national politics. The strong position of the parliamentary system led the social democrats to opt for electoral politics, thus binding them to the institutional framework of bourgeois society at an early stage. Through the network of parliamentary committees and government special commissions, the social democrats gradually adopted the 'State pespective' instead of the Marxist class-based view of politics. This, in turn, had two effects of paramount importance. For one, it led the social democrats to substitute 'Nation' for 'class' in their appeal to the people. Parallel to this, it increased the acceptability of the Social Democratic Party as a coalition partner for bourgeois parties.

It would certainly be incorrect to contest the general importance of these structural factors and their political consequences for Scandinavian social democracy. At the same time, structural analyses have weaknesses from the point of view of our inter-Scandinavian comparison. Being essentially *static* explanations, they do not offer avenues to an understanding of the variations over time in the position and strategies of the four parties. In other words, they fail to explain why Scandinavian social democracy did not converge already in the 1920s with regard to ideological development and parliamentary strategy. For the same reason, the concrete *choices* leading to similar political outcomes in the four countries cannot be understood solely in terms of social and political structure; structures do not in themselves make decisions, they only restrict the number of alternatives available to the decision-makers. Why a certain option came to prevail over others can only be understood in the final analysis in terms of concrete historical context, tactics and strategy.

This general area is the subject of the first section of the book. The chapters by Jostein Ryssevik and Lauri Karvonen examine the trends towards diversity and unity among Nordic social democrats during the first three decades of the century, culminating in the political convergence brought about by the Red-Green Crisis Agreements. In his study of the roots of the persistent Norwegian radicalism as compared to Denmark and Sweden, Ryssevik especially underlines the importance of the internal functioning of the party organization in Norway. Concentrating on the crucial shift from a 'class party' to a 'people's party', Karvonen shows that this change was by no means the result of a gradual and linear process. Rather, one discerns a roller-coaster pattern between radicalization and moderation. In the final analysis, it was the overwhelming voter response following social democratic steps towards moderation that came to reinforce the 'revisionist' course.

In the two other studies in this section, new perspectives on the development of Scandinavian social democracy are presented. In his analysis of the roots of Swedish corporatism, Bo Rothstein points to the fact that working class organizations in Sweden were given access to government-led bodies before the advent of a strong social democratic *party*. This meant that an important part of the political culture conditioning working class politics was already there when the SAP became a major force. Jan Sundberg's study underlines the importance of the social democratic involvement in local politics as a hotbed of consensualism for those party members among whom national activists and leaders were recruited. In many ways, the compromises of the 1930s were repetitions of inter-party cooperation with considerably longer traditions at local level.

Current problems

The 'golden years' of Scandinavian social democracy started with the red-green crisis agreements and reached a peak during the first postwar decades. Today, however, the social democratic parties are facing problems in elections as well as within the labour movement. The social democratic dilemma can be stated as follows. Formerly, the social democrats gathered strength from the expanding mass of workers who suffered under capitalism; today, however, their power is weakened as increasing numbers of wage-earners regard the capitalist economy as the main source of their personal welfare. During the long periods of governmental rule the social democrats managed to change the economy to a welfare society where the majority of the formerly underprivileged masses now lead comfortable lives with a modern flat or house, one or two cars, perhaps a summer cottage, and savings for an annual charter holiday to the sunny beaches of southern Europe. The new generation of workers born after World War II tend to take all the public benefits for granted while at the same time viewing government regulations as a hindrance to their individual success. Negative characteristics of public regulations are frequently associated with social democratic rule, whereas the successful reforms from the golden years having to do with income redistribution, social security, and health care may be forgotten as those generations that actively supported the reform programmes pass on.

The class identity of the workers has continuously diminished since the 1950s. Similarly, the degree of class-voting has declined and the influx of middle class voters and members has put new pressures on the social democratic party. Although the party still has a class base and a large core of stable voters the instability in elections has increased compared to the mid-1950s. The peak was reached in 1973 after the EC referendum in Denmark and Norway. New parties have emerged in the political arena, thus contributing to increased electoral volatility. The social democrats are therefore forced to extend their appeal to the middle class who lack the loyalty to the labour movement characteristic of the old generation of workers. Votes count no matter who casts the ballot, but to win votes the social democrats have to compete with the non-socialist parties with strategies and appeals similar to those of their competitors. In many respects the distinction between non-socialists and social democrats is more artificial than ever. It is more their heritage than their current activities among the electorate that separates the social democrats from the liberals.

In addition, during the golden years the labour movement became a very important channel of corporatist influence. Initially the differences were small between the two branches of the labour movement: the political (the party organization) and the economic (the unions). Today, however, the two branches are clearly separate. The functions of the party organization have increasingly focused on elections; the activity of party members is a far cry from what it once was, and membership is declining. The relationship between the unions and the party has become problematic as their interests have diverged. Most labour union members are still manual workers whereas an increasing portion of the party members are middle class citizens, often women employed in the public sector. In Sweden where the ties between the unions and the party have traditionally been strongest in Scandinavia, this liaison is now under a strong pressure of change. As of 1991 it is no longer possible collectively to affiliate labour union members to the Social Democratic Party. These changes will inevitably result in a declining membership and a loosening of union control over the party.

The social democratic parties have become *electoral parties* to a much greater extent than before and the unions are also witnessing changes. The labour unions and the corporatist channel of power was well designed to pursue the workers' aims in the industrial society. With the modernization of industrial production and the universal availability of material goods, service, and information, the traditional corporatist channel of influence became less efficient. Union membership has declined since its peak in the early 1980s. The once powerful process of centralized collective bargaining supported by the mass of members is increasingly viewed as obsolete. Today union branches compare themselves and compete with each other to gain more advantages in a negotiation game with many participants. Moreover, the path to union influence via government committees and negotiations has been attenuated with social democratic losses in elections. The social democrats form minority cabinets, join coalitions with non-socialist parties, or act in opposition. None of these alternatives entails the kind of capacity to act that the social democrats possessed in former periods when they were able to form a majority cabinet by themselves. To be sure, politics is the art of the possible; still, it seems today that the social democrats will have to reconcile themselves for many years to come to a situation dramatically different from that of the golden years.

In Part II of the book some of these predicaments of today's social democracy are highlighted. In the first of the three chapters Per Selle outlines some central ideological and organizational problems which the social democrats faced after the golden years. According to Selle, the concepts of efficiency, full employment and equality can be challenged as essentials for understanding the ongoing transformation of social democracy. In his argumentation, the social democratic ideology was dead after the postwar reconstruction period, and the traditional mode of welfare implementation, i.e. bureaucracy and centralized planning, was no longer credible either in the eyes of the electorate or to the party elite. Instead, demands for decentralization, user democracy and other non-institutionalized forms of participation have emerged, putting pressure on social democratic organization and policy formulation.

Ulf Lindström outlines a tentative theory based on what is known as the 'ghetto model' applied to the social democratic electorate. In contrast to Selle, who sees bureaucracy as a burden to social democracy, Lindström looks upon it as a reservoir which may prevent electoral losses. The work place (heavy industry) and the residential area (the working-class neighbourhood) formed 'the center of gravity' of the social democratic electorate during the golden years. Today the working-class ghettos have more or less disappeared and with them the core of the social democratic support. However, according to Lindström, the social democrats have replaced the old work-place ghetto with new groups of public employees. He sees large

8

government bureaucracies as the contemporary ghettos in which a new core of social democratic support is concentrated.

Finally, Ingemar Wörlund explores new ecological explanations of social democratic voting in Finland, Norway and Sweden. He contructs three new 'regions' according to the relative importance of jobs based on advanced technology, creativity and culture. He finds signs in Sweden of a systematic social democratic stagnation in urban 'high-tech' areas, while the periphery displays continued high levels of social democratic support. However, the findings from Finland and Norway do not corroborate this pattern, indicating that the criteria for regionalization must be developed further.

Beyond Scandinavia

As the signs of trouble for the Scandinavian social democrats began to grow pronounced in the course of the 1970s and early 1980s, democratic socialism met with spectacular success in southern Europe. After the transition from authoritarian rule in the mid-1970s, Greece, Portugal and Spain witnessed the rise to prominence of socialist parties. By 1983, the socialists had assumed office in all three countries. The same year, Bettino Craxi became the first socialist Prime Minister in the history of the Italian republic, although the PSI continued to be smaller than the communists and the Christian democrats in terms of electoral support. On the whole it seemed as if the geography of democratic socialism in Europe was being turned upside-down.

Certainly, the rise of the moderate left in Mediterranean Europe has represented the most dynamic feature of European socialism during the past decade. On the international level, the increased activity and global importance of the Socialist International is at least to some extent explicable in terms of the vitality created by the southern European socialist leaders. For the various national social democratic movements under attack from neo-liberal quarters, southern European socialism has represented the promise of a brighter tomorrow.

While the electoral record of the Spanish and Greek socialists in particular is quite impressive, it is doubtful whether the Mediterranean experience can be said to confirm the continued vitality of the 'Third Way' in European politics. True, the socialists have retained the symbols and rhetoric common to social democracy all over Europe. However, these have mainly been instruments of electoral campaigns. In office, southern European socialists have made no attempts to challenge the tenets of the capitalist system. Quite the contrary, they have endeavoured to de-regulate the economy in order to secure the undisturbed functioning of the market. State interventionism has not come to play any major part in economic policy, to say nothing of nationalization schemes characteristic of social democratic economic policy in the immediate postwar period. Similarly, unions have not found a reliable ally in the socialist governments. Rather, socialist governments have pressed the unions for major concessions in order to secure economic growth and curb inflation. All in all, the socialist policies have displayed a remarkable economic orthodoxy.

This absence of 'socialism' in the policies of Mediterranean socialist governments can at least to some extent be explained in terms of the social bases of the four parties. With the partial exception of the Spanish PSOE, the southern European socialist parties are not *workers'parties* in the same sense as the social democratic parties of northern Europe. Communist parties have won major shares of the working class vote and have maintained close ties with the unions. Thus, legislation and economic measures perceived to be 'anti-union' are not as much of a liability to the southern socialists as they would be for northern European social democrats. Rather, they can be seen as an instrument for weakening communist influence over the economy.

Moreover, the historical context in which southern European socialism became prominent cannot be overlooked when explaining the course chosen by these socialist governments. Tom Gallagher and Allan Williams note in their book, *Southern European Socialism* (1989) that

> Each of the parties assumed office at a time when their guiding doctrine was under sustained intellectual challenge with many of its central tenets, particularly where they applied to an interventionist or enabling state, falling into disrepute. The declining intellectual appeal of socialism in

10

northern Europe and its failure to be renewed by new strategies and insights that could come to terms with changing social conditions and economic recession did not go unnoticed in southern Europe.

Instead of emulating northern European social democracy, southern European socialists have turned to regional political traditions to consolidate their power. Throughout southern Europe, socialist governments have eagerly exploited the well-entrenched clientelist mechanisms at all levels of public administration. A new cast of socialist civil servants has emerged in all four countries, providing the parties with numerous channels of influence throughout the system. On the other hand, clientelism ties the parties to innumerable vested interests at local, regional as well as national level, thus restricting of the central political leadership's room to manoeuvre.

Traditional southern European *personalismo* has characterized the Mediterranean socialist parties no less than their bourgeois rivals. PASOK means Papandreou, the PSI Craxi and the PSOE Gonzales; even after his departure to the precidency, Soares continues to symbolize Portuguese socialism. To a much greater degree than in northern Europe, succession problems are at the core of Mediterranean socialist concerns. None of the parties seems to have prepared a successor well in advance. In fact, personalistic politics renders such a preparation difficult as this could be interpreted as a sign of disloyalty vis-à-vis the leader. These are a few of the themes dealt with in the two chapters on southern Europe. The authors, Einar Berntzen and Ann-Cathrine Jungar, stress the differences between Scandinavian social democracy and Mediterranean socialism in nearly all important respects; historical context, social bases, political and economic structures and cultural traditions. The gist of Berntzen's analysis concerning PASOK, the PSOE and the PSP is that there is, strictly speaking, *no* social democracy in Greece and on the Iberian peninsula; for all practical purposes, the southern socialist parties stand for *neo-liberalism* rather than for reformist socialism. Writing on Italy, Jungar underlines the repeated failure of the PSI to create a distinctive image in relation to the two major parties, the communists and the Christian democrats. Time and again, the voters have preferred 'the real thing' and voted for one of the bigger parties

11

instead. Summing up the history of the PSI in terms of those factors that made for strong social democracy in Scandinavia, she concludes that Italian socialism has failed on practically all counts.

In the final chapter of the book, Ulf Lindström presents what must be one of the very first scholarly analyses of social democracy in eastern Europe after 1989. The democratization of eastern Europe not only offers a fascinating field of study to the political scientist. To most political movements in western Europe, it represents a chance to extend their international appeal beyond their traditional domains. Nordic social democrats were among the first groups to express optimistic expectations concerning future strongholds in eastern Europe.

One year after the revolution of 1989, it would be an understatement to call these high hopes overly optimistic. In elections throughout central and eastern Europe, social democracy has scored low or negligeable figures. The exception is the only free election held in the history of the German Democratic Republic, where social democracy mustered a little over one-fifth of the vote. With *Wiedervereiningung* being the only likely future scenario, these elections could not be regarded as entirely comparable to elections elsewhere in central Europe; even as a part of the West German SDP, the East German party did more poorly than was expected. In Hungary and Czechoslovakia the social democratic alternative was flatly rejected in these first elections.

Central European social democracy failed to capitalize both on the transition from dictatorship and on the first democratic elections. During the transition, citizens' forums and various liberal groups held the initiative; in the elections, the reformed communist parties rather than the social democrats carried the day on the left. Contrary to the expectations of many western social democrats it was 'democracy, period', rather than democratic socialism that the great majority desired. Those who did not wish a total break with everything associated with 'socialism' voted for the de-Stalinized form of communism rather than for social democracy.

Labels mattered, but they are insufficient as a general explanation. The organizational and campaign activity of the central European social democrats left much to be desired in terms of realism and general appeal. Moreover, the attitude of the Socialist International was apparently problematic from the point of view of the social democrats. The SI adopted a conciliatory posture vis-à-vis the reformed communist parties of eastern Europe. This probably had a doubly negative effect from the point of view of the social democrats; it gave the reformed communists respectability and it deprived the social democrats of a profile distinct from their rivals on the left.

Concluding remarks

Democratic socialists in northern, eastern and southern Europe seem to lead existences worlds apart. Historical context and national conditions largely determine both the fate of social democratic movements, the manner in which they pursue their goals and the nature of the policies they present in government. There evidently cannot be any straightforward process of diffusion across Europe. What makes a political strategy successful is its immediate applicability in existing conditions rather than its faithfulness to an external model. The 'Scandinavian Model' was politically successful in Scandinavia because it was *Scandinavian*, not because it is the optimal model for all societies and historical contexts. Similarly, the rise of southern European socialism is best explained in terms of the ability of the Mediterranean socialists to adapt to national conditions and traditions. The clearest example of cross-national emulation found in this book does not concern Scandinavia (the Czechoslovak socialists emulating the Austrian SPÖ and the Spanish PSOE); the electorate were far from convinced.

Yet it is the international scene that will provide the major test of the future viability of social democracy. The integration of Europe will be the single most important factor conditioning the domestic politics and foreign policies of all countries studied in this book. Corporatist structures based on national consensus in Scandinavia as well as clientelist practices in southern Europe will have to adjust or even give way to common European regulations, procedures and standards. To what extent social democracy will succeed in replacing these national sources of power and legitimacy with credible transnational alliances and loyalties is a critical question to which no apparent answer exists today.

PART I
THE FORMATIVE
YEARS OF
SCANDINAVIAN
SOCIAL DEMOCRACY

Party vs. Parliament. Contrasting Configurations of Electoral and Ministerial Socialism in Scandinavia

Jostein Ryssevik

Prelude

One late January night in 1928, after several hours of heated discussions, the Central Committee of the Norwegian Labour Party (DNA) finally decided to form the first socialist government. For the labour politicians who were gathered that night the question of ministerial socialism had until that very day belonged to the realm of ideas. Although the socialists, for the first time in history, accounted the largest group in Parliament, the King's decision to call upon them to form a cabinet came as a great surprise.

Suspicion concerning parliamentary strategy was a profound trait of the Norwegian Labour Party and several of the Committee members, among them Oscar Torp and Martin Tranmæl (Party Chairman and Secretary respectively), were adamantly against any experiments in ministerial socialism. However, pressure was mounting after the parliamentary caucus had reached a positive and unanimous conclusion earlier the same day. In the final roll-call six out of sixteen members of the Central Committee opposed the assumption executive power.[1] It is part of the story that Johan Nygaardsvold, later to become Prime Minister from 1935 to 1945, left the meeting in anger when he was called upon to lead the cabinet. The choice then fell upon Chr. Hornsrud, one of the party's most experienced parliamentarians and outspoken reformists.

However, the first experiment with ministerial socialism in Norway was destined for a rather short life.[2] Eight days after the cabinet declaration was submitted, the Government was ousted from office by a vote of no-confidence. The immediate motive behind this vote was found in the straightforward and provocative statements in the opening paragraph of the declaration, but the toppling of the cabinet was also orchestrated by events and forces outside Parliament. A massive flight of capital and threatening financial crisis, as well as direct intervention by the leader of the Central Bank, were sufficient to unite the fragmented bourgeois block in a commcn effort to remove the socialists and reestablish stability.

The Hornsrud incident has been characterizes as a classic example of the dilemmas of ministerial socialism, i.e., the difficulty in combining revolutionary ambitions with minority parliamentarism. As to the question of what role a minority socialist government should assume, Przeworski offers the following choice:

> Either the party would pursue its socialist objectives and be promptly defeated or it would behave like any other party, administering the system and introducing only those few reforms for which it could obtain a parliamentary majority (Przeworski 1980, 49).

The DNA chose the maximalist strategy. Although the revolutionary implications of the cabinet's programme may be held in doubt, at least as far as the declaration is concerned, the Hornsrud episode is probably the only European example of a socialist minority cabinet directly challenging bourgeois society.

The short-lived ministerial experiment strengthened the suspicions concerning the parliamentary strategy and was heavily exploited in future party rhetoric as an illustration of the true character of bourgeois society. Edvard Bull's conclusions may serve as an example:

> The short history of the Labour Government has at least accomplished one thing; for a moment the curtain was pulled aside, giving us the opportunity to actually see the economic

16

forces at work in politics, not only to debate them. How this will effect the political orientation of the working masses over the next two years needs no prophesies, it is a daily experience in the Labour Party (Bull 1928, 201).[3]

For the revolutionaries in the DNA, the episode served as a validation of their *Weltanschauung*; real power in society was not to be found in Parliament. The experience told them to return to the trenches, to strengthen the power and ideological purity of their organization and not to dilute the class struggle by false illusions about the importance of the electoral channel.

There is a direct link between this conclusion and the distinct revolutionary turn that took place at the next Party Congress, in 1930. For one thing, the clause about the necessity of winning 'the majority of the people' was deleted. Perhaps even more significant, the congress adopted new and more restrictive guidelines in the question of ministerial socialism. To prevent a relapse of the Hornsrud incident, the congress ordered both the Central and the National Committee 'not to agree on the formation of a Labour government without the assurance that it is possible to carry out an independent political line and to effect important changes in a socialist direction' (Lafferty 1971, 128).

Scandinavian contrasts

The extraordinary character and position of the DNA in these turbulent years can only be understood if contrasted to contemporary experiences in neighbouring countries. By the time the Norwegian socialists reluctantly made their first abortive experience with the executive power, their Swedish and Danish party comrades could look back upon an extended record of ministerial socialism.

The experiences of the Swedish and Danish social democratic parties are in fact quite parallel: Both parties made agreements with, and offered parliamentary support to, liberal governments (from approx. 1910).[4] This was followed by a period as junior coalition partners (from around the end of World War I until 1920)[5] and

17

ended with several years of full government responsibility in the twenties.[6] Prior to this both the SAP and the SD engaged in extensive and unbroken, electoral and parliamentary collaboration with liberal parties. Figure 1 outlines this development.

Figure 1: The history of electoral and ministerial socialism

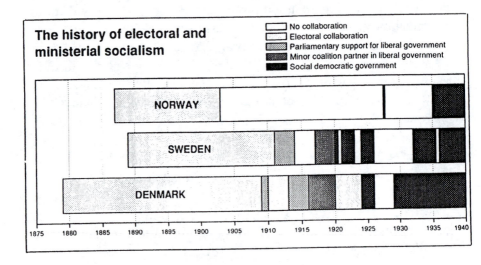

From a seemingly common point of departure (all three parties based their generic ideology on equally faulty translations of the Gotha Programme, they chose to participate[7] and they did so in electoral collaboration with the liberals) the Norwegian party was soon to diverge. In contrast to the gradual and stepwise integration of the Danish and Swedish parties into the game of parliamentary democracy, the DNA made an early break with the liberals (*Venstre*) and fostered an increasingly suspicious posture against the parliamentary strategy. Not until the mid thirties did the roads of the three parties again converge in the apparent parallelism of the so-called 'red-green crises agreements'.

Thus, in a comparative perspective, the Hornsrud incident and its immediate aftermath at the 1930 Congress, is *not* a historical parenthesis. It is the conclusion of three decades of increasing political isolation of the Norwegian Labour Party. While the social democrats in Sweden and Denmark adopted an increasingly pragmatic strategy in their efforts to achieve political and social reforms, the Norwegian party, even as late as in 1930, approached the question of ministerial socialism as a matter of principle.

Why do the roads diverge? Why did the Norwegians choose a strategy different from that of their Scandinavian sister-parties? Did the parties approach identical historical options with dissimilar methods, or was the outcome an inevitable consequence of differences in the strategic situation facing the various parties?

These are the questions to which this chapter addresses itself. In the first section three lines of explanation will be discussed:

1) the effects of late and rapid industrialization,
2) the effects of early democratization, and
3) the effects of the openness of the party organization.

The remaining sections will be devoted to the elaboration and validation of an alternative explanatory approach, emphasizing the tension and power relations between the twin 'pillars' of the social democratic party; the 'member party' and the 'voter party'. According to this approach, a major source of the Norwegian divergencies must be located in the extraordinarily dominant position of the 'member pillar' in the DNA party structure.[8]

Norwegian radicalism: three explanatory approaches

Rapid industrialization

In his contemporary and comparative study, Edvard Bull locates *one of* the causes of the DNA's radicalism in the special character of the Norwegian industrialization process (Bull 1922). Economic modernization started later but progressed faster than in Denmark and Sweden. This suddenness, accompanied by the fact that most of the new factories were located in the proximity of new hydro-electric power sources in the rural periphery, caused the major part of the new working class to be recruited from the destitute fringes of the peasant society. In short, the disruptive character of the industrialization process brought forth a working class much more susceptible to revolutionary ideas than that of the older and gradually developing class in the two neighbouring countries. This dislocated mass became the basis of the radical wing which gained control of the party at the 1918 party congress.

Supplemented by the works of labour historian Walter Galenson (Galenson 1952), the 'Bull proposition' has become part of the standard inventory of international political sociology.[9] Plausible as the proposition may seem, later comparative investigations have failed to substantiate it. Lafferty's comprehensive study of the connection between economic development and labour response in Scandinavia (Lafferty 1971) found no convincing evidence of a more disruptive pattern of industrialization in Norway compared to that of Sweden. Whether this mirrors reality or simply demonstrates the extreme difficulties associated with cross-national comparisons of aggregate statistics is a moot question.[10]

Early democratization

The second approach differs from the previous one in two important ways. First, the independent variable is sought in the political system and not in the economy; second, the effects are studied at the level of political leaders as opposed to the level of the labouring masses. Francis Castle summarizes the argument in the following way:

> It is in the different strategic choices facing the respective labour movements in the early part of this century that one can locate an explanation for the greater inclination to revolutionary activism exhibited in Norway. Paradoxically, this was largely a consequence of the earlier and more complete democratization of the Norwegian political system (Castles 1978, 20).

In Denmark and Sweden the absence of the basic prerequisites of democratic participation forced the social democrats into an extended collaboration with the liberal wing of the bourgeois block. In Denmark the principle of parliamentary government was not recognized until 1901 and the final democratization of the vote to both houses of Parliament had to wait until 1915. The Swedish resistance against threshold progression was even more stubborn. A major barrier was broken by the extension of suffrage of 1909, but the threat of a revolutionary insurrection in the wake of World War I was needed to make the Conservatives concede the parliamentary principle and accept a final democratization of suffrage.

In both countries the struggle for democracy was fought by an alliance of social democratic and liberal forces. Every battle of this prolonged struggle brought the partners closer together. What had started out as electoral collaboration before the turn of the century ended as shared executive responsibility several decades later.[11]

The Norwegian situation was strikingly different. The old regime was brought down and the parliamentary principle secured several years before organized labour entered the political arena (in 1884). Like its Scandinavian counterparts, also the DNA joined forces with the liberals in the struggle for the final extension of the franchise. But when this fight was brought to an end in 1898, only 11 years after the foundation of the party, there were no longer any common interests which could keep the alliance together.

So, while collaboration and preoccupation with issues of political reforms gradually moderated the political course of the Danish and Swedish social democratic parties, the political isolation of the DNA was a potent agency for its markedly greater inclination towards revolutionary activism. Herbert Tingsten's precise description of the Swedish party presents a picture which by and large is valid also for the Danish case:

> For several years the party [SAP] was primarily a suffrage party, supplementary to, and outshone by, bourgeois liberalism. Working for democracy strengthened the party's democratic course. One could not demand the vote, and at the same time proclaim that the revolution would come even if

21

this demand was fulfilled (Tingsten 1967, 125).

Thus, in contradiction to theories of political access, which suggest that it is *the lack of* political rights that creates frustration and radicalism, this line of explanation holds that the struggle to obtain these rights has the opposite effect. In short, fighting for democracy creates democrats.

In the comparative literature there seems to be a general consensus about the complementary nature of the previous economic and political explanations. This applies to particulary Lafferty's work which focuses on the interplay and timing of the changing factors of economic and political development. Or as one of the recent contributors puts it: '... it was the combination of an early democratization and a late industrialization that provided the conditions for a radical potential [in Norway]' (Madsen 1984, 92).

Internal party structure

The third line of explanation, represented by Ulf Torgersen's study of the role of the National Convention in the Norwegian party structure (Torgersen 1969), is less concerned with *the roots and initial causes* of radicalism. The primary object is rather to explain *how and why* the radical fraction in Norway was able to dominate and finally take control of the party, while the Danish and Swedish radical wing led a marginalized life in internal or external opposition to the dominant trend. The reason for this is found in the internal structures and power-relations of the Norwegian party organization.

Torgersen views a party-organization as a body marked by conflicting interests. But unlike the predominant trend in the party literature, the emphasis is not on the potential or actual contradictions between the elite and the rank-and-file.[12] Instead, emphasis is put on the relations between different levels of the party: the voters, the representatives (in Parliament), the member organization and the National Convention.

The DNA was largely a member-dominated party. The parliamentary caucus and its constituency were by and large subordinated to the member organization, whose interest and political outlook determined the party's strategic choices. The rules of representation to the national conventions were in addition such that they produced a constant overrepresentation of small party locals. In the period leading up to the radical take-over in 1918, it was precisely in the new and smaller branches in the periphery that the revolutionary and anti-parliamentary outlook flourished. Thus, 'the organization charter of the Norwegian Labour Party, which heavily benefitted the local association, must be considered as an important condition for the 'radicalism' of the Norwegian labour movement' (Torgersen 1969, 39). 'Branting's position was', (by way of comparison) 'based on an organization less sensitive to local idiosyncrasies' (1969, 91).

Focusing on internal party dynamics, Torgersen skips the question whether the Norwegian working class or the party elite were more 'radical' than their Scandinavian counterparts. A comparable level of 'radicalism', either in the masses or in the elite, might produce different outcomes, depending on the openness of the party structure.

Figure 2: Main features of the three approaches

Cause	Who are the radicals	Arena
Rapid industrialization	The masses	The economic system
Late democratization	The elite	The political system
Openess of party organization	Factions of the party organization	Party organization

It should be mentioned that Edvard Bull also paid some attention to the more decentralized and democratic character of the Norwegian party. The comparatively free status of the local press and the relatively frequent gathering of national conventions made it easier for the radical opposition to gain influence in the party (Bull 1922, 22).

The subsequent analysis is inspired of Torgersen's approach. The focus will be on the relations and potential contradictions between different levels of the party organization. But internal party dynamics cannot be studied in isolation. We will argue that the origins of the divergent roads of Scandinavian social democracy can be found in the interplay between the political and the organizational level or, more precisely, in how the patterns of threshold progression conditioned intra-party power relations. The analysis will proceed in two steps. First, the links between macro-political development and party strategy will be discussed. Second, the focus will shift to the intra-party level where competing interests between different levels of the organization will be highlighted.

Macro-political development

Adam Przeworski sees the advent of political rights as the crucial turning point in the history of social democracy:

> As long as workers did not have political rights, no choice between insurrectionary and parliamentary tactics was necessary. Indeed, political rights could be conquered by those who did not have them only through extraparliamentary activities.... Yet as soon as universal male suffrage was obtained, the choice between legal and extraparliamentary tactics had to be made (Przeworski 1986, 20).

This thesis of a fundamental watershed in the development of political rights represents an oversimplification of history, at least in the Scandinavian context. Consequently, it leads Przeworski to some

24

faulty conclusions about the strategic options facing the social democratic parties at different stages of this development. Political rights are not an asset which a social group either has or does not have. It is perfectly possible for a particular group to possess some political rights but to be denied others. It is also a feasible situation that some of the party's natural sympathizers have acquired the right to vote, while the rest are denied it.

Both situations were prevalent in Scandinavia for several decades. A substantial proportion of the workers were enfranchised long before the final extension of male suffrage. This was particulary the case in Denmark, where the liberal constitution of 1849 guaranteed the major part of the workers the right to participate in elections to the lower chamber (*Folketing*).[13] This was also the case in Norway (prior to the final extension in 1898) and in Sweden (prior to the 1909 reform) where at least the more affluent workers in the cities were already enfranchised. Moreover, in Denmark and Sweden the right to vote was not the only threshold that had to be changed. Long after the major part of the working class was enfranchised, the absence of parliamentary government and the existence of a non-democratic upper house prevented the transformation of votes into power.

Thus, political rights were not acquired *in a single step.* The opening of the parliamentary channel was a gradual process involving several partial victories, each providing the setting and the weapons for the next struggle. Once the parliamentary channel was opened, however incompletely, the channel could be used as a means for its own improvement. Moreover, the workers were not alone in the struggle for lower thresholds. Democratic reforms were of equal importance to the peasantry and their political instrument, the liberal parties.

Consequently, *extraparliamentary activities* were not the *only available* weapon in the struggle for democratic rights as Przeworski's schematic view leads him to conclude. On the contrary, each of the Scandinavian labour parties pinned the greater part of their faith on *electoral and parliamentary collaboration with liberal parties.*

Extraparliamentary activities were, however, considered *supplementary methods* in the efforts to achieve political reforms. The news about the successful political mass strike led by the Belgian *Parti Ouvrier* in 1893, was echoed in the Scandinavian debate and both the Swedish and the Norwegian party considered the possibility 'speaking Belgian' in the suffrage question.[14] However, the only party that followed the example was the Swedish one which organized a 'suffrage strike' in 1902. Undoubtedly the strike, which lasted for three days and involved approximately 116,000 workers, was a massive manifestation of labour power. Its effect on the tug of war in Parliament is more of an open question. The suffrage reform did not materialize until seven years later.

Przeworski is way off the mark when arguing that the use of the mass strike was never questioned.[15] The Danish party was very suspicious about the strike as a political weapon and the Norwegian and Swedish debates were characterized by hesitation. (The 1902 strike in Sweden was called eight years after the first approval.) In fact, both parties were anxious about the negative effect that a strike might have on their relationship to the liberals. Therefore, it is fair to conclude that extraparliamentary activities were only applied to the extent that they did not thwart the party's opportunities to achieve reforms through the parliamentary channel.

Until the turn of the century no major divergences can be observed in the Norwegian party's dispositions. In fact the same gradual moderation which characterized their Scandinavian counterparts is also evident in the DNA. Collaboration with *Venstre* was an inevitable part of its strategy and the existence of this relationship limited its freedom of action. However, the elimination of the suffrage question (1898) as well as the controversies over the union with Sweden (1905), changed the situation radically. The childhood years under the tutelage of *Venstre* came to an end.

The effects of the new strategic situation were soon to appear. Electoral alliances with other parties were banned at the National Convention in 1906. The same Convention also set the stage for the first major debate concerning the principles of ministerial socialism. Although the question had been a central theme in the international socialist debate since Millerand entered the Waldeck-Rousseau ministry in 1899, no formal discussions had taken place in the Norwegian party. In fact, when the question was discussed at the Amsterdam Congress of the Second International in 1904, the two

Norwegian delegates were not able to reach a common stand and split their votes. It was this behaviour that provided the immediate background of the debate at the 1906 Convention. Not surprisingly it was the freshman and would-be radical leader Martin Tranmæl who voiced the sharpest criticism against the reformists: 'Delegates who votes for 'ragout resolutions' will not do for The Norwegian Labour Party' (Lie 1988, 93).

In the years to come the DNA expended an impressive amount of energy on fence building. The party cultivated its isolation with a growing amount of suspicion and formal clauses against any form of inter-party collaboration. At the National Convention in 1909 a formal statement was made against any kind of ministerial socialism, and in 1915 this principle was extended even to the level of municipal politics (!). No social democratic mayor should be appointed without a firm majority in the local council. During this period the party also extended and formalized its control over the conduct of its MPs (see below).

Although the change of leadership at the National Convention in 1918 is generally held to be the radical turning point in the history of the Norwegian party, it may be argued that the crucial step was in fact taken twelve years earlier. It was at the 1906 Convention that the DNA set out on a course that deviated from its Scandinavian counterparts. The parties' divergent development from this point onwards might be studied under the heading *centrifugal forces*; in Norway towards increased isolation and radicalization, in Denmark and Sweden towards increased integration and moderation.

These forces may be approached from three perspectives:

    1 Effects of inter-party collaboration
    2 The nature of the issues (democratic vs. socialist reforms)
    3 Achievements (in the parliamentary channel)

It is not an invention of modern political science that cooperation with the liberals may have had an effect on the development of social democratic ideology and praxis. *Embourgeoisement* and the danger of placing ultimate socialist goals in jeopardy belonged to the standard vocabulary of contemporary left wing criticism. For the protagonists of collaboration, however, the positive value of concrete and immediate political reforms carried more weight than the potential danger of long-term psychological mechanisms. They also had great confidence in their own immunity, as evidenced by the following bold statement from *Arbetarbladet* (the chief mouthpiece of SAP):

> Shame on the party that doesn't manage to keep its coat of arms clean and shining even through the hell of parliamentarism. Such a party does not live up to the great mission of leading the people into the promised land (Tingsten 1967, 85).

In retrospect, it is obvious that the lengthy process of providing the means of completing 'the great mission' changed the vision of 'the promised land'. When the social democrats joined forces with the liberals to conquer the basic prerequisites of democratic participation, the alliance was undoubtedly regarded as highly temporary. As soon as democratic rights were achieved, the party was prepared to continue its march towards victory on its own. History played a trick on the party, however. The Swedish struggle lasted for three decades, the Danish for almost half a century. Thus, it was not collaboration *per se* that left a mark on the participants and their politics, but its lengthy character. What originated as extraordinary and conditional moderation, ended over the years as compulsory reading in the social democratic Catechism.

Turning to the second aspect, it is obvious that fighting for democracy and fighting for socialism were two completely separate issues. For one thing, it proved impossible for the social democrats to engage in a prolonged struggle for democratic reforms and simultaneously proclaim that the party's goals were not attainable within the framework of this democracy.[16] Reforming the rules of the system is a system-supporting rather than a system-rejecting activity. Eventually, democracy was gradually and almost unnoticeably elevated from the inventory of tactical weapons to the rank of principle goals. As Tingsten puts it: 'Democracy filled the ideological void left by socialism' (1967, 76).

Moreover, given a limited agenda, the preoccupation with one overriding issue gradually pushed other goals into the background. This is substantiated by the ideological immobility that plagued the

SAP around 1920. With all the democratic reforms achieved, the party had to invent a new rhetoric and a new set of goals to continue the march towards socialism. But the shift from democratic to socialist reforms was not an easy one. The party's answer to the challenge was 'socialization', but as Lotta Gröning accurately puts it, 'not now and only a little' (Gröning 1988, 180). The committee that was appointed to investigate the conditions for socialization of industry came down sixteen years later suggesting that a number of shoe factories in the Örebro region could be acquired by the state. It took a full decade and a major economic crisis to transform the 'suffrage party' into a vigilant instrument for social and economic reforms.

As for the social democratic parties' achievements and relative strength in the parliamentary channel, two significant facts are revealed by the rough historical outline in Figure 3.

Figure 3: The electoral record of social democracy

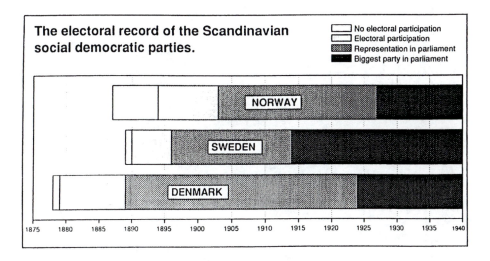

First, not only was the Norwegian party the last party to nominate candidates and participate in national elections (in 1894 - fifteen years after the Danes). It was also the last to win representation in

Parliament (in 1903 - fourteen years after the Danes) and to reach the position as the biggest party in Parliament (in 1927 - thirteen years after the Swedes). Thus, disregarding its relatively early birth, the Norwegian party was a *latecomer*. The second important observation is the extraordinarily short time that clapsed after Branting had entered the Lower Chamber of the Swedish *Riksdag* until the SAP outnumbered its competitors (only fourteen years). Thus, the Swedish party was a *'sprinter'*.

Figure 4: Absolute size of the parliamentary groups

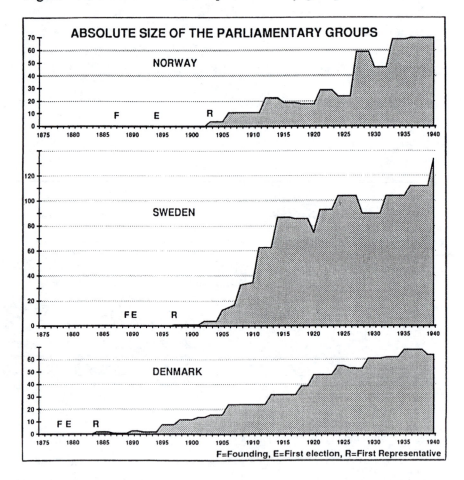

30

These observations underline the differences between the parties if we look at the detailed description in Figure 4, in which the development of *the absolute size* of the parliamentary groups is outlined. The Danish caucus shows a rather slow but steady growth without any major setbacks. The SAP had a much later entry, but multiplied with a tremendous speed during the first fifteen years of the century. Their parliamentary group grew from 1 to 87 members between 1900 and 1914. In the subsequent period there are only two major setbacks, in 1920 and 1928. These were the results of the only two elections in Sweden characterized by an outright socialist-bourgeois confrontation. The Norwegian party's road towards parliamentary maturity is, by contrast, paved with much more frustration. In fact, there is almost no growth at all in the rather long period from 1912 until the victorious election in 1927. This more or less coincides with the era of Norwegian radicalism.

The importance of this observation is revealed if we focus on this period of centrifugal political divergence between the DNA and the two other parties: the Norwegian party won 23 seats in Parliament in 1912. In the next election in 1915, the group was reduced to 19 members and in 1918 only 18 members were elected. In the same period the Danish parliamentary group grew from 24 to 39 and the Swedish group from 63 to 87. In short, while the DNA's efforts in the parliamentary channel were characterized by stagnation and setbacks, their Scandinavian comrades could look back upon a period of progress and success. To parties who based their *Weltanschauung* on an image of ever increasing growth towards a final take-over, these contrasting experiences were of utmost importance.

This is even more so if we shift our focus to the most important reason for the Norwegian deadlock. This is revealed in Figure 5 which shows the three parties' share of the vote and parliamentary representation as *relative numbers*. Again taking the year 1918 as a breakpoint, it is obvious that the parties' relative strength in Parliament does not correspond to their ability to mobilize voters. Each of the parties' constituencies counts approximately one third of the electorate. It is the electoral law, i.e. the transformation of votes into seats, that to an extreme degree works to the DNA's dis-

31

advantage. In Norway, all elections from 1906 to 1918 were run on a two-ballot system with an absolute majority provision in the first ballot. This gave the bourgeois parties an excellent opportunity to coordinate their strength and form alliances in the run-off election in which simple plurality was sufficient to secure the mandate. The figure gives a precise illustration of the system's ability to obstruct (and frustrate) the social democrats.

Figure 5: Social democracy's proportions of votes and mandates

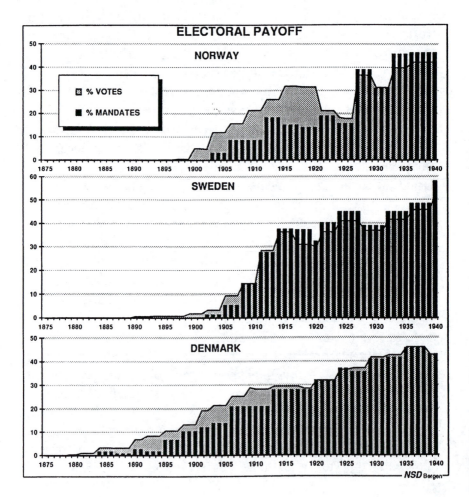

In contrast, the Danish and Swedish systems were much more responsive to the growth of social democracy. The Danish party was also underrepresented in Parliament until the introduction of PR in 1915, but in no way comparable to the Norwegian situation. In Sweden PR was introduced as part of the suffrage reform of 1909, and from 1914 onwards this system actually worked in favour of the Social Democratic Party.

Thus, in spite of the apparent democratic character of the Norwegian political system, the electoral law was a major barrier to social democratic ascendancy. There was, however, a major contrast between this threshold and the barriers that their Scandinavian counterparts were fighting to remove. As the Norwegian liberals were relatively satisfied with the existing situation, no alliance partner was available. This added to the frustration and isolation of the DNA.

In sum, the DNA's experiences in the parliamentary channel became a major source of the growing suspicion regarding the fruitfulness of parliamentary work. Our final task is to study how this experience affected the power-relations at different levels of the party organization.

Intra-party tensions

In contrast to the conservatives and the liberals, the social democratic parties were formed long before they appeared in Parliament. They emerged from embryonic and undifferentiated labour movements, and in their infancy it was difficult to distinguish the political branch from the industrial one. As the organizations grew, the division became sharper although the two branches never really separated. The relationship was kept closest in Norway and Sweden with collective membership of unions in the party organization, as well as cross-representation in the leadership of the two branches. In Denmark the relationship was less institutionalized, but nevertheless close.

This special origin has to a considerable extent left its mark on the anatomy of the social democratic parties (see Figure 6). To put it simply, they were always something more than mobilizing agents in the electoral channel. The inherent dualism between *interest organization* and *voter aggregation* was built into the party structure and constituted a constant potential for internal conflicts. On the one hand, the party was a class organization represented by a national convention that elected and delegated power to the central leadership. On the other hand, it was a group of legislators in Parliament representing and drawing their legitimacy on their constituencies of social democratic voters. It is the tension and power relations between the two pillars of the social democratic party, the 'member party' and the 'voter party', which will be in focus in this section.[17]

Figure 6: The anatomy of the social democratic party

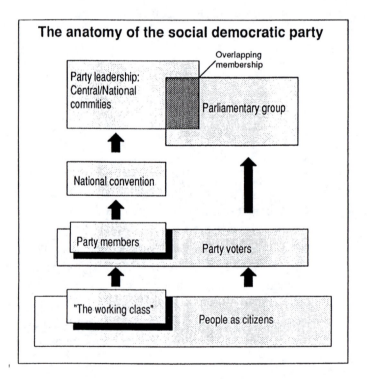

What was the nature of these tensions and in what way did the relative dominance of the two pillars influence the political course of the parties? Taking the mass-level as a point of departure, it is evident that the social democratic member organizations were never able to reach very far outside the working class proper. They evolved from the labour movements and preserved their class character through the entire study period. The electorate of the parties was, by contrast, a much more heterogeneous group. From the very beginning, the parties tried to mobilize support outside the limited strata of industrial workers and did also to an increasing degree succeed in these efforts. Thus, opposed to the 'member party' dominated by the working class, we find a 'voter party' representing a much broader and nondescript mass of 'underdogs', the urban and rural 'populace'.[18]

This contrast has an obvious parallel at the elite level. The *party leadership* represents the member organization, and their outlook and strategic choices will of course be dominated by their interpretations of this organization's interests. Although, *pace* Michels, we should not neglect the relative independence of the oligarchy, it is none-theless so that the imperative of being reelected will prevent the leadership from departing too far from the will of their organization. The *Members of Parliament*, by contrast, are elected by the social democratic voters. Although they are nominated by the member organization to fight for the party's politics in Parliament, they owe their position to their constituency. In order to be reelected, there will always be the need to please the electorate, and in order to become more powerful as a collective body to increase their representation. Thus, the mirror image of the contradiction at the mass level is the potential conflict between the twin goals of interest representation versus voter maximization at the elite level. To this observation we can of course add the conventional list of items deriving from the different environments and daily experiences of the two elites; the corridors of Parliament versus the Party Head-quarter's etc.

Based on this general model, we will suggest two propositions:

1   *The amount of internal conflict in the party depends on the*

level of integration between the two pillars, the 'member party' and the 'voter party'. At the mass level the important question is how much the composition of the constituency deviates from the membership. At the elite level, we must ask how much overlapping membership there is between the party leadership and the parliamentary caucus.

2   *Given a certain level of conflict, the overall course of the party depends on which of the two pillars is able to dominate the other.* The voter-dominated party will tend to be more moderate and have greater confidence in the parliamentary channel. The member-dominated party will, by contrast, show more suspicion of the parliamentary strategy, accompanied by a greater inclination for revolutionary activism.

The question of dominance is, among other factors a function of the size, achievements and status of the parliamentary caucus. A large group that is able to bring about practical and immediate reforms will, *pari passu*, be more influential than a small and powerless one. The question of size also has another connotation. A large group in Parliament gives positions and political outlets to a greater fraction of the party elite. It serves as a safety valve on the 'cadre-boiler'.

This brings us back to the discussion in the previous section about macro-political development and the parties' achievements in Parliament. The DNA's late appearance and subsequent frustrations in the parliamentary channel had an immediate effect on the *power relations* within the party. The striking discrepancy between the strength and ambitions of the 'member party' compared to the dwarfish and helpless character of the party's group in Parliament is a very significant trait of the DNA in the years of increased radicalism. The magnitude of this factor is clearly seen from Table 1 (which presents a condensed version of the information in Figure 4).

In the period 1911-1920 when the DNA on average commanded less than 20 seats in Parliament, the SD and SAP controlled an average of 33.4 and 76.8 seats respectively. Moreover, the two-chamber legislatures in Denmark and Sweden provided an additional arena for ambitious 'labour aristocrats'. As an illustration, the SAP held an average of 19.8 seats in the Upper Chamber during the same period.

Table 1

The average number of seats in Parliament *

Period	Denmark	Sweden	Norway
1881-1890	1.2	-	-
1891-1900	6.9	0.4	-
1901-1910	19.6	16.0	6.7
1911-1920	33.4	76.8	19.1
1921-1930	53.5	96.5	38.3
1931-1940	64.7	108.8	65.1

* In Denmark and Sweden, Lower Chamber only

However, numbers do not tell the whole story. To the crude calculations of seats we should add some qualitative observations: When the pre-parliamentary period of the DNA finally came to an end (sixteen years after the formation of the party), the breakthrough came as far from the centre of organizational strength as possible. The four mandates were all won in the northern periphery of the country, where the organizational penetration prior to the electoral victory (and for that matter also after it) was at a minimum.[19]

In fact, this represents *an extreme case of non-integration* between the two pillars of the party. At the mass level there was an immense distance between the smallholder and fishermen of northern Norway and the member organization which at this stage of development may be fully described in three words; urban, central and industrial. And, except for one of the candidates (who for a short time had served as editor of a minor Labour newspaper in Narvik), none of the fresh parliamentarians had any prior connections with the party elite.[20] No wonder the group was met with suspicion by the party leadership and had to spend its first encounter with the National Convention (1906) as targets of criticism for and lack of confidence in its records in Parliament.[21]

In Denmark and Sweden, on the other hand, the first seats were won in the capital cities by persons with leading positions in the party leadership. Moreover, the unquestioned social democratic leaders, Stauning and Branting, were also throughout their entire political career the parties' most prominent figures in Parliament. In Norway, it was the exception rather than the rule that members of the top leadership were parliamentarians. In fact the only party leader who for a short period combined his position with a seat in the legislature was Christian Holterman Knudsen (1912-1915).

This brings us to a more formal treatment of the question of *overlapping membership* between the two elite groups. As a point of departure we will argue that the influence of the 'voter party' to a large degree depends on the amount of integration at the top level of the party. If the positions in the party leadership are held by politicians who spend their days in Parliament, this will have a moderating effect on party politics. If, on the other hand, there are few overlapping memberships, this will breed suspicion and serve as an impetus to create mechanisms of control to make the parliamentarians toe the line.

At the top level of the DNA's organizational hierarchy we find a Central Committee and a National Committee, the former an executive branch of the latter. The Central Committee, whose members all had to reside in Oslo, was the real executive body of the party and usually met several times a month. The National Committee, which was the supreme party authority between the Conventions, had regional representation and met less frequently. Both Committees were elected at the Conventions, usually for a period of three years. Table 2 lists the total numbers of positions in the two committees along with information about the proportions of these positions held by members of Parliament.

The only conclusion that can be drawn from these data is that the general level of intra-party elite integration was quite low in the DNA. At no time did the parliamentarians control more than a quarter of the positions in the Central Committee; during most of the period it was of substantially less. The same is true of the larger National Committee except for the period 1912-1915 when the proportion of parliamentarians reached almost a third.

It is highly significant that this peak-level of overlapping membership inspired the National Convention to change its party statutes.

38

Table 2
Overlapping membership in the DNA leadership 1904-1936

Period	Central Committe			National Committee		
	No	MPs	%MPs	No	MPs	%MPs
1904-1906	9	0	0.0	23	1	4.3
1906-1909	9	1	11.1	19	1	5.3
1909-1912	9	2	22.2	19	2	10.5
1912-1915	9	2	22.2	19	6	31.6
1915-1918	9	2	22.2	19	2	10.5
1918-1919	9	0	0.0	19	0	0.0
1919-1920	9	0	0.0	19	0	0.0
1920-1921	9	1	11.1	23	1	4.3
1921-1923	11	2	18.2	25	6	24.0
1923	13	3	23.1	28	5	17.9
1923-1925	13	1	7.7	28	3	10.7 a)
	13	2	15.4	28	7	25.0b)
1925-1927	12	2	16.6	27	6	22.2
1927-1930	16	4	25.0	38	10	26.3
1930-1933	13	2	15.4	35	7	20.0
1933-1936	13	2	15.4	35	6	17.1

a) Period 1921-1924 b) Period 1924-1927

Since one of the National Committee's primary tasks was to control the parliamentarians, no Member of Parliament was to be elected to the Committee (Det norske Arbeiderparti 1915). The ruling was not changed until 1927, but according to the figures in Table 2, it was not always as effective as the architect behind it had intended.[22] However, the decision signals that the low level of elite integration in the DNA was not a coincidence. It was the result of a deliberate strategy to keep the party leadership as isolated as possible from the moderating influences of the parliamentarians.

Turning to Denmark, we find an organizational structure strikingly different from the Norwegian one (Dybdahl 1969). Until 1901 every Member of Parliament was by definition (!) a member of the party's General Council (*Hovedbestyrelsen*). The rest of this rather large body was elected directly by the regional member organizations, not by the National Convention as was the general rule in social democratic parties throughout Europe. From 1901 onwards, all the members of the General Council were elected by this procedure.

Table 3

Overlapping membership in the SD leadership 1888-1913

| Period | General Council | | |
	No	MPs	%MPs
1888	12	1	8.0
1890	17	3	17.6
1892	23	4	17.5
1894	23	5	21.7
1896	28	9	32.1
1898	37	12	32.4
1901	47	14	29.8
1903	45	11	24.2
1906	48	16	33.3
1908	51	16	31.4
1913	51	12	23.5

Unfortunately we have not been able to find exact information about the composition of the General Council for the entire period studied. However, the figures in Table 3 give us some indications about the amount of overlapping membership in the SD elite until 1913. The proportions of parliamentarians are generally somewhat higher than in the National Committee of the DNA, but they never exceed one third of the total membership. Our contention consequently not fully corroborated. However, it was important to notice that the MP proportion prior to 1903 was by definition a function of the party's electoral success. The very arrangement of automatic membership can in fact be regarded as a demonstration of the dominant position of the 'voter party'. The same conclusion can be drawn from the fact that the change of rules in 1901 did not lead to a major drop in the MP proportions. In addition, non-elected parliamentarians only lost their voting rights. They could still attend Council meetings. A proposal comparable to the 1915 decision in Norway was also turned down at the National Convention in 1908. Finally, the steady growth in the size of the General Council was generally a way to meet the various regional demands for central representation. It was not a method to limit the moderating influence of the parliamentarians.

The organizational structure of the SAP and the DNA was rather similar. An Executive Committee (*Verkställande utskottet*) over a Party Council (*Partistyrelsen*) served, by and large, the same functions as the DNA's Central and National Committees.[23] As for the Danish case, our information about overlapping membership remains limited. Available data are, however, convincing (see Table 4).

Table 4

Overlapping membership in the SAP leadership 1911-1918[24]

Period	Executive Committee			Party Council		
	No	MPs	%MPs	No	MPs	%MPs
1909-1911	-	-	-	23	9	39.1
1911-1913	7	6	85.7	23	16	69.6
1913-1915	7	6	85.7	23	14	60.9
1915-1918	7	6	85.7	23	14	60.9

During the period of centrifugal divergence between the Swedish and Norwegian parties, the parliamentarians were in complete control of the SAP leadership. They were dominant in the Party Council, but, even more significant, they commanded all but one of the positions in the more important Executive Committee. On top of this, Branting held the double position of party leader and leader in Parliament. In short, while the Norwegians cultivated the purity and independence of the party vanguard, the SAP leadership shuttled between Party Headquarters and Parliament. As far as elite integration is concerned, the two parties could hardly have been more different.

To complete the picture of intra-party dominance, some observations about the relative supremacy and formal independence of the leading bodies of the party should be added. In Norway the relations between the party leadership and the group in Parliament was codified at the National Convention in 1906.[25] The Convention,

41

which more or less had the character of a tribunal over the behaviour of the parliamentarians, demanded discipline and adopted severe mechanisms of control to eliminate future departures from the party line. From now on every question concerning parliamentary politics was to be discussed in joint meetings between the Central Committee and the parliamentarians, and in the case of dissension, was to be settled by majority vote.

As long as the Central Committee outnumbered the parliamentarians, these arrangements were sufficient. However, the situation changed and at the National Convention in 1915, the clause on majority voting was amended. From now on the Central or National Committees were given absolute supremacy in disputed questions. Furthermore, an additional arrangement was agreed in 1921, requiring every meeting of the parliamentary caucus to be attended by a member of the Central Committee. The party leaders' suspicion of the parliamentarians took on totalitarian features in this demand for continuous supervision.

The situation in the SAP is again strikingly different. The almost total absence of formal clauses regulating the relationship between the leadership and the parliamentarians is in fact an excellent demonstration of the comparatively low level of intra-party conflict. A diffuse formulation from 1911 stated that the parliamentary caucus *was responsible to* the party and was obliged once a year to report on their operations to the Party Council. No joint meetings were required, however, and no rules concerning the settlement of disputes were ever adopted. Ragnar Edenman's detailed study of the SAP caucus (1903-1920) holds that the group never really accepted the supremacy of the party leadership or the Convention. They regarded the Party Council as a consultative body but were never willing to bend to their decisions. He concludes:

> The fundamental questions concerning the relationship between the caucus and the party leadership were never really agreed upon. However, in practice it was always the parliamentarians' interpretations of the questions of authority that came out on top. This was reinforced by the fact that the parliamentarians little by little became dominant even in the Party Council (Edenman 1946, 285).

In short, whereas the leadership of the DNA totally dominated its MPs, the relationship in the SAP was almost the other way around. An integrated elite with positions in both Parliament and leadership was in full control of the party and made a common stand against the revolutionary and extraparliamentary agitation of the left wing opposition. In Norway, the major cleavage was not between a united elite and the opposition, but between the two pillars of the party; the 'member party' versus the 'voter party'. For several decades the 'member party' was the dominant body in this conflict.

The two parties' divergent approach to a common challenge may serve as conclusive evidence of the effects of these differences. In 1906 and 1909 respectively, the DNA and the SAP were faced with reforms implying fundamental electoral redistricting. In the SAP the reform caused an immediate adaptation of the party organization to the new electoral districts. Although revisions of the organization charter belonged to the prerogatives of the National Convention, the decision was taken solely by the Party Council. The necessity to tune the organizational structure to the needs of the 'voter party' had obviously higher priority than internal democratic procedures. As Lotta Gröning puts it:

> Changes in the organizational structure in accordance with the electoral system were self-evident. It was never an issue.... According to the party leaders, the restructuring was a natural, important and expedient way of securing an efficient and flexible instrument of mobilizing of the vote adapted to the new electoral rules (Gröning 1988, 34).

In the DNA, by contrast, even a minor concession to the needs of the 'voter party', was met by stubborn resistance from the member organization. Adaptation to the new and smaller electoral districts was accompanied by heated debates at several Congresses without this resulting in any uniform structure. Conserving an established organizational format carried more weight than the imperative of vote maximization in the electoral channel. This leaves no doubt as to how completely the 'member party' dominated the 'voter party' in the DNA.

Summary and conclusion

The origins and character of the early radicalism of the DNA is a perennial topic. Although most observers regard the change of leadership at the National Convention in 1918 as the radical turning point in the DNA's history, we have argued that the decisive steps were taken more than a decade earlier. With the early democratization of the Norwegian political system, the DNA was placed in a radically different strategic position from their Scandinavian counterparts. While the struggle for political reforms forced the SAP and the SD into prolonged collaboration with liberal parties, the early completion of the democratic struggle in Norway gave the DNA no excuses for postponing its march towards socialism. However, no natural allies were available to accompany the party on this march. Thus, the self-imposed political isolation of the DNA became a potent agency for its markedly greater inclination for revolutionary activism.

Although the constitution provided the Norwegian socialists with generous suffrage as well as parliamentary government, the electoral law worked in their disfavour. In spite of the apparent democratic character of the political system, the DNA's achievements in the parliamentary channel were thus rather meagre. This added to the frustration and isolation of the party and became a major source of the growing suspicion of the parliamentary channel.

However, macro-politics and the logic of threshold progression do not tell the entire story. Contrasting strategic situations may provide the necessary conditions for divergent actions, but not the complete and sufficient explanation. Such an explanation requires a shift of focus from the level of inter-party competition to the level of intra-party conflict. Our preliminary analysis of the relations between the twin 'pillars' of the social democratic party - the 'member party' and the 'voter party' - has justified such an approach.

Compared to their sister-parties, the DNA represents an extreme case of non-integration. An almost total absence of overlap between the leadership and the parliamentary caucus was accompanied by a considerable amount of distrust and conflict. The party cultivated the purity and independence of the party vanguard and spent an impressive amount of energy on handcuffing their parliamentarians.

Thus, a major source of Norwegian exceptionalism must be located in the extraordinarily dominant position of the 'member pillar' in the DNA's party structure.

Notes

1. Edvard Bull, member of the Central Committee and one of the party's most prominent ideologues, was in Stockholm when the decision was taken. It is said that, upon arrival at Oslo Central Station, he met his comrades with the question: 'Have you turned completely crazy?'

2. The cabinet's only important accomplishment was the release of Einar Gerhardsen (later Prime Minister) and Arnfinn Vik, who were serving prison sentences for anti-military activities.

3. This article, which appeared first in the liberal journal *Samtiden*, was reprinted and discussed in the entire Labour Party press. It served as the backbone of the party's propaganda programme over the next years.

4. In Denmark the SD supported Zahle's two cabinets (the Radical Party), the first in 1909, the second from 1913 to 1916. In a similar way, the SAP offered parliamentary support to Staaff's ministry (Liberal Party) which held office from 1911 to 1914.

5. The SD entered a government of national unity in 1916, but remained in office together with the Radicals when this grand coalition cabinet was dissolved two years later. In Sweden Branting and three other social democrats entered Edens liberal government in 1917.

6. The SAP formed three cabinets between 1920 and 1926. While the first (1920) resigned upon electoral defeat, both of its successors (1921-23 and 1924-26) fell on issues related to unemployment. The same is true for the first Danish social democratic cabinet which held office from 1924 to 1926.

7. Przeworski sees the decision to participate as the crucial event that conditioned the entire play: 'Once leaders of socialist parties decided to enter into electoral competition, the electoral system structured their future choices' (Przeworski A. and Sprague J. 1986, 2).

8. It should be emphasized at the outset that it is the variance in the commitment to electoral and ministerial socialism which is the key issue. The supplementary question, whether suspicion concerning the parliamentary strategy was accompanied by a more composite and heavily used inventory of extra-parliamentary methods, will not be discussed.

9. In Lipset's *Political Man* (1963) the Norwegian case serves as a prominent illustration of the causes of working class extremism. The same is true in William Kornhauser's *Mass Society* (Kornhauser 1960), where the example is used as a basis for generalizations about the effects of social dislocation.

10. When shifting the level of analysis to inter-municipal differences (within Norway), Lafferty was able to demonstrate a relationship between indicators of social disruption and labour radicalism (Lafferty 1971, 1974).

11. In fact, the only break in this lib-lab embracement can be found in Denmark in the wake of the 1901 franchise extension. The 'old' liberal party *Venstre* was then swapped for the splinter group *Radikale Venstre* as partner in the alliance.

12. This view is dominant in the Michels' tradition as well as in the more ideologically bent literature about the political leaders' conspiracy against the (objective) interests of the masses. Common to them all is the picture of the elite as a cohesive entity or united oligarchy.

13. The only exclusions were paupers and servants without their own household. In addition, the age requirement (30 years) was rather restrictive.

14. A resolution concerning the political mass strike was passed at The Inter-Scandinavian Labour Congress in Stockholm in 1897.

15. 'That a mass strike should be used to achieve universal suffrage was not questioned...' (Przeworski 1986, 20).

16. An interesting example of this dilemma is found in the industrial conflict in Sweden in 1909. The SAP, just about to reap the fruits of the major suffrage reform, invested a lot of energy on repudiating the accusation that the party had planned to use the strike as a weapon in the fight for political power (Tingsten 1967, 60-61).

17. There is a close relationship between this two-pillar model and the four-level model that Torgersen employs in his study. The 'voter party' contains the levels of representatives and voters, the 'member party' the levels of the member organization and the national convention.

18. At the level of socialist rhetoric, this contrast is of course reflected in the twin labels; 'class party' versus 'people's party'.

19. A fifth seat was acquired when one of the liberal candidates from Finnmark left his party and joined the DNA's group in mid-period.

20. To the geographical distance between the party leadership and their new candidates in Parliament, we can add the social distance. The group comprised a priest, a parish clerk, a peasant and a postman.

21. The parliamentarian leader, the parish priest Alfred Eriksen, was expelled from the party at the National Convention in 1912 due to his membership in *Riksmålsforbundet* (an organization defending one of the two competing language standards in Norway). Later on he joined the Conservative party.

22. An important reason for this is to be found in the timing of the National Convention compared to the parliamentary elections. The Conventions were usually held in the spring, several months prior to the elections.

23. It might, however, be important to notice that the Swedish organization was a bit more centralized than the Norwegian one. First, the SAP's Executive Committee had fewer members than DNA's Central Committee, second, the Party Council met less frequently than their comrades in the Norwegian National Committee, normally only once a year.

24. The data in this table was collected from Edenman (1922), p. 22.

25. The data about the formal relationship between the parlia-mentary group and the central leadership of DNA is based on Heidar (1974), pp. 31-4.

'A Nation of Workers and Peasants'

Ideology and Compromise in the Interwar Years

Lauri Karvonen

Introduction

The 1930s mark the period when social democracy became 'Scandinavian' in a specific sense. In many parts of Europe, democratic regimes succumbed to pressures from various authoritarian forces; in these countries, the left wing was a driving force in the polarization of society. In Scandinavia, on the other hand, social democracy found a workable solution to the dilemma of ideological distinctiveness versus practical achievements. It retained and even strengthened its position as *the* working class party. At the same time, it was able to commit itself to concrete promises; the basis of the welfare state was laid during this period. 'The Middle Way' and 'the Politics of Compromise' are well-known expressions used to portray this social democratic shift from a class party to a 'people's party'.

The crucial change in Scandinavian politics in the 1930s concerns *inter-party relations*. From a social democractic point of view, one might speak of still another reconciliation. By the end of the 1920s, social democrats throughout Scandinavia had reconciled themselves to the existing political *institutions*. They had a long record of electoral participation and parliamentary activity. In Denmark and Sweden, the social democrats had been major cabinet parties throughout the 1920s. The Tanner and Hornsrud cabinets, in Finland (1927) and Norway (1928) respectively, indicated that social democracts all over Scandinavia were also prepared to shoulder executive responsibilities.

The final step, however, was still to be taken. 'The politics of compromise' was not yet accepted as the main current of practical politics. The institutions had been recognized at least as necessary evils, but the four parties differed widely with regard to their ideological attitude to cooperation with other parties. It was in this respect that the 1930s signified a breakthrough. It is generally held that this change had far-reaching consequences for the position of social democracy and the development of the welfare state in Scandinavia (Castles 1978, 26-28; Esping-Andersen 1985, 71).

How was this crucial step taken? What were the similarities and differences between the four countries en route to this decision? What kinds of internal opposition did the parties encounter, and how was this resistance overcome? Finally, should the result be viewed in terms of national conditions, inter-Scandinavian exchange or the inexorable maturation of reformism?

These questions touch upon several propositions of theoretical value. Adam Przeworski (1987, 7-46) stresses the predetermining effect of the 'decision to participate'. Once the social democrats had decided to participate in elections they had to try to win voters beyond the working class core and seek a functioning relationship with other parties in Parliament. Elections are to be won, parliamentary influence to be maximized; this is in the nature of things. Can the deradicalization of Scandinavian social democracy be linked to a linear process of electoralization and parliamentarization? Were the Norwegian and Finnish parties in fact differently oriented towards elections and parliamentary work than their Danish and Swedish counterparts? Was there a parliamentary wing favouring inter-party cooperation and an ideological one opposing it?

Moreover, Przeworski hypothesizes that social democratic attempts to expand the electoral base beyond the working class entail a risk of losing working class support to the communists.

50

This risk becomes greater the larger the Communist Party is (1987, 104-111). It is quite conceivable that coalitions with bourgeois parties may involve similar risks; both voters and party members might choose the left exit. Was the course of moderation in the coalition politics of Scandinavian social democracy systematically related to the degree of competition from the far left? Was the danger of losing voters to the communists a major theme in the debate preceding the decisions?

It takes two to tango. Surely, what there were of coalitions and deals also depended on the bourgeois participants. Gösta Esping-Andersen holds an unambiguous view of this:

> In brief, the character of the Nordic peasantry offers the most convincing explanation of why Scandinavian social democracy has succeeded to such an extent, why the Nordic countries pioneered model welfare states and, ultimately ... came to converge politically (Esping-Andersen 1985, 88).

This strong statement needs clarification in the context of this study. Despite the crucial importance ascribed to the peasantry, it remains a curiously *static* 'background factor' in Esping-Andersen's analysis. How social democrats viewed the political role of the peasantry is, strictly speaking, not clear. Moreover, Esping-Andersen offers no account of the peasantry as a political actor. In this essay, one focus will be on the social democratic perceptions of the peasantry and the agrarian parties.

Social democrats as coalition partners

In a multi-party system, parties are always engaged in some form of parliamentary cooperation. Most of this interaction is of an ad hoc character. There is, however, also an intermediate position between temporary deals and outright cabinet coalitions. Especially in Denmark, where minority cabinets have been the rule rather than the exception, parties represented in Parliament engage in extensive deals with the cabinet. This secures the necessary majority in Parliament and gives the supporting party a channel of influence. These *forligs* were formed along two major axes in the 1920s. The conservatives and the agrarian liberals (*Venstre*) cooperated to establish a right-center current in politics, whereas the radical liberals and *Socialdemokratiet* turned to each other to form a center-left alliance. Such deals paved the way for the first social democratic cabinet headed by legendary Thorvald Stauning in 1924. It was a de facto majority cabinet until 1926, when the social democrats and the radical liberals disagreed on a tax issue and Stauning was forced to resign. Three years later, however, Stauning was able to form an outright cabinet coalition with the radical liberals. In January, 1933, the cabinet's parliamentary basis was decisively strengthened. Stauning entered into an extensive crisis agreement with *Venstre*. This deal, known as *Kanslergadeforliget* ('the Chancellor Street Agreement'), promised the farmers major subsidies as well as trade union restraint. In return, the agrarians agreed to a far-reaching crisis policy basically under social democratic leadership. In retrospect, it is generally held that *Kanslergadeforliget* represented the turning point between unstable minority parliamentarism and a long era of continuous welfare policies (Westergård Andersen 1976, 44-66; Esping-Andersen 1985, 76-77).

Though one of the major cabinet parties, the Swedish Social Democratic Party (SAP) was not involved in formalized cooperation with bourgeois parties. In fact, Swedish cabinets throughout the 1920s, irrespective of political makeup, rested on parliamentary minorities. Distinctive axes of cooperation such as those in Denmark did not come about. The cooperation between the liberals and the social democrats that had resulted in universal suffrage in 1921 did not reappear. The liberals preferred to maximize their influence through ad hoc cooperation with the right as well as the left. Their role was pivotal, which is why they could choose their partners according to the issue involved, and were able to present considerable demands to them (Stjernquist

1966, 121-122). It was the Great Depression that brought about a change. In 1932, the SAP campaigned on a platform stressing the need for a massive crisis policy. They won a new high of nearly 42 per cent of the vote and proceeded to form another minority cabinet. In connection with the parliamentary debate on their proposed crisis measures, they reached an agreement with the Agrarian Party. *Kohandeln* ('Cow Trade'), as this deal came to be called, provided strong protective measures for agriculture. The agrarians agreed to support massive public works programmes at market wages to alleviate acute unemployment. The deal secured the social democratic cabinet led by P.A. Hansson a workable majority, 218 of 380 seats in Parliament. In 1936, an outright cabinet coalition was formed between the two parties. The social democratic-agrarian axis remained, in different forms, the basis for Swedish politics up until the 1950s (Lindström 1985, 155-177; Lewin 1984, 159-199).

In Norway, cooperation with bourgeois parties was never seriously considered in the 1920s. After the Russian Revolution, the Norwegian Labour Party (DNA) abandoned its former emphasis on parliamentary tactics and affiliated with Comintern in 1919. The reformist minority left Labour to form a new Social Democratic Party. The DNA withdrew from Comintern in 1923 giving rise to still another split, as the orthodox wing formed a separate Communist Party. In 1927 the DNA merged with the social democrats, but the party remained isolated in Norwegian politics beyond the 1920s (see the chapter by Ryssevik). In March, 1935, however, following extensive social democratic proposals on economic crisis policies, the DNA and the Agrarian Party reached an agreement which included a large scale public works programme as well as extensive new subsidies to agriculture. This crisis agreement (*Kriseforliket*) proved to be the springboard to a long-lasting social democratic dominance in Norwegian politics (Lorenz 1974, 39-55; Castles 1978, 26-27).

The Finnish social democrats had an even more disadvantageous starting position than their Norwegian brethren. Finland's independence from Russia in December, 1917, was followed by a civil war between bourgeois 'Whites' and socialist 'Reds', ending in the defeat of the latter in May, 1918. Two years later, the social democrats lost a considerable proportion of their members and followers as a revolutionary party called the Socialist Workers' Party was formed. The social democrats (SDP) continued to control a majority of the socialist vote, but the communists became dominant in the unions. The SDP was up against both a hostile right wing and a large communist rival at the same time. Although no formalized deals came about, the social democrats engaged in tacit parliamentary cooperation mainly with the political center. The aim was to prevent a united front of all bougeois parties; indeed, the bourgeois parties remained split throughout the 1920s. In December, 1926, this enabled the SDP to form a minority cabinet under the leadership of Väinö Tanner. Although few social democrats described this exercise in ministerial socialism as a resounding success, it was far from the fiasco the Hornsrud cabinet in Norway proved to be. The SDP opted for a low-key strategy and stayed in power a little over a year, which was in fact more than the life expectancy of a Finnish cabinet in the 1920s (Lindman 1940). Nevertheless, the final rapprochement across the socialist-nonsocialist divide had to wait for still another decade. At the beginning of the 1930s, Finland experienced a strong right wing authoritarian current known as the Lapua Movement. Having managed to have communism outlawed, Lapua turned against social democracy and parliamentarism (Karvonen 1988, 18-29). The political and economic crisis gradually brought the Agrarian Party closer to the SDP. In September 1936 the two parties agreed on a programme emphasizing the protection of democracy as well as social and economic reforms (Suomi 1971). Six months later, they formed a cabinet together with the liberals. The *Punamulta* ('Red Soil') agreement signified an entirely new constellation in Finnish politics (Karvonen 1988 b).

Given the starting point after World War I and the record of parliamentary and cabinet participation that followed in the 1920s, one might have expected a less identical political outcome in the four countries in the short time span between 1933 and 1937. Even in this short account, Denmark stands out as the natural cradle of social democratic pragmatism in Scandinavia. The

Danish party had not only an impressive record of parliamentary activity and cabinet responsibilities; it was also well experienced in cooperation with bourgeois parties. In Sweden, there was more novelty to the deal, especially given the traditional animosity between the social democrats and agrarians. Norway and Finland are more unlikely candidates in a historical compromise, Finland because of the traumatic civil war experience and Norway due to the Comintern period of the DNA and the ensuing political isolation of the party. In sum, there was little in the position of social democracy in the 1920s that suggested the political convergence of the 1930s. In terms of historical background, the Red-Green crisis agreements appear far from self-explanatory.

The defeat of ideology?

Denmark

Social democrats in Denmark have worried remarkably little about questions of an ideological nature. This is all the more surprising because Danish social democrats, quite unlike their Scandinavian brethren, received pervading ideological impulses from Germany. In fact, large portions of the Gotha and Erfurt programmes were directly translated into Danish and adopted as party platforms. At the same time, the overwhelming concern of *Socialdemokratiet* was with practical matters - social and political reforms, economic conditions and electoral progress. Ideology remained a convention rather than a guiding instrument (Togeby 1968, 7-10; Bryld 1976, 128-130)

The seemingly effortless development towards the Red-Green compromise of 1933 can not be separated from the ideological flexibility evident in Danish social democracy already in the 19th century. To a large extent, what there was of ideological - 'leftist' - resistance against cooperation with bourgeois parties was removed already at that time. In 1889, the question of electoral cooperation with the Liberal Party split the social democrats and led to the exclusion of the 'revolutionaries' (Bertolt et al. 1954, 194-208). The importance of this incident can hardly be over-estimated; the party leadership considered cooperation with the liberals important enough to risk a party split.

The final battle over the question of cooperation versus con-frontation was caused by the 1915 constitutional revision, which introduced universal suffrage into Denmark. A radical wing largely identical with the youth organization of the Party demanded a shift to a purely social democratic electoral strategy. The party leadership replied that the question of electoral alliances was a practical, not an ideological matter. The 1916 Party Congress in fact explicitly gave its blessing to the idea of a coalition cabinet with the radical liberals. The youth organiza-tion kept attacking the party for its support of a radical liberal cabinet, especially the fact that Stauning had joined the cabinet as Minister of Controls. The 1919 Party Congress finally decided that enough was enough. The youth organization representing some 11,000 members was excluded from the party and went on to form the Danish Communist Party (Bertolt et al. 1955, 34; Bryld 1976, 44-45).

Thus, by 1920 *Socialdemokratiet* had fought two battles over cooperation with bourgeois parties. In both instances, the party leadership had preferred to let the radicals go.

Consequently, Danish social democracy in the 1920s displays all the features associated with a reformist party. The parliamentary cooperation with the radical liberals remained basically unquestioned. In the ideological debate, an increasing consensus manifested itself about the nature of the party; the Social Democratic Party was a *people's party* rather than a class party. The daily newspaper *Social-Demokraten* commented on the 1924 Party Congress as follows (Togeby 1974, 208):

> Social democracy has through fifty years of growth and maturation increasingly become a People's Party. The political and social course which from the very beginning was our ideal attracts increasing numbers of people...also from outside the circle of the actual wage earners.

56

In connection with the 1929 election campaign, this theme was echoed by Stauning in a radio speech (Togeby 1974, 208):

> ...it is now seen more clearly than before that this party is the real People's Party. It is the party whose programme is designed to the advantage of everyone doing useful work - be it intellectual or physical.

This ideological development proceeds without noteworthy internal opposition throughout the 1920s and into the following decade. It is paralleled by a similar pragmatic and conciliatory attitude in specific areas, including agriculture, where private ownership of land is acknowledged as the self-evident foundation. Hitler's *Machtergreifung* also moderated the traditionally restrictive social democratic attitude to defence spendings as well (Westergård Andersen 1976, 77-78).

It is therefore not much of a surprise that *Kanslergadeforliget* stirred little ideological debate among Danish social democrats. The agreement was seen as yet another deal in a series of parliamentary compromises in which the social democrats had been involved for several decades. Nevertheless, it is evident that they were aware of the need for a rapprochement with the agrarians, a party which was all but uncontested as a representative of Danish farmers. The driving force was not only the need to create a functioning crisis policy. There was also a risk that the extreme right wing would gain support among the farmers (Lindström 1985, 137). It was equally imperative for the Agrarian Party to act resolutely in the face of an increasingly volatile electorate.

The economic depression and the fascist threat must be seen as the immediate forces behind the Red-Green compromise in Denmark. The deal as such was not a source of ideological disagreement among social democrats. The party hardly risked an internal split over this issue. The decisive battles over deals across the socialist-bourgeois divide had been fought - and won - years ago. The response of the voters was enough to convince any remaining sceptic. In 1919, when the final split over coali-

57

tions occurred, *Socialdemokratiet* had 28.5 per cent of the vote. In 1924, when Stauning first took office with radical liberal support, the party's share had increased to 36.6 per cent. Two years after *Kanslergadeforliget*, after a campaign based on the famous working programme 'Denmark for the People', Stauning led his party to an all time high of 46.1 per cent of the vote. The appearance of the communists in Parliament in the 1930s only served to strengthen the social democratic commitment to the mainstream of Danish politics (Svensson 1974, 136-142).

In a similar vein, *Kanslergadeforliget* did not entail any basic reappraisal of the agrarians as political actors. There was simply no doubt about the democratic nature of *Venstre* among the social democrats; the absence of such assertions in the empirical material cannot be interpreted in any other way, nor was there a widespread impression that *Kanslergadeforliget* was a historical turning point in the relations between the two parties. The deal was based on the notion that workers and farmers had partly converging interests in the area of crisis policy. In 1934, Stauning characterized the agreement by saying that the cabinet 'has made use of the agrarian *Venstre* to produce appropriations for crisis policy'(Samråd i kristid, 31). An understatement or not, these words implied that the parties would continue with 'politics as usual' once the crisis had been weathered.

Sweden

The immediate background of interwar politics in Sweden was strikingly similar to the Danish situation. In 1917, the liberals and the social democrats formed a coalition cabinet which was to carry out the final democratization of the Swedish form of government as well as to institute several major social reforms. The youth organization of the SAP opposed this cooperation vehemently. The result was that a major part of the organization left the SAP to form a more radical party. Some 10,000 members, 15 MPs and two party districts were lost to the 'revolutionaries' (Elvander 1980, 46; Gröning 1988, 158).

From here on, however, the ideological course of Swedish social democracy diverged from that in Denmark for many years to come. The 1920 Party Congress came to an unprecedented degree to be dominated by the question of socialization. This new ideological orientation was quite prevalent among the congress delegates, although it was apparent that 'socialization' meant a variety of things ('guild socialism', 'state control, 'cooperatives' etc.) to them. The comprehensive programme revision which ensued was studded with Marxist slogans:

> Social democracy... wants to restructure the economic organization of the bourgeois society totally and to carry out the social emancipation of the exploited classes...
> This goal cannot be attained without political struggle. Social democracy therefore wants to... organize the exploited classes... attain political power and... carry out the socialist organization of society (Tingsten 1941, 251-252).

The 1920 programme set the stage for the ideological course of the 1920s, and it was therefore also central from the point of view of coalition politics. Turning to factors that made this development different to that in Denmark, the sheer *potential* for profound ideological discourses can hardly be overlooked. In contrast to Danish social democracy, the SAP had a long intellectual tradition. Its leadership had been and still was dominated by intellectuals and academics. Branting, Karleby, Wigforss, Sandler and Möller are names of theoreticians and political influentials at the same time. Secondly, the disagreement with the liberals in the 1917 cabinet came to coincide with the definite breakthrough of mass democracy in Sweden. Irritation with interparty cooperation was matched by the prospect of a rapid development towards a socialist majority in Parliament (Tingsten 1941, 241). Finally, the fact that social democratic losses to the far left had been much more substantial in Sweden than in Denmark (the Swedish communists mustered an average of 5.4 per cent of the vote in the 1920s compared to 0.4 per cent in

Denmark) may have made the SAP wary of ideologically novel moves.

However, this ideological preoccupation left limited traces in practical politics. The social democratic minority cabinets that ruled between 1920 and 1926 (with the exception of Trygger's conservative cabinet in 1923) emphasized their role as a 'popular national government'. The bills put to Parliament concerning social and economic reforms were at all times within the confines of what bourgeois parties at least were prepared to debate seriously. Ideologically central issues were avoided with reference to the impossibility of creating majorities for such reforms. In a couple of important cases concerning socialization and industrial democracy the cabinet appointed investigative commissions with representatives from the various parties. These commissions proved to be extraordinarily tenacious; the Socialization Commission sat from 1920 to 1934 without achieving anything concrete. At social democratic party congresses, these commissions were frequently referred to by the party leadership: 'We have to await the report of the Socialization Commission'. It is difficult to escape the impression that the commissions were a conscious strategy on the part of the cabinet (largely identical with the party leadership) enabling them to have their cake and eat it. They pacified the party congresses demanding socialist reforms; at the same time, they were far from revolutionary spearheads in the eyes of bourgeois parties.

By 1926, however, social democratic minority cabinets had reached the end of their tether. They had clashed with the nonsocialist parties concerning unemployment policy. Their minority position had gradually disclosed the distance between ideology and reality. Moreover, the unquestioned leader of the party and a long time prime minister, Hjalmar Branting, had died in 1925. In opposition, the SAP gradually moved towards a more radical posture. This change was evidenced at the 1928 Party Congress in the form of a more confrontationist attitude vis-à-vis other parties. At the ideological level, one innovation may be noted. In a parliamentary speech in 1928, party leader P.A. Hansson coined the expression People's Home (*Folkhemmet*). He likened the State to a home:

> The foundation of the Home is the spirit of community and togetherness. The Good Home has no privileged or underprivileged members, no favorites or stepchildren... Applied to the great People's and Citizens' Home this would mean the abolition of all social and economic barriers which now divide the citizens into privileged and underprivileged, ruling and dependent, rich and poor... The Swedish society is not yet a Citizens' Home (Tingsten 1941, 307-308).

The novelty of this rhetoric lies in the emphasis on the *State*. It is no longer the exploited masses but the State that is to have economic power in society. Furthermore, 'class' has increasingly been replaced by 'the People' or 'the Citizens'. This change did not, however, signal a willingness to compromise with other parties. Quite the contrary, in the 1928 elections they were challenged more clearly than before with far-reaching demands concerning expropriation of private property and radical tax reforms (Hamilton 1989, 166-167).

This was to be the last time that the SAP campaigned with socialization as a major theme. The party lost fourteen of its 156 seats in Parliament, while the conservatives grew from 109 to 122 seats. But it was *not* the last time that the 'People's Home' and the 'Good State' were to be central themes.

It was clear that it was the economic radicalism rather than the new emphasis on the People and the State that had repelled the electorate. Hansson now embarked on a straightforward critique of ideological orthodoxy: it was high time to abandon the idea of a class struggle. The label of a People's Party was to be the only trade mark of the party, and social democrats should do their utmost to win over the peasants and the middle class to the party. Although this self-examination was evident immediately after the 1928 defeat, the more orthodox line by no means lost all of its support. In 1931, when a report from the Socialization Commission was discussed, an influential faction stressed socialization as a leading principle for the SAP. When the Great Depression hit Sweden, the SAP had reached an ideological stalemate. The 'People' and the 'State' hinted at a new ideological era, 'Socialization' lingered on as a definite cleavage between the SAP and bourgeois Sweden.

The stalemate was to persist for another two years. On the one hand, the party proceeded to design a parliamentary proposition concerning a comprehensive crisis policy with special emphasis on massive government relief work to alleviate unemployment. On the other hand, a sizable faction in the party insisted that the depression offered a historical chance for a transition to socialism. The parliamentary proposition was defeated, but it became the basis for the 1932 election campaign. Hansson managed to present the bourgeois rejection of the crisis measures as the main campaign weapon against them:

> In the face of the resistance of the bourgeois majority against this democratic policy, we appeal to the Swedish People. We appeal for support for a policy which will give effective aid to the needy and the oppressed. Let us unite behind a political course which wants to defend and advance democracy in all areas to secure the common good, irrespective of group or class interests (Tingsten 1941, 337).

Both the Party Congress and the subsequent election campaign were vague regarding socialism and socialization. Tingsten: 'In 1932, just as in 1920, the Socialization Commission worked as a kind of ideological substitute for socialization' (1941, 339). The capitalist system was given the blame for the crisis, and a socialist future was alluded to in vague terms. At the same time, the necessity to act *now* to meet the crisis was underlined.

The response of the voters was unambiguous. The SAP reached a new high of 41.7 per cent of the vote, whereas the conservatives and the liberals suffered bitter losses. As the agrarians made considerable gains, there was no clear electoral basis for a bourgeois front. The SAP re-entered cabinet politics and proceeded to present an expanded version of its crisis policy to Parliament.

The initial bourgeois response indicated that all three parties were intent on defeating the proposition as well as the cabinet. In the course of the negotiations, however, a palace revolution of sorts took place within the Agrarian Party; party leader Olsson of Kullenbergstorp was de facto dethroned, and the agrarians entered into bilateral negotiations with the cabinet. The social democrats were indeed accomodating; among other things, the tax on margarine, refuted as an absurdity by the 1932 Party Congress, was included in the deal. On 18 June 1933, the crisis agreement was passed by a clear majority in Parliament (Nyman 1944, 22-73, 87-88; Lewin 1984, 180-184).

The deal having been concluded, Hansson engaged in an extensive rationalization of the new alliance. He found it extraordinarily important that two large parties which had previously fought each other had come to an agreement on crucial issues. Social democrats and agrarians represented the two main productive groups in society. 'Nothing is more natural than a collaboration between these two great segments of the citizenry, who share a democratic character and a love of freedom'. Moreover, Hansson pointed to the cooperation between the 'working segments of the population' as a *leitmotif* of SAP ideology over many years (Tingsten 1941, 361).

What he did not mention was that the deal in fact had *substituted parties for classes*. Certainly, social democratic programmes and manifestos had been envisaging the unification of workers, small farmers and the urban middle classes for quite some time. The premise had been, however, that this unification was to be carried out within the framework of the SAP. In terms of inter-party relations, it implied a zero-sum game; other parties would lose voters and the social democrats would gain the majority necessary for the socialist transformation of the society.

The deal with the agrarians was, in an accentuated manner, the work of the cabinet and the parliamentary group; this is even more true of the Agrarian Party. What followed in terms of a theoretical rationalization was nothing less than an ideological *fait accompli*. It had not been preceded by either a renewed orientation towards inter-party cooperation or a reappraisal of the Agrarian Party as a political actor. Like a bolt from the blue, this party emerged as the *Ersatz* of the 'farming population', united with the social democrats through its 'democratic character and love of freedom'. *Tout est pour le mieux dans le meilleur des mondes possibles!*

Norway

It is only with the benefit of hindsight that we can concentrate on the DNA when analysing the ideological development of *social democracy* in Norway before the mid-1930s. The 1925 programme is a far cry from the reformist approach:

> The Norwegian Labour Party is a communist party. It sees as its mission the organization of the working class in order, by the means of class struggle, to both defend the daily interests of this class and to carry on the struggle until the working people have become masters over the means of production and free from capitalist exploitation... (Lorenz 1972, 184).

Throughout the 1920s, Norway was a politically polarized society. The left wing, divided though it was into three parties until 1927, was dominated by a revolutionary line totally unacceptable to bourgeois Norway. When the reformist wing of the DNA rejoined the party that year, it was not the result of any noticeable reorientation towards reformism on the part of the DNA. Rather, the driving forces were the unions (Elvander 1980, 75). The political division of the working class had been very problematic from their point of view. Originally, the idea was that all three parties should unite under the auspices of a new Labour Party. The communists (NKP) refused to accept the terms of the deal, which left the DNA and the Reformists as parties to the unification. The Unification Congress of 1927 was preceded by

64

widely differing demands from these two wings as well. Although these were far from settled, the unification entailed some clear concessions on the part of the revolutionary wing. Party leader Oscar Torp underlined that the unity of the organization was more important than 'all theories, doctrines and dogmas'. The principal programme adopted by the congress took a major step towards a more parliamentary attitude, as the main goal of the party was to

> ... win the entire working population and thereby the *majority* of the people for its socialist world view (Lorenz 1972, 178, emphasis in original).

The parliamentary elections held later that year gave encouraging results. In 1924, when the DNA and the social democrats had run on separate tickets, their share of the vote had added up to 27.2 per cent. Now, the DNA won no less than 36.8 per cent of the vote; at the same time, the communists were losing support. As the three bourgeois parties failed to agree on a cabinet solution, the DNA, by now far the largest party, announced its willingness to form a minority cabinet. This decision was preceded by considerable disagreement in the DNA. Characteristically enough, the cabinet was to be led by Hornsrud, a spokesman of parliamentarism, whereas the cabinet *programme* was designed by Edvard Bull who was against this experiment in ministerial socialism. This declaration stated flatly that the objective of the DNA was to achieve a socialist society in Norway. The cabinet was aware of the fact that, being a minority cabinet, it lacked the means to do this immediately. Nevertheless its activity would be aimed at preparing such a transition in the future (Bull 1947, 309-310).

To be sure, this preamble was followed by eleven paragraphs on concrete measures against unemployment and for the advancement of, inter alia, agriculture. But the shock of the introductory formulations was more than enough for bourgeois Norway. The conservatives, liberals and agrarians united against this 'class government', and threw Hornsrud out of office. Far from being a step towards moderation, the cabinet episode strengthened the opponents of parliamentarism in the DNA. The next party congress held in 1930 was characterized by a growing suspicion against the parliamentary strategy. The programme adopted deleted the 1925 characterization of the DNA as a communist party. On the other hand, parliamentary participation was reduced to merely one among a host of instruments of class struggle. Nothing in the 1930 programme hints at the intrinsic value of democratic participation, let alone inter-party cooperation. In fact Lorenz points out (1972, 186) that the 1930 programme bears witness to an attempt to forestall communist criticism. References to 'experience from Marxist struggle in all countries' and the necessity to utilize 'the organized power of the entire working class' are examples that clearly reflect anticipated criticism for class compromises. What made the 1930 programme most controversial, however, was the fact that the cautious 1927 formulation on a parliamentary emphasis ('to win the majority of the people') was deleted (Bull 1947, 315-316).

Like the cabinet programme of 1928, the 1930 party programme was *gefundenes Fressen* for the bourgeois parties. In the elections held in October, 1930, they depicted the DNA as a champion of a 'Russian situation' and of a one-party dictatorship. The DNA lost twelve seats, and its share of the vote fell from around 37 to less than 32 per cent of the vote. The communists fared even worse, losing half of their electorate and their parliamentary representation *altogether*.

The mutual exclusiveness of revolution and parliamentarism has rarely been portrayed as distinctively as in the post-election Norway of 1930. What followed in terms of an ideological debate bore a striking resemblance to Sweden in particular. For those who doubted the benefits of cooperation between classes, the State now became the instrument through which social democrats could gain power. Ole Colbjörnsen coined the expression 'nation-wide industrialization' (*nasjonal fabrikkreisning*). Through government measures, the Norwegian social structure was to be rapidly altered in favour of the DNA. Other debaters, in particular Halvar Lange, stressed the need to win the rural population for the party; this was the only way to gain a parliamentary majority. It was time to accept the notion of the DNA not as a class party but a People's Party of all 'working classes' (Kjeldstadli 1978, 122-135).

The ensuing debate must be one of the most meticulous scrutinies of rural class structure ever performed by a political party. At least seven different agricultural classes were found to exist, and even among independent farmers one could distinguish between five or six different strata. While a consensus gradually emerged concerning the need to engage in cooperation with rural segments, the actual delineation of the DNA's potential rural allies remained diffuse. Most debaters stressed the gap between farmers with medium-sized and large farms on the one hand and the working classes on the other (Kjeldstadli 1978, 46-59).

Meanwhile, an important change took place in the attitudes of the labour unions. Their confidence in direct action gradually crumbled in the face of the economic depression and government repression. By 1932, they were prepared to accept the so-called Boycott Laws proposed by the agrarian cabinet. These entailed severe restrictions on union actions. Simultaneously, the unions explicitly renounced extra-parliamentary actions. The altered position of the communists was an important precondition for this reorientation. They had not only lost their seats in Parliament; their influence among the unions had also waned considerably. The social democratic majority no longer needed to wage a two-front war in the labour market (Lorenz 1974, 23-25).

The 1933 Party Congress has been called the 'Great Reformist Congress of the DNA' (Lindström 1985, 168). Revolutionary strains were conspicuous in their absence, and the ambition to 'gain the support of the majority of the people' was reinstated as a central goal.

Moreover, there was a general consensus about the need for government measures to combat the economic crisis. A comprehensive crisis plan became central in the electoral campaign of 1933. At the same time, suggestive electoral posters portraying a worker and a farmer shaking hands under the heading 'Democracy' were distributed throughout the country. The response of the voters was overwhelming: 22 new seats and a new high of more than forty per cent of the vote. At the same time, the *entire* bourgeois bloc suffered losses. The social democrats declared that they were entitled to form a cabinet. However, as none of the bourgeois parties was prepared to support a social democratic cabinet, the result was a liberal minority cabinet under the leadership of Johan Mowinckel. This cabinet came to sit a little over a year. Its crisis policy received increasing criticism from the farmers. Meanwhile, the DNA's parliamentary group, and Johan Nygaardsvold in particular, was seeking parliamentary backing for a social democratic cabinet. Kjelstadli (1978, 295) underlines that this took place independently of the party executive which did not believe in the prospect of a social democratic cabinet. As the liberals were the cabinet party and an alliance with the conservatives was out of the question, Nygaardsvold was left with the agrarians as the only possibility. In March, 1935, the agrarians and the social democrats joined forces to defeat Mowinckel's budget proposition. Four days later, Nygaardsvold formed a social democratic cabinet. The cabinet launched a comprehensive crisis plan, including an extra budget of 34 million *kroner* for agriculture, forestry and the fisheries. A new sales tax, a traditional agrarian proposal hitherto rejected as a 'poor man's tax' by the DNA, was to provide a financial basis for the plan. *Kriseforliket* gave the social democratic cabinet a de facto majority, but the cost in the form of concessions to the agrarians was considerable.

The Red-Green compromise of 1935 was highly surprising in view of the previous antagonism between the parties. In 1931, a leading DNA activist had characterized the agrarians as 'our fiercest and bitterest enemies'; two years later, the agrarians were found to be the very core of reactionary politics (Kjeldstadli 1978, 294-295). Naturally, the about-face in 1935 had to do with the need to counteract the depression as well as the threat from the extreme right wing. Still, the change would not have been possible without some essential ideological factors.

The major ideological change preceding *kriseforliket* was, of course, the return to an openly declared parliamentary strategy at the 1933 congress. This not only influenced the voters; it also gave the parliamentary group a stronger platform. Here, it is important to note that the parliamentary caucus in Norway, as opposed to the Swedish case, was clearly separated from the party leadership (Bull 1959, 124-125). This lack of overlap made it possible for the parliamentary group to pursue negotiations which would have been extremely difficult for the party executive to market to the DNA organization. Thus, the risk inherent in the deal was not taken by the DNA leadership personally. Finally, the debate on 'State socialism' and on winning the rural population had opened the door to entirely new issues. Although nothing had been said about inter-party coalitions, the agreement could be presented in terms of this preceding debate. As in Sweden, the compromise came to be the 'operationalization' of an ideological discussion based on the notion of a purely social democratic strategy.

One can hardly speak of a reappraisal of the Agrarian Party before the 1935 agreement; in fact, the social democrats largely refrained from such declarations even after the deal had been concluded. The democratic orientation of the agrarians had long been acknowledged by social democrats, but this was more often interpreted in *negative* rather than in positive terms: the agrarians harboured 'parliamentary illusions'. This was positive insofar as it made them less susceptible to fascism but negative since they were blind to the 'real nature' of power in a capitalist society (Kjeldstadli 1978, 110-111).

What Nygaardsvold did in 1935 was not a *result* of a new social democratic strategy. Rather, it was an instrument by which a new strategy was brought about. It was an independent move on the part of the parliamentary group of the DNA; its acceptability was open to testing. The 1936 election provided that test, and the result (42.5 per cent of the vote) was in favour of Nygaardsvold. At the same time, the economy picked up considerably. To what extent that improvement was due to *Kriseforliket* will remain a moot point. As for Nygaardsvold, he had acquired an aura of success which was hard to resist.

Finland

The socialist defeat in the 1918 Civil War made the situation in Finland radically different from the rest of Scandinavia. Bourgeois Finland was likely to meet anything resembling a socialist movement with uncompromising resistance.

Those social democrats who reorganized the SDP after the Civil War had explicitly renounced any attempt at armed revolution and remained personally outside the war. From the beginning, therefore, the 'new' Social Democratic Party had a number of influential leaders committed to reformism and parliamentarism. The leader of this orientation was Väinö Tanner.

As early as 1919, the social democrats were negotiating with the liberals with a view to forming a coalition cabinet. The SDP had done surprisingly well at the elections held that year (80 out of 200 seats). Moreover, the party had cooperated with the political centre to produce a republican form of government instead of the monarchy propounded by the conservatives and the Swedish Peoples' Party. However, these negotiations led nowhere, partly due to the social democratic demands, partly because of a fear of reprisals from the right wing (Soikkanen 1975, 338).

The demands which had been too far-reaching for the liberals reflected the fact that the reformist wing had gradually been joined by a more radical group in the SDP. In fact, there was a clear attempt at a communist takeover in 1919-20. This internal conflict entailed a temporary programmatic radicalization clearly manifested at the 1919 Party Congress. Among other things, participation in cabinets could be considered only 'under exceptional circumstances' (Kettunen 1986, 289-290). Moreover, a 'left-right' division was created inside the party even beyond the showdown with the communists. Nevertheless, the majority took an uncompromising stance towards the communists, who left the party in 1920 to form the Socialist Workers' Party.

A 'centrist' movement in the SDP (as opposed to the reformists as well as the communists) had wanted to avoid the split by making concessions to the communists. In the party as a whole, it failed to convince the majority. However, the social democratic leaders followed this strategy in the labour union movement. At the 1920 Trade Union Congress, the communists were allowed to take over all the leading positions. The unions became part and parcel of the communist movement for the entire decade (Viitala 1988, 40-41, 159).

Gradually, reformism gained ground at the ideological level. The 1922 Party Congress abandoned several Marxist dogmas, including the theories of impoverishment and the collapse of capitalism. More importantly, it was underlined that small farming, including small-scale forestry, was to be based on private ownership. Later that year, a communist proposal for an electoral alliance was unanimously rejected (Soikkanen 1975, 399-407). The 1922 elections gave the left somewhat more than the social democratic share of the vote three years earlier (39.9 as compared to 38 per cent). The social democratic share was 25.1, while the communists got 14.8 per cent of the vote.

However, the opposition against Tanner had by no means disappeared. At the 1926 Party Congress, 53 delegates wanted Tanner re-elected as Party Chairman. 52 delegates voted for Matti Paasivuori who, although no outspoken 'Marxist', lacked a clear reformist profile. Based on the feebleness of his support, Tanner withdrew his candidacy. Paasivuori was elected; moreover, K.H. Wiik, the leading Marxist theoretician of the party, was elected Party Secretary.

Tanner's withdrawal from the chairmanship increased the distance between the parliamentary group of the SDP and the party organization at large. In Parliament, Tannerian reformism was largely unquestioned, and the social democrats continued their policy of ad hoc cooperation with the political centre and the Swedish Peoples' Party. The aim of this cooperation was mainly to keep the bourgeois parties divided among themselves and to support centrist cabinets against the conservatives. The nonsocialist parties did indeed remain divided, and in December, 1926, their stalemate resulted in a social democratic minority cabinet led by Tanner. The decision had been preceded by feelers directed towards both liberals and agrarians, but neither of these parties seemed willing to join forces with the socialists (Lindman 1940, 15-16).

The Tanner cabinet was not uncontroversial in the SDP, but one can hardly speak of a determined opposition against 'ministerial socialism', either. The attitude was rather one of 'wait and see'. Meanwhile, internal working groups were busy with questions typical of Scandinavian social democracy at that time. Socialization, state socialism, pacifism and defence policy were some topics which gave rise to resolutions at party congresses. The late 1920s brought clearly diverging lines of development to the parliamentary and internal party arenas. In the former, the SDP operated from a clearly reformist platform seeking ad hoc support from the liberals, the agrarians and the Swedes. Communist opposition to the Tanner cabinet - for instance, in the form of the wave of strikes in 1927 - only added to this moderation in cabinet and Parliament. In the internal arena, a gradual shift towards a more theoretically Marxist position took place, though with numerous deviations from the orthodox line. The 1930 Party Congress portrayed this paradoxical development clearly. On the one hand, Tanner regained a definite hold of the party organization by, inter alia, handpicking the new chairman (Kaarlo Harvala, one of his closest associates). On the other hand, the new Party Platform stressed the socialization of major industries and large agricultural estates, and linked the threat of war to the capitalist system (Soikkanen 1975, 499-506).

Meanwhile, reality intervened! In 1929, the social democratic labour union activists finally left the communist-controlled Trade Union Congress and formed a network of separate social democratic unions. Shortly thereafter, an anti-communist wave pervaded the country in the form of the Lapua Movement. Lapua rapidly gained momentum, and it was initially welcomed by the entire bourgeois Finland. In a fairly direct manner, Lapua dictated cabinet formations and influenced the outcome of the extraordinary elections of October 1930. These elections produced the parliamentary majority necessary for the enactment of the 'Communist Laws', which rendered all communist organizations, including their labour unions, unlawful. The SDP was left as the sole contender on the left wing of Finnish politics (Rintala 1962, 164-190).

The position of the social democrats vis-à-vis Lapua was openly critical from the start, although they underlined that the preceding subversive activity of the communists should be given part of the blame (Tanner 1966, 107-109). Having had communism legislated out of politics, Lapua started to attack social democracy and the parliamentary system as a whole. The centrist, notably agrarian, support for Lapua diminished sharply. When the movement was outlawed in 1932, after what looked like an attempted coup, only the conservatives were willing to continue supporting Lapua (Karvonen 1988, 34-35).

The Lapua years clearly brought the defence of parliamentary democracy to the fore in the SDP. As such, parliamentarism had hardly been questioned by social democrats in the 1920s; those who remained in the SDP did so because they had renounced a revolutionary course. Now, however, the Lapua challenge to democracy became the *overshadowing* concern. It became the theme of the 1933 Party Congress, which preceded the victorious parliamentary elections later that year (from 66 seats in 1930 to 78 seats and 37.3 per cent of the vote in 1933). In relation to bourgeois parties, the SDP continued its previous line. It gave its support to cabinets that were critical of Lapua while doing its utmost to forestall pro-Lapua fronts in all bourgeois parties. This strategy was highly successful. In particular, the long-lived cabinet (1932-35) led by liberal T.M. Kivimäki depended on this tacit social democratic support (Jääskeläinen 1977, 535).

The defeat of Lapua and the electoral success of the SDP led to social democratic demands for cabinet participation. Meanwhile, the agrarians became increasingly critical of Kivimäki's crisis policies. Signs of a rapprochement between the two parties started to appear in 1933-34, as individual debaters in both parties began to advocate a 'coalition of workers and peasants' (Soikkanen 1975, 584; Leinonen 1960, 248-251). Until the landslide victory of 1936, however, Tanner preferred the considerable leverage the Kivimäki cabinet's dependence on the SDP gave the party. In September 1936 the SDP and the agrarians agreed on a joint program stressing the protection of democracy against 'all forms of subversive action', and providing for major social reforms. The social democrats agreed to increased defence spending and to a postponement of a comprehensive unemployment insurance, whereas the agrarian concessions included reduced protective tariffs on agricultural products. When President P.E. Svinhufvud refused to appoint a cabinet including socialists, the SDP and the agrarians joined forces to replace him with agrarian Kyösti Kallio in the presidential elections of February, 1937. Kallio promptly proceeded to appoint a Red-Green cabinet led by liberal A.K. Cajander as a compromise and a mediator between the 'big two' (Suomi 1971; Hufvudstadsbladet, March 13, 1937).

In the ensuing debate, both parties stressed the popular and democratic character of the new cabinet. In a speech a year after the *Punamulta* coalition was appointed, Tanner described its basis in the following manner:

> As a matter of fact, the two main groups [workers and farmers] spring from the same roots. The present working class has just recently, or at most a couple of generations ago, emerged from the farming population (Tanner 1966, 201).

The *Punamulta* agreement was preceded not so much by a reappraisal of the Agrarian Party as by a clearer social democratic stand concerning the defence of democracy as a basis of all political activity. The SDP had rarely questioned the democratic character of the agrarians; rather, the antagonism had been based on a notion that the party was a defender of the class egoism of the farmers (Tanner 1966, 188). Between 1930 and 1936, Tanner openly declared that a major strategy of the SDP must be to encourage agrarian opposition against the extreme right wing; the key to victory over fascism lay with the Agrarian Party. As to the idea of a coalition per se, the reorientation was more 'historical' on the part of the agrarians than of the SDP (Paavonen 1987, 139).

In Finland, social democracy faced stronger competition from the extreme left than in the other Nordic countries. In terms of ideological concessions to revolutionary socialism, the party split marks a turning point. As long as the revolutionary wing remained within the SDP, the leadership was willing to go part way towards meeting its demand. After the split, reformism rapidly became the main guideline. In the ideological debate after 1920, there is next to no reference to communist competition. Rather, the abyss separating the two parties was stressed. After 1930, the SDP had a unique position as communism had been legislated out of Finnish politics altogether.

Comparisons

Patterns: one, several or none?

Between the bird's-eye view of the macrosociologist and the pedestrian perspective of much of historiography - the one viewing the Red-Green compromises as inevitable products of a structural logic and the other not recognizing the existence of a generic Red-Green deal - there is plenty of room for comparative analyses sensitive to *both* the need for generalizations and the differentia specifica of each case. The road to the agreements was not uniform in the four countries; on the other hand, several interesting regular features can be noted.

In our description of the *ideological* path to the Red-Green coalition, Denmark certainly stands out as the deviant case. Since 1919, there was no major change at the ideological level that could have constituted either a prerequisite for or a hindrance to deals across the bloc distinction. *Kanslergadeforliget* was of major importance as a practical platform for social democratic strategy. However, it would have had little principal bearing had the other three countries not followed suit. Their route to the deal was much less self-evident, and they display some interesting similarities between themselves.

The table depicts a chronological sequence; chronology is not necessarily causality. Nevertheless, it is clear that the break with the communists was one major prerequisite of the social democractic minority cabinets of the mid- and late 1920s. Moreover, the fall of these cabinets was causally related to the ensuing radicalization in Sweden, Norway and, to a lesser extent, in Finland. From there on, the pattern is fairly identical in these three countries. Irrespective of whether the electorate was actually reacting to the programmatic radicalization of the parties, it is hard to *interpret* the setbacks of 1928-30 in any other way. By the same token, the landslides of 1932-33 following the reformist offensive could only be interpreted in favour of a growing ideological moderation. The fact that all four parties did better than ever before in the elections following the Red-Green agreements was the final argument for the superiority of the reformist approach. Electoral success and ideological orthodoxy seemed mutually exclusive.

In Sweden and Norway, as well as in Finland, the fall of the minority cabinet was connected with or parallel to bitter labour conflicts. One precondition of the growing social democratic moderation was the waning of union activism after these clashes (Åmark 1988, 62-63; Lorenz 1974, 22-25; Luoma 1967, 182-183). In all three countries, unions retreated to defensive or more conciliatory positions; in the Finnish case, the ban on communism wiped out the main branch of the union movement, leaving the small social democratic unions as the sole contenders in the field. Paradoxically enough, the offensive strategy of the employers, amounting to a more or less violent repression in Norway and especially Finland, was a central prerequisite of the Red-Green alliance; it enfeebled one major source of potential opposition against a collaborative social democratic posture.

In Finland and especially in Norway, the link between the party organization and the parliamentary caucus was much weaker than in Denmark and Sweden. This 'weakness' was an important key to the Red-Green deal, particularly in Norway. What was carried out 'by the party' with a conspicuous involvement on the part of the party leader in Denmark and Sweden, was in Norway and Finland much more of a back room deal between parliamentary

Table 1
Ideology, response and compromise:
the road to the Red-Green deals

	Denmark	Sweden	Norway	Finland
Break with revolutionaries	1919	1917	1923	1920
Minority cabinet fall	1926	1926	1928	1927
Radicalization?	None	1928 party congress	1930 party congress	1930 party congress
Voter response	Growing support	1928 electoral disaster	1930 electoral disaster	1930 bourgeois landslide
Reformist offensive?	No clear change	1932 campaign	1933 party congress	1933 party congress
Voter response	Growing support	Landslide 1932	Landslide 1933	Landslide 1933
Red-Green deal	1933	1933	1935	1937
Voter response	All-time high 1935	All-time high 1936	All-time high 1936	All-time high 1939

elites. Stauning and Hansson could rely on the loyalty of the party organization to a much greater degree than could Nygaardsvold and Tanner. In Norway, the 'parliamentarians' needed more distance to the 'ideologues' of the party organization in order to be able to approach the agrarians at all.

Nevertheless, no reformist leader could operate entirely independently from the ideological debate. Here, a fascinating pattern emerges in the form of the 'second best solutions' in Sweden and Finland, as well as in Norway. Those who advocated 'socialism' were placated with 'state involvement' (in Sweden also with reference to the Socialization Commission). The debate on winning the agrarian population for the party was utilized when the agreement with the Agrarian *Party* was rationalized. These concepts, originally couched in Marxist thought, were used as stepping stones for a quite radical deviation from the Marxist path.

Diffusion?

Kanslergadeforliget 1933, *Kohandeln* 1933, *Kriseforliket* 1935, *Punamulta* 1936/37. When similar things happen in neighbouring countries, the comparativist should be aware of *Galton's Problem*, the possibility that the similarities may reflect a process of diffusion from one country to another (Naroll 1965). To what extent were the Red-Green compromises a result of emulation between the countries?

The series of agreements easily complies with the requirements for potential diffusion: a sufficiently similar innovation, a credible time lag, awareness of the innovation, a high level of contacts, and references to other countries prior to the crucial decisions (Nyman 1944, 28; Bull 1959, 123; Soikkanen 1987, 17). Moreover, inter-Scandinavian cooperation had been strengthened through the creation of the Nordic Social Democratic Cooperation Committee in 1932. From the beginning, the cooperation between farmers and workers was one of the main themes in the Committee's work (Blidberg 1984, 9-18, 31-38; Samråd i kristid, 30 ff.).

Still, *Kanslergadeforliget* would have remained just another Danish deal had there not been a pressing need for Swedish social democracy to create a strong platform for its crisis policy and a way out of an ideological impasse. It is for this reason that the SAP had to portray *Kohandeln* as a historical turning point, which stands out in rather clear contrast to the matter-of-fact attitude of the Danish social democrats. For their Norwegian and Finnish

78

brethren, faced with a similar situation, these two deals radically increased the acceptability of the idea. With every deal concluded and evaluated inside the party, the trade unions and at the polls the next one seemed less of an ideological deviation.

While it is clear that the four parties influenced each other, diffusion must not be seen in isolation from the internal conditions prevailing in each party; the *Eigendynamik* of diffusion should not be exaggerated.

Conclusions

The analysis of Scandinavian social democracy reveals that decisions about coalitions are normally not *preceded* by clear changes at the ideological level. In fact, coalitions and compromises as such require a degree of secrecy and uncertainty alien to ideological declarations. For this reason, inter-party deals tend to assume the character of *faits accomplis* from the point of view of the ideologue. Once realized, however, coalitions require extensive rationalizations also in ideological terms. These crucial decisions therefore often *shape* ideology instead of being conditioned by it. The extent to which they have such effects depends largely on their success in concrete terms, in the form of electoral gains and institutional outputs.

On the other hand, ideology can clearly *retard* the process towards inter-party cooperation. The radicalization of the SAP, the DNA and the SDP towards the end of the 1920s certainly restricted the manoeuvering space of those social democratic leaders who already at that time considered alliances with bourgeois parties. Equally important, it had a repelling effect on potential partners.

Przeworki's proposition about the logic of parliamentary participation finds much support in the Scandinavian case. Participation leads to system acceptance, the pursuit of goals through Parliament calls for deals and coalitions. Still, the stalemate between ideology and political *Praxis* had no self-evident solution in Sweden, Norway and Finland around 1930. The Great

Depression and its political repercussions were indeed the factor that 'came to rescue social democracy out of its ideological dilemma' (Tingsten 1941, 331); this statement is even more valid for the DNA and the SDP than for the SAP. The crisis gave the parliamentary wing a chance to 'try it their way'.

Przeworki's idea about the electoral trade-off between social democracy and communism receives no clear support in our analysis. The Swedish and particularly the Finnish social democrats faced much stronger communist competition than did the DNA. Still, they drew a much clearer ideological line vis-à-vis communism than did their Norwegian comrades. The communists failed to profit electorally from the de-radicalization of social democracy; to the extent that communism made any gains, they were totally dwarfed by the repeated landslide victories of the social democrats. In fact, the electoral success of the 'class compromise' was perhaps the strongest argument in its favor.

The position of the Scandinavian peasantry - Esping-Andersen's main explanatory factor - certainly stands out as an important aspect of our analysis. Again, however, Denmark is somewhat of a deviant case. On the one hand, *Socialdemokratiet* never seriously attempted to reach out to the farming population at large; the average Danish farmer was effectively outside its reach due to the structure of Danish farming. On the other hand, there was no abyss between protectionism and free trade separating the farmers and the workers in Denmark. Elsewhere in Scandinavia, small farming was much more prevalent, thus constituting a theoretically acceptable addition to the social democratic electorate. Also, the protective tariffs for agriculture constituted a barrier between social democrats and agrarians in Sweden, Norway and Finland. The following three conclusions are mainly applicable to these three countries:

1   Having entered the road to 'socialism via popular majority', social democracy must, because of the sheer number of small farmers, give due consideration to this class.

2   The agrarian parties were dependent on their parliaments for crucial decisions concerning subsidies, duties and

prices. Partly for this reason, they were the 'parliamentary party par excellence'. This was always recognized by the social democrats. When the political and economic crisis of the 1930s made the 'protection of democracy' a crucial issue for social democracy, the two parties were brought closer together.

3   The agrarians were the party most interested in government regulation of the economy. After the social democrats moved away from grand socialization schemes to government crisis policies, their approaches to economic policy more or less coincided.

However, none of these 'causes' must be interpreted in a deterministic fashion. To be sure, they influenced those politicians who negotiated the deals, and they were used as rationalizations when explaining the agreements to the electorate as well as to the party organizations. Still, it was the domestic and international context that gave the compromise of the 1930s its historic significance. Whatever the causal background of the Red-Green deals, these deals compared favourably both to the domestic political stalemate of around 1930 and to the collapse of democracy in much of Europe between the Wars. The ideological barriers at home were dwarfed by the massive polarization between the Left and the Right in the international environment.

Social Classes and Political Institutions: The Roots of Swedish Corporatism

Bo Rothstein

Introduction

Since the beginning of the 1970s, the concept of corporation has been at the center of the discussion about how the Scandinavian (and some other) welfare states should be understood (cf. Cawson 1986; Rothstein 1987b). All Scandinavian polities rank high on any index. They all have strong interest organizations on the producer side of the economy, and there is a firm institutionalization of cooperation between interest organizations and the state. This corporatist political culture takes many forms, one of the most significant being that interest organizations are not seen as 'private' organizations situated outside the state in what could be called civil society. Rather they fulfil a function as transformation belts between civil society and the state, and even if they are not public organizations they are mostly seen as having some kind of official status. They participate directly at all levels of government and are formally represented in many public bodies.

In general, interest organizations are not seen as a problem for the state. On the contrary, they are a part of the solution to problems. Political problems and crises are to be solved by an extended collaboration between state and interest organizations, not, as in the Anglo-Saxon polities, by the state attacking the organizations. This political system, if it may be so called, takes different specific forms and varies somewhat between the Scandinavian countries. The aim of this study is to increase our understanding of how this system was once established. It does so by taking a closer look at the most corporatist of the Scandinavian countries - Sweden. The question asked is why (and how) such a political system was established.

The roots of Swedish corporatism

The theoretical starting point is that the various forms and mechanisms of political government, of which corporative government is one particular type (cf. Rothstein 1987a), may be regarded as *institutionalized systems*. The specific way they originated has an important explanatory function. This line of thought implies that once political *institutions* have been established, they have an inherent inertia. As political structures they are hard to change, and they leave their imprint on the national political culture over a long period, i.e. on the very thinking about what politics is, how it should be conducted and what is politically possible or impossible (Douglas 1987, 45; March and Olsen 1984; Mouzelis 1988; Ridley 1975; Skocpol 1985; Therborn 1978). This approach means that institutional analysis is considered primary in relation to various forms of strategic decision analysis.

Examples of the importance of such institutionalized systems are political party systems (two-party vs. multiparty systems), election systems (majority vs. proportional representation) and various forms of public-sector administrative systems (federal vs. central). Once institutions of this kind have been established in a polical sytem, they tend to influence the political culture for a long time. The Scandinavian states have rightly been described as countries characterized by unified, strong, dominant special-interest organizations (Heclo and Madsen 1987; Micheletti 1984; Therborn 1987). Today these organizations assume a very prominent role in the political process and are also formally represented on the lay boards that govern many public agencies (Rothstein 1988a). Despite these strong and uniformly organized interests, many observers say that Swedish political culture is characterized by pragmatism and the willingness of opposing and relatively evenly matched interests to bargain and compromise (Korpi 1983; Heclo and Madsen 1987; Therborn 1987). Some also argue that, at least during certain periods, dominant interest organizations have paid greater heed to the general interest than to their respective special interests in Swedish politics (Olson 1982). It has also been shown that when representatives of a strong special-interest organization take seats on the boards of public agencies, they tend to distance themselves from the demands of their own organization in favour of what they perceive as the best interests of the agency or the public (Rothstein 1988a).

Whatever meaning one attributes to the concept of 'corporatism', it is clear that Sweden, as well as the other Scandinavian countries, ranks high on the international list in terms of the role that organized interests assume in the political system (Lembruch 1982; Cawson 1986). The present report argues that this political culture - so strongly characterized by pragmatic negotiations and agreements between the government and strong organized interests - can largely be explained by the way in which these interests were drawn into or demanded to be represented in various public agencies at the beginning of the modern political era.

We must seek the roots of Swedish corporatism in the late 19th century. At that time, Sweden was characterized by late but very rapid industrialization. In Marxist parlance, we were thus at the threshold of a new mode of production. It is typical of such historical situations that there are no established political-legal mechanisms that can deal with the new kind of dominant social conflicts generated by the new production system. Existing political institutions appear insufficient for the new types of social classes. In every historical situation there is also a political system, a polity, of some kind. How this polity chooses to act when confronted by new types of societal conflicts may be assumed to play a decisive role in the shape these conflicts will take and how intensive they will be (Birnbaum 1988, 6).

Although the structure of the fundamental conflict is determined by the production system in question, the fundamental assumption here is that the form of institution created to handle these conflicts is not. There is room both for genuinely actor-determined or other non-structural explanations. In the *formative historical moment*, where the superstructure is empty, so to speak - i.e. no firm political-legal institutions for conflict resolution have yet been established - there is considerable room for variations between how public institutions are shaped in different political systems (cf. Anderson 1974; Ashford 1988).

This is not the place for an exhaustive presentation of the debate on corporatism (cf. Cawson 1986). What should be stated here is that I do not intend to use the concept of corporatism to characterize a whole political system. Instead, the concept is used at a lower level of analysis to describe those political institutions in which the public sector, together with organized interests, shapes and implements various policies. The establishment of these kinds of corporative political institutions has been explained as the result of concessions by legislative and other public-sector bodies or as responses to demands presented by strong organized interests. Given their strength, these organized interests have had the potential to block various legislatively based reform initiatives. They have also been able to demand influence and/or representation in various public institutions (Lowi 1969; cf. Offe 1985; Lauman and Knoke 1987). The mirror image of this discussion is the idea of a strong public sector (or 'strong state') which creates loyal special interest-based organizations from above, in order to facilitate the implementation of certain programmes and measures (Schmitter 1974). By analyzing the *background, organizations, motives and effects* of the first corporative institutions in the Swedish polity, we can preliminarily test these different hypotheses. The question is whether it was strong special interest organizations that demanded representation in the public sector or a strong public sector that created loyal partners from outside the public sector.

The background: Solving the 'labour question'

The first proposal about the establishment of a corporative agency in the Swedish public sector was presented by a special public commission of inquiry known as the Workers' Insurance Commission as early as 1888. The Commission believed that, to the extent legal technicalities permitted this, the state had an obligation to try to reduce the insecurity 'of the role assumed by manual labourers who are solely dependent on their labour'. According to the Commission, the reason why the state should intervene to protect workers was that because of the new use of machinery, the labour processes had become so complex that an individual worker was incapable of understanding or controlling them. It was thus incorrect to argue that the best interests of both parties could be assured by letting them freely reach their own accords on working conditions. The Commission pointed to the relatively weak and dependent position of wage laborers vis-à-vis capital. It argued that workers lacked the ability to evaluate the possible risks that working conditions posed them. Workers, the Commission argued, were forced to accept the jobs that existed, regardless of the physical risks they were subjecting themselves to. In addition, legislation in this field was necessary because - unlike the funds provided by a capitalist - the labour that a worker agreed to provide to his employer was physically inseparable from the worker. The Commission thus said that there was an unequitable relationship between capital and labour caused by the difference between them and by their respective connections with the production process (cf. Offe, 1985, ch. 8).

To resolve these problems, the Commission recommended that a state labour inspectorate be established and that a mandatory system of public occupational accident insurance be introduced. According to this proposal, the system would be administered by a new government agency specially established for this purpose, to which a corporatively structured advisory body consisting of 25 people would be attached. Aside from technical experts on insurance, it would also include 'representatives of different social classes'. In addition, disputes concerning insurance settlements would not be decided by the existing courts of law, but by a board specially appointed by the government. This board would consist of an impartial chairman, a physician, an engineer *plus two employers and two workers*. The board's decisions on insurance cases would be final.

The recommendations of the Workers' Insurance Commission were not backed by Parliament, however. Instead, a new public commission of inquiry was appointed in 1891. Known as the New Commission on Workers' Insurance, it presented largely the same arguments as its predecessor in favour of state intervention to resolve the 'labour question' but recommended somewhat different legal cum technical solutions. The Commission felt that an additional reason for

87

state regulation was that the accelerating industrialization meant a rapid increase in the size of the working class. At the same time, the patriarchal responsibility that employers had previously assumed for their employees was disappearing because of the special character of the industrial labour process. According to the Commission, the insecurity felt by individual workers about their chances of economic survival during illness or old age could easily make them feel 'ill will and dissatisfaction with the existing social order'.[1]

The Commission admitted that its proposal for mandatory workers' insurance interfered with the prevailing principles of economic freedom and personal responsibility. According to the Commission, its recommendation would indeed reduce personal freedom because the state would take away the right of the individual to dispose of part of his property. In addition, the individual's personal feeling of responsibility would be reduced. This would affect his thrift and power of initiative in ensuring his own economic security. But, the Commission reasoned, the principles of freedom of contract and economic freedom were only justified *if the interests of the individual and society coincided*. If this was not the case, and if unrestricted freedom of contract was instead harmful to both the individual and society, the Commission reasoned, there was then no obstacle in the Swedish legal system to coercive state intervention.[2] The commission recommended that the insurance system in question should be administered by a central state agency which would have under it local 'corporations or so-called boards, in which all interests would be represented'.[3] These local corporatively structured boards would be responsible for making decisions on the crucial issues of the reform - who would be entitled to insurance, who would have the right to receive a pension and under what conditions, the size of pensions and insurance fees, etc.[4]

The recommendations of the *New Workers' Insurance Commission* did not receive the support of Parliament either. However, its proposal did not fail because of its recommendation that the reform should be administered partly by corporative institutions, but because of political opposition to the idea of social insurance as such. In 1902, when a *Conservative* government pushed through the first public social insurance system in Sweden (accident insurance for workers), it proposed that a corporatively structured *workers' insurance council* consisting of five employer and five worker representatives be attached to the national agency that would administer the reform. Parliament adopted the reform itself, but rejected the proposal to establish a workers' insurance council. What triggered the disapproval was not, however, the thought of corporative influence on insurance administration as such, but the technically complicated way in which representatives would be chosen under the reform proposal. On the contrary, a number of MPs critical of the proposal felt that the establishment of such a council would be of great value.

The first corporative institutions in the Swedish political system appeared instead at the local political level. Beginning in 1903, municipalities and cities established public employment offices (i.e. labour exchanges) whose boards were structured on a corporative basis, with fifty per cent employers and fifty per cent workers under the chairmanship of a neutral public official. These employment offices were not tied to specific occupations or industries, but were designed to provide information about all types of work, free of charge. The development of these institutions was rapid, and by 1907 such corporatively structured public employment offices had been established in all major cities. This development differed markedly from the general European pattern, in which control over the employment offices usually rested either with employer organizations or with the trade unions. On the Continent, the question of control over the labour exchanges had become a major source of conflict between the two sides. The reason was that control of the labour supply is obviously of pivotal importance to both unions and employers in the event of industrial conflicts. By controlling the employment offices, trade unions can make their strikes and boycotts much more effective. They can for instance demand that those who seek jobs must be union members and they can force strike-breakers out of the labour market. On the other hand, if the employers control the employment offices, they can recruit people willing to work, i.e., strikebreakers, thereby reducing the significance of strikes, while using the employment offices to winnow out undesirables (union activists, strike leaders etc.) from the work force. Elsewhere in Europe, the struggle for the control of employment office operations was therefore at times very bitter indeed (Rothstein, 1985; 1988b).

In Sweden, however, developments took a completely different path. As early as 1903, to be sure, the Swedish Employers' Confederation (SAF) was interested in establishing its own employment offices as a weapon against the trade union movement. Officials from the Confederation were sent to Germany, where they collected information about how employers had gained major advantages vis-à-vis the trade unions by controlling employment office operation. But probably because they organized relatively late, Swedish employers had no practical opportunity to set up their own employment office network before the issue was resolved in Sweden around 1907. That year, Parliament approved state grants to the locally established publicly operated employment offices. As a condition for such grants, the employment offices were required to have corporatively structured boards, to observe unconditional neutrality in the event of industrial conflicts and to agree to provide information on all types of work free of charge, i.e. exactly the principles established by local initiatives in 1903.

It may be added that at first not only employers but also the social democrats were suspicious of the publicly operated employment offices. In Parliament, Party Chairman Hjalmar Branting spoke against the proposal to give state grants to these offices. He argued that because local political bodies in cities were not elected by universal suffrage, there was a great risk that the employment offices would act in favour of the employers. The social democratic press warned that the offices might be utilized to facilitate the employers' recruitment of strikebreakers. Very soon, however, opposition to the publicly operated employment offices from both the labour movement and the employers disappeared. From 1907 on, the fundamental principles behind their operations were never questioned by either side (Schiller 1967; Rothstein 1988b).

The principles that came to govern the publicly operated employment offices, i.e., a corporative structure, neutrality and cost-free service, had been adopted at national level by a series of *Employment Office Conferences*. The national Board of Trade - the government agency responsible for commercial and industrial issues - organized such meetings beginning in 1906. The Board invited representatives of the local publicly operated employment offices to these conferences. Although they were a temporary phenomenon, the conferences were probably the first corporative institutions in the modern sense at national level in Swedish politics. At the last of these gatherings, arranged in 1912 (it was the last because its work became permanent under other auspices; see below), the delegates agreed to work toward a rapid expansion of their programmes. The chairman of both the Swedish Employers' Confederation (SAF) and the Swedish Trade Union Confederation (LO) were among the conference participants.[5]

The concept of corporative representation rapidly took root in Swedish politics. The National Insurance Office, established to administer the public system of accident insurance that was introduced in 1903, requested permission in a 1908 message to the government to establish a separate workers' insurance council on a corporative basis.[6] In 1909, a commission of inquiry that presented its recommendations for changes in workers' protection legislation also proposed the establishment of a corporatively structured advisory body.[7] Not until 1912, however, was the first permanent national corporative body established in the Swedish civil service system. This happened when a separate National Social Welfare Board was established by Parliament in 1912. In addition to its board, composed of civil servants as was traditional, it appointed two separate assemblies for employers and workers, as well as a corporatively structured *social welfare council* divided into four different sections.

At first the task of the National Social Welfare Board was somewhat vague, but it is clear that the so-called 'social welfare question' was in fact the labour question. In other words, a whole new social class had emerged, and its insecure working conditions constituted a problem for the country. The public commission of inquiry that recommended the establishment of the Social Welfare Board maintained that 'in contemporary society, human labour has become a commodity, so to speak, the supply and demand of which are subject to fluctuations and which consequently have a value that is uncertain and dependent on circumstances'.[8] According to the commission, this led to the concentration in cities and other large labour markets of 'a lot of individuals who never become rooted and

91

never feel completely at home in any particular spot or even in the country as a whole'.[9] Widespread poverty was thus not the focus of the government agency-to-be. For instance, the proposed National Social Welfare Board would have no connection with public poor relief, which was handled by local authorities. Nor was the creation of the new agency related to the introduction of any social reform. Instead, its establishment appears more to be the result of the state's general desire to build up its capacity and expertise, thus gaining an overview and better information about the problems caused by the 'labour question'.[10] According to the Commission, it was increasingly urgent to do so, given the speed and complexity that characterized the growth of the 'labour question'. But there was also another reason:

> The more clearly the dangers of industrialism became evident even to the most capable and most irre-proachable workers - and the more strongly manual labourers saw themselves as a closed class in relation to employers and other groups of citizens - the more clearly the national dangers of this situation became discernible. The rising level of public education then gave workers the means to clarify for themselves and others the source of their worries, the organizational system gave them the collective power to work on behalf of their own interests, and in national elected bodies, these interests are being asserted by a growing number of direct worker representatives....The feeling of solidarity that has emerged among the working masses, in itself praiseworthy, is limited to themselves and they do not appear to wish to extend it to the whole society in which they share responsibility and play a part. This obviously poses a national danger, which must be removed in the common interests of everyone. Everywhere the government therefore faces the difficult task of mitigating conflicts of interest and repairing the cracks that are opening in the social structure.[11]

Although the proposal to establish the National Social Welfare Board encountered some opposition at the 1912 session of Parliament, there was no comment whatever about the recommendation to create

92

corporatively structured bodies attached to the Board. The idea that corporative institutions were needed had apparently become generally accepted in Swedish politics. Two 'worker representatives' had participated in the task of devising the actual proposal for how the Social Welfare Board would be organised. The Swedish Employers' Confederation, which submitted its written comments on the government bill to establish a Social Welfare Board, approved the creation of both the goverment agency as such and the corporative institutions that would be associated with it.[12]

In the following year, another new social welfare agency was established: the National Pensions Board, which was also furnished with an advisory, corporatively structured body. Before 1920 another two corporative agencies were established in Sweden: the National Industrial Injuries Insurance Court and the Work Council. Neither of these was merely advisory. On the contrary, they were institutions resembling courts of law, and their decisions were final. The former was entrusted with deciding issues related to the public system of occupational accident insurance, the latter with issues related to the law that mandated an eight-hour working day. Neither the proposals to set up these agencies nor their corporative structure led to any debate in parliament.[13]

Organization

The result of this early corporative political culture was three different types of institutions. First, a number of corporative institutions had a purely advisory function vis-à-vis public agencies (for example the Social Welfare Council of the National Social Welfare Board). Second, the National Social Welfare Board also selected two delegates from its labour and employer assemblies to participate directly in the major decisions of its governing board. The chairman of the Swedish Employers' Confederation (SAF) and the Swedish Trade Union Confederation (LO) were appointed to these positions. Third, there were agencies resembling courts of law (the Labour Council and the National Industrial Injuries Insurance Court) whose task was to make decisions on the interpretation and enforcement of existing legislation. The usual pattern was that they consisted of equal numbers of worker and employer representatives, plus lawyers. The chairmanship was held by one of the lawyers.

Some of the early proposals for corporative institutions involved fairly complex systems for choosing representatives. The institutions actually established, however, did not use these selection systems. Instead, representatives of *special-interest organizations* were appointed by the government (for national agencies) or by locally elected assemblies (e.g. for local employment offices). In practice, this was probably of no great importance because there are strong reasons for believing that in choosing representatives, public bodies always complied with the recommendations they received from dominant special-interest organizations. There is also reason to assume that both worker and employer organizations attached fairly great importance to representation in these bodies. As their representatives on the governing board of the National Industrial Injuries Insurance Court, the Social Democrats appointed their Chairman, Hjalmar Branting. To be sure, Branting was a member of Parliament. Nevertheless, he represented the 'workers' side' in a corporative agency. As for the latter agency, the Trade Union Congress (LO) succeeded in pushing through without opposition a rule that only national union confederations above a certain size were entitled to be represented. The motive, in all likelihood, was to exclude competing union organizations such as the syndicalists and communists from representation.[14]

Motives: Flexibility, legitimacy and the public interest

What, then, were the arguments behind the establishment of all these corporative bodies at that time? Why could not civil servants or, for that matter, members of Parliament, handle the 'labour question'. The first proposal for a corporative workers' insurance council in 1888 contained no arguments at all. It was apparently considered completely natural at the time to use a corporative system in these contexts. Three arguments, above all, that emerge from later sources are: a) the need for *flexibility* in the actual implementation of social reforms, b) the need to *legitimize* programmes in the eyes of those groups for whom the reforms were intended and c) the desire to transform special-interest organizations so that they would also pay greater heed to the *public interest*.

The demand for flexibility is related to the difficulties of using legal technicalities to regulate social reforms with a sufficient degree of precision. Taking social insurance regulations as an example, it turned out to be difficult to adapt them to volatile labour market and social conditions. It was simply too complicated for the provisions of the law to specify who should be included in the insurance system and who would be entitled to receive what insurance compensation under what circumstances. As early as 1893, the *New Commission on Workers' Insurance* believed that 'as...indicated, it is not possible to set these limits in such a way that all doubt as to whether or not a person is entitled to insurance is eliminated in every single case'.[15] To prevent unreasonable consequences from arising from the enforcement of the law in individual cases, it was necessary to design the regulations so that they permitted a fairly broad degree of discretion in their concrete implementation. This was also the argument behind the establishment in 1919 of a corporative National Industrial Injuries Court to decide cases of this type. When the law on the eight-hour working day was passed, it contained various exceptions for certain types of companies and manufacturing operations. It also included provisions to apply for waivers. Because of this desire for flexibility in enforcement, the law was worded in a fairly general way. To decide how it would be enforced in individual cases and how waiver applications would be evaluated, the above-mentioned corporative *Work Council* was created. When the law on the eight-hour day was enacted by Parliament in 1919, Östen Undén, the social democratic government minister who introduced it (and who was also a professor of law), said the following:

> Given the criticism that has been expressed here.... that the law contains too many exceptions, I would like to close by pointing out that in itself, it is not an ideal method of legislation to make the provisions of the law so narrow and so lacking in opportunities to adapt to practical life as these speakers seem to have intended. On the contrary, I believe that to the extent that the new Work Council will win public confidence through its enforcement of this legislation, it is

conceivable that there will be a desire to place additional powers in the hands of the Work Council.[16]

This room for manoeuvre in implementing reforms, necessitated by the demand for flexibility, could of course be filled by different forces. One argument against letting the general court system decide these cases was that it could not be expected to handle them with the necessary speed. If decisions were appealed through all levels of the public court system, an unacceptably long time would pass between a work injury and final settlement of the case, for instance. Court-like corporative institutions such as the National Industrial Injuries Insurance Court were believed to be capable of working with the speed required in these areas.[17]

Another argument against letting courts of law or regular civil servants handle discretionary aspects of implementing these laws was their lack of expertise on the special conditions characterizing different aspects of the 'labour question'.[18] It was pointed out that corporative bodies could give 'increased life and intensity to the administration (of the law) and prevent it from becoming too rigid'.[19] Implementation required expert knowledge (medical and technical) but above all, it required a knowledge of what specific effects different ways of enforcing and interpreting the provisions of a law might have. *The corporative principle of representation would allow a balancing of interests to replace formal juridical interpretation of the law as a decision-making method.* Furthermore, corporative bodies could take initiatives and make proposals for changes in legislation and public administration that might be justified on the basis of their actual enforcement experience.[20]

Another pivotal argument for establishing corporatively structured institutions was that this form of organization was considered capable of increasing the level of understanding and knowledge of their work among the groups they were intended for. By offering such groups representation in the responsible public agencies, it was hoped the implementation of reforms could achieve a greater degree of legitimacy. Decisions on how to interpret these reforms often had a very intrusive effect on individuals or groups.[21] It was believed that the manner in which reform programmes were implemented might also trigger social conflicts. The commission of inquiry that proposed the establishment of the National Social Welfare Board thus argued that:

> For its part, the Commission firmly believes that such 'councils' should be more necessary and useful in the social welfare field than in almost any field of public administration, because social welfare matters are difficult to resolve and involve strong confrontations between different interests.[22]

Others pointed out the great need for continuous contacts with both workers and employers. In its 1908 letter to the government requesting permission to establish a corporatively structured council on workers' insurance, the National Insurance Board maintained that such a council would cause both employers and workers to become more interested in the work of the National Insurance Board. At the same time, this agency would gain 'knowledge of different opinions among those members of the public most closely affected by the work of the Board'.

Finally, it was argued that corporative institutions might bring greater understanding and insight into the general problems of a given field. Because representatives of organized special interests were being asked to make decisions together with civil servants and experts, it was hoped these representatives 'would act as guardians not only of special interests but also of the interests of everyone, of society as a whole...It should certainly be expected that a representative body structured according to these principles, official and thus functioning with a sense of responsibility, should provide valuable support for the new social welfare administration'.[23] By taking part in corporative institutions, the labour movement - with its emphasis on opposition and mobilization - would thus learn the noble art of political government.

Impact

As for the boards of the local employment offices, it is generally accepted that their corporative structure was particularly instrumental in giving this institution a dominant position in the Swedish labour market (see Rothstein 1986, 1988b). In a 1916 statement to the government regarding the work of the publicly operated employment offices, the National Social Welfare Board declared that 'no objection has appeared from any quarter against the organizational principles on which the publicly operated employment offices are based'.[24] On the contrary, the Board believed that these principles were precisely what had helped the offices to grow and had strengthened the confidence in their work felt by employer organizations and unions, 'which in our country have fortunately abstained from utilizing the referral of jobs as a weapon in the social struggle, [in a way] which in Germany has partially distorted the whole employment office issue.' The board also observed that

> Despite the sharp social and political conflicts that have emerged in other areas of public life between members of the employer and worker camps, on the boards of the employment offices the same persons have, in the experience of the National Social Welfare Board, continued to cooperate faithfully in the interest of objectivity.[25]

One of the officials at the National Social Welfare Board who was responsible for overseeing the employment offices said in a 1920 article, after concurring with the above statement, that 'it appears as if this form of organization had a number of advantages over the majority principle that rules politically elected assemblies ..In any case it is outstandingly suitable for institutions where society needs the direct participation of the parties in the class conflicts'.[26] In addition, there was no criticism whatever of the work of the publicly operated employment offices at any of the annual parliamentary discussions of state grants to these offices from 1907 until 1940, when the state took over the offices entirely from the local goverments (see Rothstein 1986).

In 1926 there was an overall evaluation of the National Social Welfare Board's corporative institutions, i.e. the system of worker and employer representatives and the Social Welfare Council. As for the representative system, i.e. 'the right of the respective chairmen of the Swedish Trade Union Confederation and the Swedish Employers' Confederation to participate in major decisions of the agency's board, the National Social Welfare Board declared the following:

> The purpose of establishing the representative system was undoubtedly to give the National Social Welfare Board the necessary immediate contact with the main organizations in its most sensitive field of activity - the labour market and its organizations. The choice of representatives was therefore not, as some people have later claimed, based on political or parliamentary considerations...instead the Board selected persons who enjoyed a particularly high degree of confidence from employers and workers, respectively, and were suited to represent their interests. The fact that persons in such a position became representatives with the approval of their organizations, on the other hand, imposed on them an obligation to regard themselves also as representatives of the public.[27]

The National Social Welfare Board also noted that the contacts its top officials had made as a result of the representative system had been of great importance. It also pointed to the importance of the informal and confidential deliberations that the head of the National Social Welfare Board occasionally had with one or both representatives on particularly sensitive issues. For these reasons, the Board strongly opposed the abolition of the representative system, and it was retained. The report also stated that

> the system of worker and employer representatives has been and remains of value to the public, because it has made it possible to sweep away prejudices and create understanding of the measures undertaken by the state with regard to the legal or actual relationship between employers and workers. It is also useful in contributing towards smoothing out conflicting interests in a relatively flexible fashion within its field of operations, even at an early stage of the discussion of an issue.[28]

Table 1 shows the frequency of participation by union and employer representatives in the board meetings of the Social Welfare Board between 1913 and 1919.

Table 1
Union and employer participation in Board Meetings 1913 -1919[29]

Year	Number of meetings	Number of issues
1913	48	118
1914	39	85
1915	48	90
1916	20	42
1917	17	20
1918	15	21
1919	4	21

It is worth adding that the above report indicates that the union and employer confederation representatives not only participated in discussions of broad issues but also, to a great extent, in concrete decisions made by the various departments of the Social Welfare Board. As the table shows, the chairmen of the Trade Union Confederation and the Employers' Confederation thus met nearly every week, joining with the Board's civil servants in the task of shaping and establishing Sweden's social welfare policy. In the above statement, the Social Welfare Board explained that the decline in the number of meetings and issues (see Table 1) in which the labour and employer representatives took part was not due to a decline in their interest in or the need for cooperation. Instead, the reason for their intensive cooperation during the first few years was the need to create practices and precedents while laying the foundations of Swedish social welfare policy. The gradual decline in the number of recorded formal meetings was offset, the Board declared, by an intensification of informal contacts. An additional reason for the decline was that the labour and employer representatives sometimes chose to participate only in the actual formal decision. The reason for this was that they did not want to commit themselves to a particular stance on issues on which they might have to make decisions later in another capacity. It should be added that the two representatives participated in decision-making on far more issues than the minimum required by the agency's instructions. This was because, according to the statement of the Social Welfare Board, it 'was regarded as being of great value to the Board to gain the support of the representatives' experience and judgement'.

The Social Welfare Council attached to the National Social Welfare Board and which consisted of four sections - each with 15 members - met less often than the board plus the LO and SAF representatives. Because many of its members were not resident in Stockholm and because of their large number, it was considered a fairly costly and complicated matter to call a meeting of the sections. The frequency of meetings can be seen from the following table.

Table 2
Meetings of the Social Welfare Council 1913-1919[30]

Year	Number of meetings	Number of issues
1913	8	15
1914	5	9
1915	5	9
1916	8	4
1917	2	3
1918	2	5
1919	12	17

In the above statement, the National Social Welfare Board maintained that it had found the Council's input valuable 'not only thanks to the expertise it has contributed to the handling of issues, but also because a more detailed awareness of the contents and purpose of issues could be communicated through members to circles interested in a particular issue, with the aim of eliminating prejudices, preventing misunderstandings and awakening understanding'.

As for the work of the Work Council and the Industrial Injuries Insurance Court, there is nothing to indicate that they did not function to the satisfaction of the state as well as the employers and the trade unions. The usefulness of the existing law on working hours was debated at regular intervals in Parliament until the end of the 1930s, but no criticism of the Work Council's work emerged. The other court-like institution from this period, the Industrial Injuries Insurance Court, lasted in its original form dating from 1919 until the 1970s.

Conclusions

What conclusions can be drawn from this early corporative institutionalization of the Swedish political system? First of all, it is obvious that the principle of corporative representation was established well before the principle of democratic representation in Sweden. Several decades before the introduction of universal suffrage, it seemed uncontroversial to appoint working-class representatives to national administrative agencies. In formal terms, too, the corporative principle was introduced before the democratic principle - in 1903 in local government administration and between 1906 and 1912 in national administration. Second, it should be observed that the 'labour question' was the factor that gave rise to the introduction of corporative insitutions. 'The poor', a large general category of people who posed a bigger problem than the proletariat in both numerical and social welfare terms, were never considered for any representation.

The above indicates that it was the *organization* of the working class and the resulting potential threat to the existing society that made it necessary to give workers some kind of representation in the political system. Third, it is important to observe that the principle of corporative representation first emerged on the *output* side of the political system, i.e. at the administrative level. This part of corporatism is often neglected in modern literature. What appears to have made such representation necessary was the difficulty of achieving the requisite precision by using the tools available to elected bodies (general legal provisions), given the flexible and complex social conditions that characterized the 'labour question'. If the legal rules were made sufficiently exact, they often had unreasonable consequences when applied in practice to individual cases. Further-more, conditions in the area of desired intervention were so change-able that it was quite difficult to predict all the situations in which a law could, or should, be applicable. It was thus necessary to make the legal provisions less precise in order to achieve the necessary level of flexibility in applying them. This, in turn, gave the agency charged with implementing the policy fairly large room for mano-euvre. It can be argued that with this type of legislation, policy is actually shaped at the administrative level.

How this room for discretion at the implementary stage was utilized was of crucial importance to the way that the groups who were the targets for a policy would perceive the legitimacy of public regulations. This is an assumption based on the concept that the legitimacy of a government action is both a scarce and a necessary resource and is not exclusively - or even mainly - based on the wording of general legal provisions. Instead, the legitimacy of political intervention is determined by the way it is implemented in invidual cases.

Instead of giving the usual, legally trained, civil servants this dis-cretionary power, Parliament chose to give it to the organizations, the members of which were to be the chief beneficiaries. If this argument carries any weight, it points to an important element of the power relationships between elected bodies and organized interests - that the power of elected bodies is limited by the character of the instruments at their disposal, namely the passing of general laws.

Lastly, it should be noted that it was not a particularly strong state that created loyal interest organizations with whom they could control the emerging working class, nor was it particularly strong interest organizations that demanded representation within the state. On the contrary, it seems like corporatism was created by an insecure and reluctant state in order to increase its information and capacity to deal with the 'labour question' (Birnbaum 1988, 5 - 6). Especially interesting is the fact that the request for corporative representation in some cases came from the traditional corps of civil servants.

As for the long-term effects of this early corporative institutionali-zation in the Swedish polity, a few comments are in order. First, it is worth noting how rapidly the principle gained general approval from all parties concerned. As for the role of the employment offices, they are especially interesting because they comprise the organizational embryo of what would later become an 'active labour policy' unique to Sweden (Therborn 1986; Rothstein 1986, 1988b). The principles established in 1903-07 still apply. Corporative institutions were apparently effective in terms of giving legitimacy to their work. Similarly, we should not underestimate the importance of the fact that at the national level, the chairman of the Trade Union Confederation and the Employers' Confederation met practically every week in a joint effort to help solve everyday public-sector problems related to implementing various programmes to resolve the labour question. At the local level, we can only speculate about what impact it had when representatives of organized labour and the employers together succeeded in dealing with the often intricate problems of employment office operations.

This image of early cooperation and consensus in (certain portions of) Swedish politics must at least supplement the traditional description of this area as one characterized by extremely tough social and political conflicts. It is thus possible that the pragmatism, the willingness to bargain and compromise and the absence of conflicts in matters of principle said to characterize Swedish postwar politics have their origins in the institutionalization of corporative bodies that began back in the late 19th century.

Compared to other European labour movements during the formative interwar period, Scandinavian labour can be characterized as more reformist, more integrated into society, less suspicious of the state and bureaucracy, and more collaborative, willing and able to forge alliances and compromises with other forces in society. Accordingly, Scandinavian labour has been less inclined to contract into a self-sufficient ghettoized existence and, most critically, into a subaltern notion of politics. The public policies the Scandinavian labour movements pursued during this period, in particular their social policies, were mostly universal and general, i.e., directed towards the whole population, in contrast to developments on the Continent where social policies were usually directed to narrow class-defined groups. One could say that what singles out the Scandinavian Social Democratic parties during the interwar period is that they were able to develop a hegemonic notion of politics, in which they viewed themselves not as a subaltern, isolated group or class in society, but as the dominant social and political force, destined to take overall responsibility for the nation. This was especially significant during the economic crisis of the 1930s, in which the fate of the Scandinavian labour movements stands in sharp contrast to the fate of their compatriots in the rest of Europe. The political compromises they were able to strike were of immense importance, not only for preventing a fascist development and avoiding the split and dissarray that became the fate of the British labour movement, but also because the political development that took place proved the social democratic parties were the natural party of government in these countries, able to save the nation and provide secure government during hard times. One possible explanation for this unique Scandinavian route is the early development of corporatist structures as shown above. This development demonstrated that collaboration with capital was possible, at least in some cases; that compromises could be struck to the advantage of workers' interests; and that the state and bureaucracy need not be just 'a committee for handling the common affairs of the borgeois class', but could also be used to protect the interests of the working class as well. If this line of reasoning is correct, the explanation for the unique character of Scandinavian labour should be sought not only in the development of social and economic factors in the Scandinavian societies, but also in the specific character of the Scandinavian *states* during the formative period of the modern labour movements.

Notes

1. Arbetareförsäkringskomiteens betänkande. 1. Utlåtende och forslaga. (Report of the Workers Insurance Commitee 1. Statements and proposals). Stockholm 1888, p. 4.

2. Idem.

3. Nya arbetareförsäkringskomiténs betänkande. 1. Utlåtande och förslag (Report of the New Workers Insurance Commitee. 1. Statements and proposals). Stockholm 1893.

4. Ibid. p. 25-29.

5. Ibid. p.101.

6. Ibid. p.11.

7. Government Bill, 1902, no. 15, p. 26.

8. Socialstyrelsens arkiv, Arbetsmaknadsbyrån. Arbetsförmedlingarnas historia. Riksarkivet (Archives of the National Board for Social Affairs, the Labour Market Bureau, History of the Labour Exchanges. National Archives). Stockholm.

9. Riksförsäkringsanstaltens arkiv: Utlåtande med förslag rörande ändring av vissa delar av lagen angående ersättning för skada till föjld af olycksfall i arbetet, avgiftet af Riksförsäkringsanstalten den 10 januari 1908. Riksarkivet (Archives of the National Insurance Board, Statement and proposal concerning changes of part of the law regarding indemnification in work accidents, given by the National Insurance Board 10 January 1908. National Archives). Stockholm.

10. Betänkande afgifvet den 9 december 1909 af den av Kungl. Maj:t den 20 januari 1905 tilsatta kommittén för revision av lagarna angående skydd mot yrkesfara (Statement given 9 December 1909 by the Royal Commission established on 20 January 1905 in order to review the law on work-related accidents). Stockholm 1909.

11. Departementalkommitterades betänkande nr 5. Civildepartementet II. (Report by the Commission on the Organization of the Ministries, no. 5. Ministy of the Interior II). Stockholm 1912. p. 4.

12. Ibid. p. 5.

13. Idem.

14. Departementalkommitterades betänkande... (Report by the Commission on the Organization of the Ministries..) p. 6.

15. Government Bill, Record of the Swedish parliament, 1912, no. 108, p. 224.

16. Government Bill, Record of the Swedish Parliaments, 1913, no 298; 1919 (Autumn Session) no. 10; 1919 no. 333; 1917 no. 228, 1916, no. 111.

17. Nya arbetarförsäkringskomitén .... (Report by the New Workers Insurance Committee...) p. 103; Ålderdomsförsäkringskommitténs betänkande. *Report by the Old Age Insurance Committee* no 5, Stockholm, 1915, p. 94f.

18. Records from the Swedish Parliament. Second Chamber, 1919, no. 9, p. 31.

19. Government Bill, 1916, no. 111, p. 95.

20. Idem.

21. Departementalkommitterades betänkande ... Report by the Commission on the Organization of the Ministries ... p. 164.

22. Ibid. p. 166, and Government Bill, 1902, no. 15, p. 16.

23. Arbetarförsäkringskommitten... (Report by the Workers Insurance Committee) p. 101.

24. Departementalkommitterades betänkande... (Report by the Commission on the organization of the Ministeries....) p. 166.

25.   Idem.

26.   Government Bill, 1919, no. 247.

27.   Sosialstyrelsen, underdånigt yttrande angående statens medverkan för
       befrämjande av den offentliga arbetsförmedlingen m.m. den 17 april
       1916. Socialstyrelsens handlingar, Riksarkivet. (Statement by the
       National Board for Social Affairs concerning the collaboration by the
       State.

28.   Idem.

29.   Järte, Otto. 'Ett steg mot arbeidsmarknadens centralisering', in *Sociala
       Meddelanden*, 1920, s. 564.

30.   Socialstyrelsens handlingar, Social rådets protokoll, Riksarkivet.
       (Archives of the National Board for Social Affairs, records from the
       Social Council, National Archives). Stockholm.

Participation in Local Government: A Source of Social Democratic Deradicalization in Scandinavia?

Jan Sundberg

Scope and problem

The aim of this study is to discuss to what extent social democratic participation in local government has helped to deradicalize the active rank-and-file members. The debate on social democratic deradicalization goes back to the period around 1920 when the parties adopted programmes that were the most Marxist and offensive in their history. Today, their once radical socialist ideology is deradicalized and preoccupied with different short term interests; the once dynamic party organization has lost its spirit of solidarity and collective activity. The once offensive strategy has been replaced by a defensive attitude of wait-and-see. Given these changes, the social democrats are now facing electoral setbacks and declining membership activity (Selle 1991; Lindström 1991; Offe 1983, 225-246; Esping-Andersen 1985; Elvander 1980; Przeworski 1986; Przeworski and Sprague 1986; Touraine 1986, 165-167; Panebianco 1988).

The process of deradicalization is well documented but has not been analyzed systematically. Different studies show that class aspects are considered less than before in party programmes, in party manifestos, and in party newspaper editorials. Party propaganda has become vague, appealing to general groups common to all parties or to specific but ideologically diffuse groups (Helenius 1969, 27-136; Elvander 1980, 219-255; Pekonen 1990, 81-95; Karvonen 1990; Bilstad 1986; Bell 1960; Tingsten 1963; Heidar 1980). However, there is an almost total lack of information about the way in which the process of deradicalization has proceeded in local politics. Does participation in local government have a deradicalizing effect on those party members who hold a local office?

William Lafferty has investigated the degree of radicalism among the members of those Norwegian social democratic party branches which in 1918 held more than 30 per cent of the seats in local municipal councils. The results of the study show no relationship between local government participation and immunity against radicalism (Lafferty 1971, 271-274). On the contrary, observations from Finland and Norway strongly indicate that experience of local government politics has a moderating effect on the participating members (Soikkanen 1975, 470-475; Kettunen 1986, 285-287; Torgersen 1969). These studies are based on written party documents and therefore not afflicted with operational and statistical problems always connected with ecological analyses.

In sum, what there is of empirical data provides no clear clues as to the causal relationship between radicalism and participation in local politics. Below, we shall approach the problem by discussing relevant theories of deradicalization and their shortcomings.

Theories of deradicalization

The process of deradicalization as explained in the theoretical literature is by no means a simple one. Four different theories can be distinguished: the theory of 1) bureaucratization is exclusively based on the internal life of the party, whereas the theory of 2) transgression seeks the explanation in the competition for votes between parties in the party system. The theory of 3) institutionalization is a combination and a development of these two frameworks. Finally the theory of 4) power integration comes closest to our perspective insofar as it looks for explanations in the public institutions that hold power. In the following discussion the first three theories will be presented and evaluated briefly.

The concept of *bureaucratization* is problematic since it has been used in a wide variety of senses to describe size maximization, loss of control, efficiency and inefficiency, among many other things (Albrow 1970; Lane 1987, 1-31). However, if we follow Robert Michels, bureaucratization simply means that the party organization grows and that the administration is run by professionals (Michels 1962). According to Michels, upward mobility from worker to party bureaucrat automatically drains ideologigcal convictions. It seems likely that party bureaucrats wish to maintain the existing administrative order primarily because all drastic changes may threaten their positions. A contrasting view has been presented by V.I. Lenin who sees the employees (i.e. bureaucrats) in communist parties as the vanguard of the working class whose mission is to agitate and lead the masses to carry out a revolution (Lenin 1972; Lundquist 1982).

The concept of *transgression* introduced by Robert Michels and renamed by Adam Przeworski to *electoral socialism* 70 years later implies that in order to maximize their influence in Parliament, social democrats must seek electoral support outside the working class. Sooner or later, this will undermine their support among workers (Michels 1925, 25-26; Michels 1962, 334; Przeworski 1980, 38-41; Przeworski 1986; Przeworski and Sprague 1986; Esping-Andersen 1985). Thus social democratic parties face an electoral dilemma; if they want to gain power in Parliament they have to broaden their electoral appeal and this will result in a dilution of socialist ideology. The argumentation seems logical and reasonable but social democrats need not necessarily to broaden their electoral appeal to obtain power in Parliament. For instance, the Scandinavian social democratic parties gained power in the 1930s by entering into arrangements with agrarian parties without a prior broadening of their class appeal (Karvonen and Lindström 1988; Lewin, Jansson and Sörbom 1972, 163-188;

111

Wörlund 1990, 49-56; Thomsen 1987, 92-106).

Institutionalization is seen by Angelo Panebianco as the main determinant of party transformation, including deradicalization; he talks about a stepwise change over time in three phases (Panebianco 1988). The development is seen as a smooth linear process where the one step follows the other. The main argument against this interpretation is that institutionalization is per definition a result rather than a determinant of deradicalization because the process is determined by the environment and not by determinants within the organization (Selznick 1957, 5; Selznick 1966, 256-257; Parsons 1954, 143 and 239; Huntington 1968, 8-24). Philip Selznick, who originally developed the concept, sees the process of institutionalization emerging when organizational goals or procedures tend to achieve an established, value-impregnated status (Selznick 1966, 256-257). An organization, Selznick argues, is a tool and a rational instrument to achieve a goal, whereas an institution is a natural product of social needs and pressures characterized by responsiveness and adaptation (Selznick 1957, 5). Thus, social democratic parties may well be institutionalized, but this is by definition a result of changes in the environment and not a product of an autonomous process named institutionalization.

As the present study focuses on participation on the local levels, however, the theories of *power integration* seem more promising than the other three orientations presented above. The notion of power integration originates from Robert Michels' well-known statement: 'Political organization leads to power. But power is always conservative' (Michels 1962, 333). Originally, the statement stems from the idea that a working class organization promotes dissimilarity and gives power to its most talented members. The power-holding leaders are, according to Michels, prone to become conservative because they want to maintain their power and this can best be done under a status quo.

Michels has received strong support from Poul Meyer who has divided the active party members into two separate groups according to their mode of activity. The first group consists of members who participate in meetings, in party study circles, and are active volunteers in electoral campaigns. The second group, in contrast, consists of appointed representatives who fill the boards in the local associations, and of a smaller group who are representatives at higher levels in the party hierarchy. In addition, the two types of party activists can be differentiated according to their degree of radicalism. Those members who are active as individuals are more inclined to be radical because they have no responsibility for the organization and there is no prestige involved in their party work. In contrast, those members who are appointed representatives at different levels in the party have a responsibility for the organization and there is also prestige involved in their leadership role (Meyer 1965, 75-77). Therefore Meyer concludes that the appointed representatives are less inclined to be radical and they have an interest in trying to moderate ideological strains that might threaten the homogeneity of the party.

Morerover, the theory of power integration does not exclusively apply to the dynamics of internal party life. Its main application has to do with situations where working class party members have attained power through a public office. It is a well documented fact that where the working class was denied full political citizenship, strong radical movements developed. Conversely, the more the working class organizations were accepted into the political and economic order the less radical their ideological profile became (Lipset 1983, 1-18; Tingsten 1963; Bell 1960, 401; Mannheim 1936, 218). If access to the political and economic order offers the participating working-class members income, status and power, then in the process they will become a privileged group which resists radical political change (Lipset 1983, 1-18).

Implicitly, this argumentation supports the impression that it is the party leaders who personally gain from access to power. Also it indicates that the leaders become conservative whereas this is not the case with rank-and-file members who are supposed to maintain their radicalism in the absence of power and influence. However, no such rift has been visible in the social democratic parties, which indicates that the rank-and-file members received their share of power as well. Seymor Martin Lipset has emphasized this problem that is mostly overlooked. The development of workers' organizations permits the most politically active members to increase their income, status and power which makes them a privileged group and a force for moderation. If the workers manage to achieve public power and improve their social situation through their political organizations, they will be potentially less radical in a crisis situation than a comparable stratum that lacks the same means (Lipset 1983, 1-18).

Given these theoretical elements we can hypothesize that the more access to municipal power the active working class members get through their party organization, the more they are inclined to become deradicalized. The discussion that follows first examines the changing role of the social democratic local branches, followed by the process of politicization of local government, the changing role of the local politican, and finally the theoretical repercussions raised by the findings.

The changing role of the local branches

The social democratic parties were created as a means for working class members to change the political and economic order in society. The mass membership was the very strength of the party organized in local branches throughout the country. At local levels, the branch was the centre for membership activity and provided the means for members to share municipal power. The social democratic branches were characterized by an internal activity surpassing all other parties. According to Henry Valen and Daniel Katz, the local party association has three main functions:

1. It activates the ordinary member and makes it possible for him or her to participate in the decision-making process within the organization.
2. It organizes election campaigns at the local level.
3. To some extent it participates in the decision-making

process at the local governmental levels (Valen and Katz 1964, 63).

We shall discuss the first and the second function in relation to local social democratic branches. The most radical period for the social democratic parties in Scandinavia followed the introduction of proportional representation resulting in party splits and the emergence of communist parties (Karvonen 1991). More interesting is the fact that the social democratic youth organizations played an important role in the process of radicalization and fractionalization. The members of the youth organizations were active but in general lacked the responsibility of an appointed representative to a much higher degree than the active members in the party branches. In line with Meyer's theory, the youth or student organizations have played the role of a radical opposition culminating in the referendum on Danish and Norwegian membership in the Common Market (Bjørklund 1982; Elvander 1980, 193-204).

Furthermore, the whole hierarchy in social democratic parties is built on the principle of representative government. Even in the smallest local branches, decision-making lies in the hands of a board chosen by the members of the branch. Size is essential in direct democracy as a form of self-government. Most of the local social democratic branches were small enough to apply successfully the principles of direct democracy and self-government, and in Jean-Jaques Rousseau's terms, this would be the best means of preventing power from being concentrated in a minority of citizens (Rousseau 1968). Rousseau's ideas were well-known to the architects of the social democratic model of organization. Nevertheless, the principle of representative democracy was introduced from the very beginning at all levels in the organization independently of the size of the unit. Representative government transfers power of decision from the ordinary members to the representatives and enables a large hierarchial organization of control to be built up.

The membership of the local branches was usually defined in geographical terms. However, in Norway, in contrast to Den-

115

mark, Finland and Sweden, also trade union, womens' and youth associations were included. In larger cities and municipalities, the concentration of local branches was considerable whereas the smaller municipalities often lacked the full range of branches. In 1923, 27 per cent of the municipalities did not have a social democratic branch due to the party split (DNA Beretninger 1923). Very soon, however, the social democrats managed to build a network over the entire country. This network of local branches was a necessity when the social democrats began to nominate candidates to municipal council elections. When social democratic branches had spread to most municipalities in Scandinavia, a new period began with sudden decreases accelerated by the comprehensive municipal amalgamations in Denmark and Sweden. These amalagamations did not have similar effects on membership size. The considerable decline in membership in Denmark is much more complicated (Sundberg 1987, 17-38: Sundberg 1989b, 288-311; Elklit 1990; Togeby 1990). In Sweden and Norway the local labor union members are still collectively affiliated to the social democratic party, whereas in Denmark and Finland only individual members are included.

The branches listed in Table 1 underwent a considerable change during the period from the early 1900s to the late 1960s. Originally they were created by and for the workers, but with their increasing access to local power, the nature of the branches changed. The branches led a relatively autonomous organizational life before their involvement in local politics. According to Maurice Duverger, the nature of activity in political parties can be divided into three categories: community, association, and order. Community and association refers to the 'Gemeinschaft' and 'Gesellschaft' types of social groups. In Duverger's argumentation, the social democratic parties belong to the community category because their class base is a natural 'Gemeinshaft' link. In addition:

A community is not created, it is discovered. One does not really become a member of a community: one belongs to it automatically, willingly or unwillingly. One is born into a

116

Table 1

Social democratic branches in Scandinavia since 1921
(five-year averages)

	Denmark	Finland	Norway	Sweden
		year/N		
	1908/180	1916/1625	1913/962	1910/334
1920	859	1147	1733	944
1921-25	954	1115	1014[1]	1075
1926-30	1021	1270	1155	1463
1931-35	1141	1148	2170	2057
1936-40	1282	1149	3450[2]	2435
1945	1345	1115	3559	2612
1946-50	1360	1392	3759[3]	2787
1951-55	1356	1376[1]	2915[4]	2805
1956-60	1303	1479[2]	2254[5]	2701
1961-65	1231[1]	1363	1952[6]	2483
1966-70	1086[2]	1343	2487[7]	2159[1]
1971-75	764[3]	1379	2228[8]	582/1744[2]
1976-80	688[4]	1491	1920[9]	278/2595
1981-85	682	1497	2129[10]	282/2875
1987	683	1472	2300[11]	284/2432

Denmark: 1) 4-year average; 2) information exclusively from 1969; 3) 3-year average; 4) 3-year average.
Finland: 1) 3-year average; 2) 2-year average.
Norway: 1) 3-year average; 2) 3-year average; 4) 4-year average, 5) 4-year average; 6) 2-year average; 7) 2-year average; 8) 2-year average; 9) 3-year average; 10) 2-year average; 11) figures from 1988.
Sweden: 1) 4-year average; 2) 3-year average, due to a organizational reform in 1970 whereby the workers' communes became the municipal central organization of the local branches.

Source: Party data listed in Arbejderbevægelsens Bibliotek og Arkiv in Copenhagen; *Puoluetilastot* 1899-1942, Annual party reports 1943-1987, Sundberg 1989a, 37; *Det Norske Arbeiderparti, Beretninger* 1913-1987; *Socialdemokraterna: Verksamheten 1987.*

community and does not escape from it. Being part of one's family, one's village, one's country, and one's race is natural and involuntary (Duverger 1978, 125).

Given these criteria of social democracy, the difference between appointed representatives and ordinary members existed in the form of an oligarchical order between leaders and dependents. More important is the fact that in the very beginning, the members were on the same baseline concerning social class, formal education, and experience in politics. An appointment to the local executive committee presented a great challenge and entailed a process of intensive education. Through rotation among the appointees, a considerable proportion of the members became involved in running the local branch or some other ancillary or associated organization within the labour movement. This implies that with a 'Gemeinschaft' solidarity prevailing there was no room for rifts within organizations, only between them. However, the 'Gemeinschaft' solidarity is no longer the dominant party culture; instead the 'Gesellschaft' type of organization has gradually become the prevailing form. According to Duverger, the 'Gesellschaft' or association type of party organization is characterized by the following qualities:

> It is created because it is in someone's interest to create it: instead of being based on neighbourhood, geographical proximity, or blood relationship, the Association is based on interest. Membership of the group is founded here on the advantages obtained from it (Duverger 1978, 125).

The local branch has lost many of its functions in the course of this cultural change. Its educative and social functions have all but disappeared; little debate is conducted on political programmes and organizational matters; very little money is raised through the local organization. The local social democratic branch is no longer a branch in the original sense; rather, it is a local association similar to those of the non-socialist parties. The social democratic organization has increasingly assumed a character typical initially of other parties; an electoral machine characterized by competition within the party as well as by competition with other parties. In other words, a nucleus of members com-

118

pete for the positions of trust in the party hierarchy and in the process of candidate selection prior to elections. In contrast, during elections the parties compete with each other to obtain the votes of the increasingly volatile electorate, no matter where they come from.

Today between 10 and 16 per cent of the electorate in Scandinavia are party members. Of these, only a small minority are appointed as representatives in the party organization. In addition, survey studies show that the mode of activity in the party organizations has changed since the 1950s. Those who take part in campaign work personally are as few as before, but members were more active in attending party meetings in earlier periods. Today, they prefer to express their aims through direct activities, via interest organizations, by contacting mass media, or by personally contacting politicians and bureaucrats (Elklit 1990; Togeby 1990; Peterson, Westholm and Blomberg 1989, 81-129; Holmberg and Gilljam 1987, 65-68; Aardal and Valen 1989; Pesonen and Sänkiaho 1979, 155-160; Sundberg 1989a; Sundberg 1990, 41-43; Rokkan 1970, 352-361; Valen 1972, 21-25; Martinussen 1973, 43-52; Olsen and Saetren 1980; Kristensen 1980, 31-61). In addition, the social democrats have ceased to be the indisputably largest party organization, and the degree of local membership activity is no longer highest in the social democratic party. Finally and most important, the social democratic party has ceased to be an offensive force in politics parallel to the organizational transformation from a 'Gemeinschaft' solidarity to a 'Gesellshaft' association.

Municipal government as a school of political deradicalization

The history of local self-government goes back to the middle ages. In the nineteenth century, the ties to the church were broken and a smooth process of democratization was begun with the introduction of representative government (municipal councils), proportional representation, and universal suffrage. In the inter World War period, the role of the municipalities began to change with the rapid increase in public welfare tasks. Today the municipalities are responsible for primary education, social welfare, communications, primary health care and culture. However, before discussing the deradicalizing effect of running municipal government in Scandinavia, we must first evaluate earlier studies on this issue.

The idea that large masses of citizens should participate in public decision-making goes back to Jean-Jacques Rousseau and his book 'Le contrat social' which has had a decisive impact on the development of democratic theory. Rousseau strongly underscores the educative function of participating in decision-making (Rousseau 1968).

Rousseau strongly influenced Alexis de Tocqueville and his book 'De la Démocratie en Amérique'. de Tocqueville's concepts of freedom and political participation are particularly interesting because he relates them to the notion of local democracy:

> Local institutions are to liberty what primary schools are to science; they put it within people's reach; they teach people to appreciate its peaceful enjoyment and accustom them to make use of it. Without local institutions a nation may give itself a free government, but it has not got the spirit of liberty (de Tocqueville 1988, 63).

He goes on to illustrate the effects of active participation in local government with an example from New England:

> The New Englander is attached to his township because it is strong and independent; he has an interest in it because he shares its management; he loves it because he has no reason to complain of his lot; he invests his ambition and future in it; in the restricted sphere where within his scope, he learns to rule society; he gets to know those formalities without which freedom can advance only through revolutions, and becoming imbued with their spirit, develops a taste of order, understands the harmony of powers, and in

the end accumulates clear, practical ideas about the nature of his duties and the extent of his rights (de Tocqueville 1988, 70).

John Stuart Mill has evaluated and developed de Tocqueville's notion of participatory democracy at the local level. According to Mill, democracy at the national level has a heavier impact on the citizens' minds than on their behaviour; it affects their thoughts without creating a sense of responsibility. For the majority of the people, democracy merely means a passive acceptance of certain ideas.

Local democracy is different because the citizens not only vote in elections but stand a realistic chance of becoming elected. By holding a public office, the appointees learn to take responsibility for society at large and to act democratically for the common good. In Mill's view, people are exclusively concerned with their own problems, but with their involvement in local government they learn a sense of collective responsibility and abstain from pursuing their own interests. It is only by participating in local government that citizens learn about democracy. To learn democracy is like learning how to write or swim; the skills come through practice, not through instruction. By practicing small scale popular rule, people learn about democracy at national level; therefore, holding an office in municipal government is a school that provides an entrance ticket to national politics (Mill 1910, 346-359).

We would argue that the education of the participants proceeds in two phases. First, in the party organization, the working class members learn to apply the technical skills of party politics and to take responsibilty for the organization. With these skills acquired at party organization level, they continue their education as office holders in municipal government. This second step extends their responsibility and power from the narrow category of party members to cover all citizens in the municipality. The first stage may stimulate the educated towards radicalization, but at the same time they will become prepared to hold public office and this will necessarily moderate them in the long run. In

Duverger's terms, this second stage integrates the participants into a *community*. If that were not the case, then parliamentary democracy would not work.

Social democracy and local government

Social democrats were not involved as municipal councillors - apart from a few exceptions - before proportional representation and universal suffrage were introduced. Prior to these reforms, councillors in towns were almost exclusively elected from the non-socialist party tickets, whereas most of the rural municipalities were run by councillors from non-party lists (Palme and Lindberg 1962, 98-107; Hjellum 1967, 17-51; Kuusanmäki 1987, 386-403). However, with the introduction of proportional election of councillors and universal suffrage, a new era began in the process of politicization. Tables 2, 3, 4, and 5 illustrate how the process of politicization proceeded in the four Scandinavian countries.

The time spans in Tables 3 and 5 start from 1945 and 1938 respectively, although the criteria of representative democracy had been fullfilled already in the late 1910s. In Finland the process of politicization started already with the first free local government elections in 1918. However, politicization was one-sided since it was almost exclusively the social democrats that made use of the opportunity to nominate candidates for elections. Not until the 1950s and 1960s did the non-socialist parties participate to the same extent as the social democrats. In Sweden, the development was different because there were no local councils until 1937 in the majority of the municipalities. These small municipalities were run by a public assembly to which all citizens eligible to vote had full access; in other words, these communities at least formally came close to Rousseau's ideal of direct democracy.

Direct democracy seems to be a very effective method of keeping political parties out of the government. The Norwegian system of plural voting had a similar effect on parties. Therefore, it was in the interest of the social democrats to introduce repre-

Table 2
The politicization of municipal elections in Scandinavia:
Denmark, 1909-1985

	Party lists %	Other lists %	Total %	Councillors N
1909	24.9	75.1	100	9 897
1913	34.3	65.7	100	10 038
1917	43.0	57.0	100	10 166
1921	64.4	35.4	100	10 313
1925	57.0	43.0	100	11 329
1929	58.0	42.0	100	11 403
1933	57.5	42.5	100	11 425
1937	58.6	41.4	100	11 371
1943	62.6	37.4	100	10 569
1946	61.8	39.2	100	11 488
1950	60.4	39.6	100	11 499
1954	60.2	39.8	100	11 505
1958	58.8	41.2	100	11 529
1962	58.0	42.0	100	11 414
1966	57.0	43.0	100	10 005
1970	82.9	17.1	100	4 677
1974	85.8	14.2	100	4 735
1978	86.6	13.4	100	4 759
1981	88.8	11.2	100	4 769
1985	89.9	10.1	100	4 773

Source: *Statistiske Meddelelser* and *Statistiske efterretninger*

sentative government and proportional voting at local levels. The
social democrats were the most active of all parties in politicizing local elections after the introduction of proportional representation. Compared to other parties, the social democrats had a
great advantage in their nation-wide organizational networks of
local associations. No other party could compete with a similar
mass organization. Tables 6, 7 and 8 compare the number of
municipalities in which the social democrats, conservatives, liberals and agrarians nominated candidates in Denmark and Norway.

The local social democratic branches were most active in
nominating candidates to municipal elections and in running local

Table 3

The politicization of municipal elections in Scandinavia: Finland, 1954-84

	Party lists %	Other Lists %	Total %	Councillors N
1945	62.3	37.7	100	10 201
1947	62.3	37.7	100	10 659
1950	66.2	33.8	100	12 236
1953	79.4	20.6	100	12 236
1956	81.6	18.4	100	12 361
1960	91.4	8.6	100	12 408
1964	89.4	10.6	100	12 325
1968	94.1	5.9	100	11 856
1972	96.4	3.6	100	11 191
1976	97.5	2.5	100	12 739
1980	97.9	2.1	100	12 777
1984	97.6	2.4	100	12 881

Source: Sundberg 1989c, 33-38; Municipal election statistics since 1968.

governments. In Finland prior to 1945, it was almost exclusively the social democrats who contested the local elections while parties on the right were content to support independent non-socialist lists. Even in 1945, according to estimates, approximately 70 per cent of all non-socialist councillors were elected from non-partisan lists (Sundberg 1989a, 78-88). Electoral data from Norway resemble the findings from Finland. During the whole history of democratic local elections, the social democrats have been by far the largest party in Norway. In 1937 the Norwegian non-socialist parties clearly lagged behind in nominating candidates to party lists in local elections. The conservatives were extremely passive at the beginning of the period, and now they are almost as active as the social democrats. Not until universal suffrage was introduced in the Danish Parliament did the degree of politicization in the local elections increase considerably. Although the Danish social democrats were most active in politicizing the municipal elections, the Liberal Party and the

Radical Party spread their organizational activity very early on to the rural municipalities. The differences between the large parties almost vanished with the considerable municipal amalgamations in 1970.

Table 4

The politicization of municipal elections in Scandinavia:
Norway, 1913-1987

	Party lists %	Other lists %	Plural voting %	Total %	Councillors N
1913	38.2	19.2	41.9	100	13 457
1916	43.7	17.6	38.7	100	13 747
1919	47.4	30.7	21.9	100	13 964
1922	53.5	28.6	17.9	100	14 444
1925	49.5	32.0	18.5	100	14 654
1928	54.1	30.7	15.2	100	14 799
1931	58.4	29.7	11.9	100	14 932
1934	61.9	30.7	7.4	100	14 975
1937	66.1	30.0	3.9	100	15 056
1945	66.1	29.7	4.2	100	15 094
1947	69.2	26.5	4.3	100	15 086
1951	73.3	23.6	3.1	100	15 232
1955	76.9	21.1	2.0	100	16 418
1959	80.3	18.4	1.3	100	16 348
1963	85.1	14.0	0.9	100	14 343
1967	90.4	9.3	0.3	100	13 523
1971	89.9	9.9	0.2	100	13 392
1975	90.6	9.2	0.2	100	13 545
1983	95.2	4.9	0.1	100	13 806
1987	93.3	6.7	0.1	100	13 648

Source: Norwegian Social Science Data Services (NSD)

The late entrance of non-socialist parties into local elections cannot exclusively be explained by the lack of organizational resources. In smallest municipalities, the local council work was

125

Table 5
The politicization of municipal elections in Scandinavia: Sweden, 1938-1985

	Party lists %	Other lists %	Total %	Councillors %
1938	70.7	29.3	100	38 863
1942	70.0	30.0	100	39 748
1946	77.3	22.7	100	40 188
1950	99.4	0.6	100	32 983
1954	99.2	0.8	100	33 048
1958	98.9	1.1	100	32 877
1962	97.6	2.4	100	32 282
1966	98.5	1.5	100	29 546
1970	97.5	2.5	100	18 327
1973	98.4	1.6	100	13 236
1976	98.6	1.4	100	13 247
1979	98.3	1.7	100	13 369
1982	98.5	1.5	100	13 500
1985	98.5	1.5	100	13 500

Source: Municipal election statistics

Table 6
Party lists in Danish local elections, 1909-1966
(rural municipalities)

	1909 %	1913 %	1917 %	1921 %	1925 %	1929 %	1933 %	1937 %
Social Democrats	19	28	35	67	63	66	75	82
Conservatives	8	14	16	25	21	21	22	21
Radicals	12	25	28	50	45	45	43	43
Liberals	20	32	37	62	54	54	52	48
N = (municipalities)	1137	1144	1151	1170	1290	1299	1304	1297

Continues

	1943 %	1946 %	1950 %	1954 %	1958 %	1962 %	1966 %
Social Democrats	84	81	80	79	78	76	74
Conservatives	25	23	21	20	18	21	27
Radicals	44	40	38	37	34	31	27
Liberals	54	52	51	51	49	49	46
N = (municipalities)	1188	1302	1301	1300	1298	1267	1018

Table 7
Party lists in Danish local elections, 1909-1966
(urban municipalities)

	1909 %	1913 %	1917 %	1921 %	1925 %	1929 %	1933 %	1937 %
Social Democrats	88	95	93	100	97	94	93	98
Conservatives	47	49	44	70	68	61	60	68
Radicals	49	58	65	82	79	76	74	79
Liberals	44	54	43	65	62	60	55	56
N = (municipalities)	73	74	75	76	85	84	85	84

Continues

	1943 %	1946 %	1950 %	1954 %	1958 %	1962 %	1966 %
Social Democrats	99	99	99	99	100	100	100
Conservatives	84	82	81	79	79	80	83
Radicals	86	73	72	71	66	54	51
Liberals	67	74	74	73	79	78	79
N = (municipalities)	76	85	85	85	86	86	86

Source: Bentzon 1972 and Danish Data Archive
Social Democrats = *Socialdemokratiet*; Conservatives = *Konservative Folkeparti*; Radicals = *Radikale Venstre*; Liberals = *Venstre*.

characterized by a high sense of community between the councillors. This observation coincides with the discussion of participatory democracy in Rousseau, de Tocqueville, and Mill, and also generally with the debate on size and democracy; small units are seen as more likely to generate loyalty to a single integrated community (Dahl and Tufte 1973, 4-16). To be a councillor was an appointment of trust with a relatively high status and rarely attainable for anybody but the local elite. The social democratic councillors did not challenge the sense of community even when they won a majority of the council seats. No 'Commune de Paris' was founded in any of the heavily industrialized municipalities. The social democrats preferred to enter deals with, for instance,

Table 8
Party lists in Norwegian local elections, 1937-1987

	1937 %	1945 %	1947 %	1951 %	1955 %	1959 %	1963 %
Social Democrats	92	88	90	90	91	91	91
Conservatives	-	15	22	31	44	52	62
Liberals	40	41	44	48	50	55	59
Agrarians	37	24	31	36	44	53	64
N=(municipalities)	747	744	744	744	744	744	732

Continues

	1967 %	1971 %	1975 %	1979 %	1983 %	1987 %
Social Democrats	96	98	99	99	100	100
Conservatives	75	75	75	94	96	94
Liberals	77	74	56	65	72	67
Agrarians	78	83	84	87	88	87
N=(municipalities)	451	444	445	454	454	448

Source: NSD

Social Democrats = *Det Norske Arbeiderparti*; Conservatives = *Høyre*; Liberals = *Venstre*; Agrarians = *Bondepartiet*, since 1959 *Senterpartiet*.

the foundry proprietors, by offering them the position of chairman of the local government administration or other consensual agreements (Soikkanen 1966, 483-492). Why did the social democrats choose consensus and not conflict in the municipal councils?

Clearly, the limited organizational resources of the non-socialist parties would have rendered an extensive participation in local elections difficult. However, there was also a clear ideological strategy behind the decision not to participate via party lists; a non-political council was seen as the best weapon against social democratic influence in local politics. This strategy has much in common with the conservative ideology which strongly opposes all efforts to enlarge the arena of politics in society. Another very common strategy was to nominate common non-socialist lists against the social democrats (Bentzon 1972; Hjellum 1967, 17-50; Sundberg 1989a, 78-103).

The municipal programmes of the social democrats from the period before World War II were pragmatic, but they strongly emphasized the enlargement of local self-government and the development of social welfare programmes (Arbeiderpartiets kommunepolitikk 1931; Kettunen 1986, 285-287). Marxist doctrines contained little in the way of solutions to municipal problems. Nevertheless, when social democrats demanded more efficient local welfare measures, the non-socialists frequently saw this as a radical, ideologically motivated strategy.

When the non-socialist parties became fully represented in the local councils, the political culture changed from a predominantly local consensus towards an institutionalized order of competition. Local politics had become nationalized and followed similar swings in voting behaviour as in national elections. Much more than earlier, the municipalities are today miniatures of the national Parliaments (Thomsen 1984, 288-297; Aardal and Valen 1989, 287-309; Holmberg and Gilljam 1987; Sundberg 1989a).

Characteristics of the local politician

Studies show that members of the local social democratic branches actively discussed local problems and gave instructions to their councillors. Gradually, however, participation in the municipal councils and boards began to dominate the work of the party activists at the expense of internal party work. Especially after World War II, when the non-socialist parties put pressure on the social democrats through their massive entrance into local politics, the social democratic activity in municipal government was strengthened. This change in the focus of political activity resulted in a concentration of organizational activities moving from internal party work to representation in local government (Bergh 1987, 76; Kettunen 1986, 195-197; Lindström 1989, 96-100). In addition, in most cases those who ran in the local elections also held leading positions in the local party branches, and this tendency became most conspicuous among the social democrats (Wallin, Bäck and Tabor 1981, 1-179; Hoikka and Kiljunen 1983; Ruusala 1972; Bentzon 1981; Larsen and Offerdal 1979; Offerdal 1976, 30-61). It was the local party leaders who were primarily recruited as councillors, followed by other prominent party activists. With the extensive municipal amalgamations in Sweden and Denmark, the number of appointed representatives in the municipal councils and boards was reduced.

This presents the local party branches with a major challenge, because the positions have lost much of their attraction. Practically all active party members are involved in running municipal government today. The activity in the branch has decreased to a minimum between elections. Many party members are still very active but their activity is performed outside the local branch. They represent the party in municipal government as well as in other types of organizations. Moreover, formerly the councillors were the local elite. Today, on the other hand, the position is seen as a duty rather than as a reward.

In essence, the social democratic branch used to provide the political schooling; the main activity took place within the party. This role has been replaced by the municipal government where most of the party members perform their political activity today. The decreasing membership activity in social democratic parties is a serious problem which has received much attention (Elvander 1980; Esping-Andersen 1985). The phenomenon of passivity has been characterized by Peter Blau and Marshall Meyer as follows:

> We generally no longer govern our voluntary organizations: we simply join them, pay our dues, and let experts run them. As a result, we have less and less opportunity for acquiring experiences that are essential for effective participation in democratic government (Blau and Meyer 1971, 167).

The development seems at least partly to go back to what de Tocqueville and Mill once advocated and to the main way in which non-socialist MPs received their political education ever since the nineteenth century. The trend did not change with the entrance of parties into Parliament and municipal councils. Still practically all MPs have started their political careers as councillors in municipal government. Similarly, most of them have been representatives in local party organizations, whereas a minority of the MPs were members of the party elite. Only new and successful parties have to recruit candidates with a very narrow political experience (Sköld and Halvarson 1966, 397, 455-459, 474-477; Soikkanen 1966, 633-639; Noponen 1964, 250-255; Damgaard 1977, 106; Eliassen and Ågotnes 1987).

The differences between social democrats and other parties have decreased in this process. In all parties it is local politics that directs the activity rather than vice versa. To be a local politician today is to follow very elaborate public regulations; this activity strongly dominates ideological goals. Pressure from the public is even stronger due to the rapidly increasing number of municipal employees who outnumber the locally elected positions. Perhaps more important is their high level of education and specialization which gives them competence far above that of the local politicans. The contemporary local politican has a complex role at the intersections between different pressures. In sum, the role of the politician today is problematic, diversified, and lacks clarity compared to the situation when the first social democrats were elected as councillors. Earlier, the social democratic party was the given platform of access for working class members to gain political influence and power in municipal government. Now many approaches are open, either to influence through the traditional 'parliamentary' way, by becoming a bureaucrat in municipal administration, by becoming an opinion leader in the media, or by taking part in grass-roots activities. The most rational way is to combine the different means of influence, and this is the most common approach today among party members as well as among other activists. The party is no longer the only platform, it is one of many actors controlling power.

Conclusions

Four basic perspectives can be found in the literature on social democratic deradicalization. In this study the theory of power intergration is applied with emphasis on the deradicalizing effect of participating in local government. The theoretical model was originally developed to explain deradicalization in national politics. Implicitly the model presupposes that it is exclusively the party elite that is deradicalized and not the rank-and-file members. According to this theory, there will always be a latent possibility that a rift may arise between the party elite and the rank-and-file members. In addition, the process of deradicalization is suggested to be linear.

The degree of radicalism in the party programme seems to vary according to the organizational strength and the degree of responsiveness among the holders of municipal and central government power. The degree of responsiveness may range from total rejection to full governmental access. Between the extremes lies a period of partial access which refers to the step-by-step democratization of elections and Parliament, followed by full access to parliamentary power without any regulations or discrimination. The social democratic parties may adopt three different strategies in pursuing their political aims. They can take a radical-offensive, a reformist-offensive or an adaptive-defensive standpoint.

Table 9 demonstrates that the social democratic parties may choose different strategies, as was the case in Norway up to the early 1920s compared to Denmark and Sweden. However, the electoral system in Norway up to 1918 directly discriminated against the social democrats and favoured their non-socialist competitors openly. The Finnish electoral system of 1906 gave the social democrats free access to Parliament but the actual political power was in the hands of the Russian police state. In addition, changes in accessibility do not automatically transform party strategy; this was the case with the Norwegian social democrats, who maintained their radicalism for some years after the elec-

Table 9

Social democratic strategies in four different situations

The party becomes:	System responsiveness:			
	No access	Partial access	Full acc. Parliament	Full acc. govt.
Radical/ offensive	E.g. Finland prior to 1919	Norway until early 1920s		
Reformist/ offensive		Sweden until 1921; Denmark until 1915	Scandinavia until mid-1930	'Golden Years' 1935-70
Adaptive/ defensive				Since early 1970s

toral reform. In contrast, the process of radicalization did not spring directly from a situation of rejection or partial access. It was rather the result of a relatively long process, in which a growing political force had practically no choice but to threaten the system after years of unsuccessful demands.

With the full access to Parliament and later to government, the doors were opened for an offensive reformist strategy where the parliamentary system took over the role of the party organization as a means of change. The golden years is a story of success for social democracy, but the comprehensive reforms tied up most of the organizational efforts in monitoring the implementation of laws, decrees, and resource assignments concurrently with the public administration undergoing a comprehensive expansion. The change from offensive to defensive strategy took place as it became insufficient to undertake reforms by the traditional public means. Neither the party nor the government bureaucracy could provide new alternatives. The initiative was lost and the social democrats had to adapt to the environment even though their ally in reform work - the public sector - has been designated as the roots of stagnation.

If the period of radicalism, including offensive reformism, started around 1920 and was definitely terminated in the late 1960s, the same is not automatically valid for local politics. With the democratization of municipal government, the access to local power was fully open for social democracy, but it was never used as a means for implementing local socialism, not even when it won a numerical majority in the councils. During that time the local conflicts were only marginally affected by the cleavage structure of national politics. In Table 10, the main characteristics are summarized for the period when the local social democratic branch was directed by a 'Gemeinschaft' solidarity and the municipalities were run in a traditional non-politicized way.

Table 10 summarizes the types of context that the members of local social democratic branches met when they entered municipal government in the first decades of the twentieth century. First of all, the non-socialist strategy of excluding party politics from municipal councils had a desired effect on the well organized and radical social democrats. In general, the social democrats responded by a cautiously offensive programme demanding very modest social reforms which were seen as radical by the non-socialists but seldom challenged the state of consensus. Most of the administrative work was done by the councillors and the elected representatives on the boards, and this effectively trained the social democrats in how to run local government. Perhaps more important is the fact that the less educated working class councillors acquired local power and status through the social democratic party and that they gradually became respected by the traditional power-holding elite.

It seems obvious that the theories of power integration have overestimated the deradicalizing effect of access to parliamentary power. In this paper, deradicalization is seen as the process through which the party organization is transformed from an offensive to a defensive position. In that process the organization ceases to be a means of change and becomes institution-

Table 10
The characteristics of social democratic branches and municipal governments during the early days of local democracy.

	The social democratic branch	The municipal government
Membership	large	many elected positions
Units	many large branches	many small municipal governments
Members	working class	the local elite
Order	'Gemeinschaft' solidarity	low degree of politicization
Involvement	solidarity	honorary task
Activity	high	low
Mode of activity	voluntary and self-sacrificing	elected duty
Doctrine	offensive	consensus
Ideology	radical reformist	status quo
Dominant actors	oligarchical working class rule	layman rule
Degree of bureaucracy	very low	low

alized. The departure to integration begins when the means of change is transmitted from the party organization to public administration. Thus, according to this argumentation it is not enough to obtain political access to parliamentary power. The theory of power integration must be enlarged to comprise executive power. Thanks to new missions generated by offensive party demands for reforms, public administration grows, gains

135

more control, and most important, is given power that hardly can be managed through elections, parties, and Parliament.

What about today? The most important observation when comparing Table 10 to Table 11 is that the social democratic branches have changed in so many respects that they can now be called local associations rather than branches. Their organizational life is no longer autonomous to the same degree as before when the 'Gemeinschaft' solidarity prevailed. Clearly, when the municipalities were amalgamated in Denmark and Sweden it had immediate organizational effects. The social democrats adapted the number and size of the local associations to the drastic change in the number and size of municipalities. The activity in the local associations is low between elections. The rational and self-interested party member is, however, often very active but the activity is focused on running local government which is not effectively controlled by the local party association. Previously the political initiative came from the branch, whereas now it is in the hands of the professionals in local adminstration, in close collaboration with the local politicans. The role of the local representatives is no longer an honorary task allocated to the elite. The representative has become a skilled politican specialized in some sector of the municipal adminsitration. To be a local politician is not very attractive today, the position is loaded with work and contains few incentives. The degree of bureaucracy has increased radically and the bureaucrats are much more skilled than the politicans.

All in all, the situation is problematic for the local party association which is now closely integrated with the local government. The internal activities remaining are nominations, election campaigns, and group meetings before important council session. The involvement in district level and national level party congresses is weak and concerned with appointments to the representative bodies rather than with ideological aims. Briefly, party actions are not directed by short or long-term programmes as before. The actions are, rather, a result of random events occur-

136

Table 11
The characteristics of social democratic local associations and municipal governments since the 1970s

	The social democratic local association:	The municipal government:
Membership decline	smoothly diminishing	periods of rapid
Units	periods of rapid decline	periods of rapid decline
Members	blue and white collars	the local mediocricity
Order	'Gesellschaft'	high degree of politicization
Enrolment	self-interest	self-interest
Activity	low	high
Mode of activity	voluntary but rational	elected obligation often self sacrificing
Doctrine	defensive	offensive
Ideology	adaptive	reformist
Dominant actors	white and blue collar oligarchy	professional rule
Degree of bureaucracy	low	very high

ring at all levels in the party hierarchy and mostly initiated in connection with running the state, county council, or municipal government.

In sum, deradicalization as suggested at the outset is closely connected to power integration; public bureaucracy has replaced the party organization as an instrument of change. The phenomenon, as it developed in Scandinavia with a very decentralized public administration, has opened access to the integration of more or less all active members in the party hierarchy. For the active rank-and-file members, participation in municipal government functions as schooling in politics and a platform on which to build their political careers, whereas the active role of the local party association has diminished along with waning radicalism. The social democratic parties of today resemble the liberal parties in their organizational functions as well as in their ideology. This is yet another feature which suggests that the socialist-nonsocialist distinction has lost most of its meaning.

Notes

I am indebted to Rolf Danielsen, Tore Grønlie, and Ulf Lindström of the University of Bergen and Lauri Karvonen of Åbo Academy for their comments on an earlier draft of this study. The Norwegian Social Science Data Service (NSD) and the Danish Data Archive (DDA) have provided me with data and computer runs.

PART II
CURRENT
PREDICAMENTS

The Idea of Equality and Security in Nordic Social Democracy

Per Selle

Introduction

> Socialism seems to me to have two main dimensions, the use of governmental power to give a better life to the poor and to workers, and to do this in particular by reducing the power of ownership of the means of production. Below I discuss this dilemma, but clearly Norway has come a good deal farther in giving a good life to the poor than in reducing the power of capital (Stinchcombe 1979, 1).

In a recent interview with the German author and social democrat Günter Grass, ideas were unveiled which we would like to make our own. He says:

> I find social democratic politics as pursued in Scandinavia, The Netherlands and Germany one-sided. In these countries social democracy has continued to develop towards the welfare state, the social state. It seems to define the world in purely materialistic terms, just like capitalism. Decisions were always aimed at material improvements, at answer economic questions. Now we are experiencing the importance of other areas that do not fall within the scope of social service: the importance of the cultural components (Günter Grass 1990, 35).

If 'the cultural components' are taken in their broadest sense, Günter Grass is here stressing central features of the historical heritage of social democracy while at the same time pointing to the important challenges now facing social democracy. Moreover, in a very interesting (if not exactly original) comment, Grass asserts the view that one of the main reasons social democracy is not interested in overriding cultural issues is related to the major schism in Europe which resulted in the Reformation, and thus in the varying strength of the more puritanical way of life. This is an ideology and a way of life found first and foremost in the northern parts of Germany, in the Netherlands, in Scandinavia and in England, that is to say, those countries where capitalism was first successful, and which later became the heartland of social democracy. Seen in this light, social democracy is a Protestant rather than a Catholic movement, and, says Grass:

> (p)uritanism does not take much pleasure in art and prefers to focus on profit, security, cleanliness and social conventions. Art is so wonderfully irrational, exuberantly pointless, but necessary all the same. Pointless and yet necessary, that's hard for a puritan to understand. A puritan only wants art if it gives him something to live by, furnishes him with some deeper moral, a guidebook to life (p. 35).

Let us therefore set out from this universal and strong emphasis on the material, the efficient and the instrumental aspects of social democracy. Przeworski, one of the main theoreticians on social democracy, claims that *efficiency, full employment* and *equality* are essential if we are to understand the historical distinctiveness of social democracy (Przeworski 1987, 241). This is a general view, but the difficulty is that the exact meaning of equality is never clarified. This paper takes as its point of departure the view that if we are to understand social democracy as a historical phenomenon, we should start with the concepts of *'efficiency', 'full employment'* and *'security'*, and although this sounds more or less the same, we shall soon see that this is not the case. One of the main objectives is to show that this prevailing emphasis on 'equality' prevents insight, it prevents us from penetrating into what is typical of social

140

democracy. On the other hand, the term 'security' (or the prevention of marginalization), which is clearly distinct from the concept of 'equality', is of great help. The question will also be raised whether full employment is as fundamental a hallmark of social democracy as the other elements, or whether this just arises out of the others and should be considered more a means rather than a paramount goal.

Social democracy is now undergoing a major ideological and organizational transformation process. We must go right back to the 1930s to find anything similar. How can new groups of voters be reached (absolutely essential if genuine governing power is really being sought) without losing already existing voters? Social democracy is moving away from being a system that does not work any longer, but its ultimate destination is not yet certain. As in the period prior to Keynes, there is no alternative economic model - the meaning of the term 'alternative' would have to be considerably expanded to allow the argument that social democracy is today able to pursue an alternative economic policy. In this *open* and confused situation, it is worth trying to pinpoint some of the features that are typical of social democracy, features that are so universal that they were valid in the beginning and must be valid now and in the future if social democracy is to remain social democracy.

This chapter is divided into three main parts. First we will discuss in general what social democratic 'equality' really means, and consider this in conjunction with the demand for efficiency and full employment. Then we will look at the way in which this 'equality' is represented and institutionalized in our most important welfare institutions. The final section of this paper will deal with the challenges social democracy is facing today, and will discuss the directions in which social democracy may turn while still retaining contact with its historical traditions. The situation in Norway is our point of departure, though our main views also have relevance to the situation in other Nordic countries.[1]

What is social democratic 'equality'?

If the term 'equality' is to be used in a discusion on social democracy as a historical phenomenon, something must be said about the type of equality being discussed. At all events, an attempt must be made to differentiate between *equality of opportunities* - seen here as a combination of formal equality and equality of resources (see Hernes, 1974), and *equality of results*. If one is talking primarily about equality of opportunities, one is saying very little, because so few people would oppose this that there would hardly be room for variation in societies without feudal traditions and strong Catholic institutions. Nevertheless, this does not prevent there being substantial differences of opinion as to how far one is to go, that is to say, what conditions should be introduced so that one feels that an acceptable level of equality of opportunities exists. If, on the other hand, one means *equality of results*, or at least a *genuine* redistribution, one must demonstrate exactly where this has taken place. Good studies showing that social democracy has pursued a policy in which wealth is taken from the rich and given to the poor, which must be the broad definition of redistribution, are, to put it mildly, hard to find. In addition, the term 'redistribution' is also one of those concepts without clear boundaries, concepts which can be read with a variety of meanings to suit individual purposes. Certain types of redistribution would probably find more or less universal support; however, and more important, we can easily envisage forms of organization that stress redistribution without emphasing equality. Redistribution is not equality, even though it may be possible to make it sound that way.

It is our view that the idea of equality, meaning equality of results, has never held an ideologically strong position in social democracy. It is more like a myth, with strong interests engaged in sustaining that myth. It cannot be assumed a priori that the idea of equality is much stronger in Norway and in Scandinavia in general than in other parts of the world and that this to a certain degree explains the unusually strong support for social democracy in the northern countries. It is an empirical question and must be treated as such. I believe, and most of it is *belief* since so little *empirical* research has been done in the matter, that it is the material premises that historically have made it difficult for most of us to become much richer than others. This was also the situation before social democracy made its appearance on the scene. Because we have no history of wealth, this does not imply that we either ideologically to a much greater degree than others are averse to wealth, or that we to any extent have formed organizations to prevent the development of inequality, either financially, socially or culturally.

After social democracy entered into an alliance with the capitalist production system in the 1930s, *efficiency* and *productivity* have held absolutely central positions in the social democratic view of society. At the same time, and as a part of this process, social democracy chose to allow itself to become integrated into society, that is, it accepted the parliamentary system and thus the 'bourgeois' state. After all, social democracy advanced as it did not because less was to be produced, but rather because more was to be produced through a more rational and economic system which at the same time guaranteed people *fundamental rights* in their work situation and also in other respects. The demand for efficiency and rationality was *more* pronounced in social democracy than in any other political movement at this time. The Conservatives as a political party, for instance, at any rate for as long at the conservative cultural and moral values were exerting a substantial influence, were far more open to 'irrational' local elements while opposing extensive dismantling of the social hierarchy. This prevents talents from emerging and hampers genuine competition. In addition, substantial unemployment was accepted because for a long time it could be interpreted as a law of nature. Social democracy was thus far less 'fatalistic', far less controlled by its environment, and thus more expansive and with a will to intervene and to control. In other words, social democracy accepted less 'slack' in the system, and certainly in its golden era (1945-1970) - and probably even today, even though the internal debate now concerns degree - it was and is a 'technocratic' party of growth.

The view on unemployment is an important element here. Nothing was considered to be more of a waste, from the point of view of society, and at the same time, nothing was considered a greater indignity, seen from the point of view of the individual. *In a way, the view on unemployment joins together the view of society with the view of the individual*, and it is not possible to understand social democracy without understanding the role played by work. Productive work is what makes a person whole, and at the same time it leads to increased prosperity for society in general. If labour's role in society changes fundamentally - and many claim that it is now doing so (viz. the various theories about the post-modern/post-materialistic society) - this may suggest that the view on unemployment may also change without it being possible to claim that social democracy thereby has broken fundamentally with the past. Preventing unemployment may have been more a means than an end; it may have been a 'reflection' of more fundamental circumstances. We will revert to this later.

Economic efficiency and full employment have been far more important than redistribution and equality. As we see it, redistribution - to the extent this has actually taken place - has been more a result of a conflict of interests within a constantly more 'corporative' structure than an integrated part of a planned social democratic structure. Redistribution is something that first and foremost refers to the nature of the relationship between classes and social groups. Social democracy has only to a small extent stressed the alteration of such relationships through active intervention to make us all more alike. However, what has been stressed, and this is another matter altogether, is the development of institutions and regulations which are to prevent any form of *marginalization* of ordinary folk. So far, full employment has been the principal means of preventing marginalization, for ensuring that neither labourers nor smallholders should ever again find themselves in a situation reminiscent of that existing for many years between the two World Wars, and also before World War I for that matter. Full employment does not imply redistribution in the sense of moving power and status relationships between groups. Rather it guarantees 'ordinary' people a position where others cannot treat them in an arbitrary manner. In other words, it renders politics decent by creating social security.

The Norwegian social scientist Ottar Brox (1988) has propounded an interesting theory on why there is so little marginalization in our system. He emphasises the *complementary* and balanced development in the relationship between town and country, where the Nygaardsvold policy' (i.e. the crisis agreement and the absolute acceptance of parliamentarism) made the rural alternative more attractive through the use of state mechanisms. The alliance between town and country was a good alliance for the nation, irrespective of whether it was planned or not. The coordinated effort meant that the towns did not grow too rapidly, thus strengthening the market position of workers in the towns. At the same time, rural society continued to be *open*, i.e. many people were qualified to carry out most of the jobs, and this in turn provided flexibility, this was an absoultely vital quality. It was this flexibility that helped to prevent marginalization, perhaps first and foremost because it prevented long-term unemployment and thus ensured at least a modicum of security. Perhaps it is possible to claim that the prevention of marginalization, that is to say the promotion of security, is of greater fundamental importance than guaranteeing full employment at any time. Marginalization is first and foremost promoted by long-term unemployment. Thus the existence of a certain amount of unemployment does not in all circumstances suggest the failure of social democracy, while marginalization of major groups of the population *always* indicates this.

In the years prior to the last World War, preventing marginalization was the same as *integrating* the working class into society by eliminating absolute poverty (which actually belongs to the post-war period). The social democratic strategy was built on political democratic participation parallel to - at least in an interim period - the establishment of alternative social democratic institutions. These establishments were necessary in order to strengthen social democracy's position as a social and political movement, while increasing the self-respect of those taking part. Whether social democracy historically speaking to a greater degree than other parties has supported the ideas of a genuine *participatory democracy* compared to a more *paternalistic view of democracy* is an important question which cannot be discussed in detail here. What is certain, however, is that the paternalistic features have been strong, and stronger in some countries than in others (e.g., Sweden). However, these features became weaker over time, and were much reduced after the 'social democratic' and centralized control model started to loose its legitimacy at the beginning of the 1980s. It is now one really starts talking about *user democracy* and *decentralization*. When it no longer is considered legitimate for society to intervene, i.e. the 'social democratic' state, people must themselves intervene. Paterna-

145

lism is on the way out.

What we consider to be fundamental in the social democratic ideology, or in the view of human beings, if one will, is that ordinary' people are to be masters over their own lives.[2] 'Ordinary' people were to (are to) be entitled to a new form of *personal autonomy* which few earlier had been interested in giving them, and which they themselves had not thought they could achieve. In other words, the right to security must be fought for. However, this does not presume equality either ideologically or institutionally. Such rights may well be envisaged within *hierarchical* systems - for instance where Catholicism, with its stress on responsibility, holds a strong position - systems where structurally given differences are felt to be as natural. Alternatively, they may be envisioned in societies with sharply delimited sub-cultures which have relatively fixed boundaries between themselves and their surroundings, but in which there do not need to be hierarchical relationships between the various sub-cultures. What first and foremost separates (separated?) the social democratic view of welfare from the 'Catholic' view is a far less fatalistic outlook on the individual and thus on society, a view which says that we do not always need to have large numbers of marginalized and poverty-stricken people among us. It is possible to intervene to manage social developments. The aim is to promote an 'open' society, a more mobile society without large marginalized groups and sharp barriers between various layers of the population.

Do our welfare institutions promote equality?[3]

When we take our point of departure in the characteristics of our welfare institutions, it is because these are so well suited to shed light on the social democratic 'view of equality'. This is because the main responsibility for shaping these institutions is largely ascribed to social democracy, and with some justification. This is perhaps the area where we most expect to find social democratic values reflected in the shape of society's institutions. But as in the rest of our economy and community life, our institutionalized welfare schemes are not designed to promote equality, i.e. to alter the relationship between social groups or classes. They safeguard the rights which promote

146

security, without actually promoting *real* social redistribution (Kuhnle and Solheim 1985). We must all have the same right to institutional care. If someone breaks a leg, that leg is to be set quickly no matter who the patient is. We consider it natural that such care should not be linked to production, status and ability to pay. But this is not really a question of redistribution in the ordinary sense of the word, but rather that preferential treatment should not be given to different categories of patients with the same complaint. Some rights are more universal than others, but that does not imply redistribution. In my opinion, this is necessary in order to enable this type of system to be seen as *decent*. It constitutes a universal demand for fairness. It is not easy to ascertain whether social democracy in such fundamental issues differs from other systems, that is to say, whether social democracy is promoting quantitatively more than others, or whether social democracy is promoting something that is also *qualitatively* different. It is my feeling that there is a strong argument for the first approach.

Most of our welfare schemes are designed to prevent our losing what we have succeeded in acquiring if anything were to go wrong, irrespective of what these acquisitions or benefits may consist of, and particularly if such loss is due to no fault of our own. This is why some people receive higher unemployment and sickness benefits than others, and why some people receive higher pensions than others. But in Scandinavia and in a few other places in the world we all receive a pension when we are old, even if we have not been gainfully employed, and we all receive unemployment benefits and sickness benefits in proportion to what we would otherwise be earning. Of course, this can be considered redistribution, because the funds for this must originate somewhere, but it is not a true redistribution that changes the relative strength of various social groups. It seems to be more appropriate to stress the *element of decency* in these schemes, i.e. combinations of fairness and socio-political goals. *The institutions* are there for everybody, they are *collective and universal*, but *the solutions* are *individual*. We must all have equal access to the institutions, this is what creates security, but we do not all receive the same benefits from them. In other words, the institutions do not redistribute wealth by taking from the rich and giving to the poor. However, they do prevent both the 'poor' and the 'rich' - at any rate in the short term - from suffering a reduction in their circumstances if an unexpected situation should arise. If this is redistribution, it must be redistribution in the sense that an advance contribution is made towards a service that may not be required, so that this service may perhaps be provided to someone else. Of course, the same applies to private insurance schemes.

Most people probably feel that it is only natural that our institutions should create more security than equality. This is because equality is stressed more in the *sphere of care* than in the *sphere of production*, though even this is not always the case any longer. Martinussen (1988) demonstrates at least one thing in his analysis of the welfare state, and that is that there is a fundamental difference between people's views on production and their views on caring. Although everybody must naturally be entitled to receive the same treatment for the same illness, irrespective of address or status (though it does not always work quite like this in practice), no one should try to suggest that the same wages should be paid for all types of work, or that people should not be rewarded according to the amount of effort they put into their work.

In a discussion on the relationship between the sphere of production and the sphere of caring, caring for the elderly is of particular interest, because this lies at the intersection of these two spheres. Many of us, when we become old, need both a new home and either short-term or long-term care. Caring for the elderly deals with the way in which we spend the last years of our lives. This caring thus differs fundamentally from other 'caring schemes' within health and social welfare. If we do not suffer from a chronic complaint, most of our contacts with the health services consist of *entering the system in order to leave it again.* Care of the elderly, on the other hand, is directly linked to our *general* way of life, and thus to the standards and rights we have earned in the sphere of production, or on the market, if one will. Many, therefore, find it easier to accept a greater degree of inequality here. If this is not so, it may be an indication that the elderly are not considered to have the same value as other people, because it is felt that different rules should apply than at earlier stages in life. At the same time, care of the elderly is perhaps the one area in which social democracy really will have to pursue a new line of policy if some large groups of the elderly are not to be marginalized, while at the same time other large groups of the elderly will be among those with the decidedly highest standards of living. Demands will no doubt be made for new forms of property and capital taxation, issuing formidable challenges to social democracy. The choice facing social democracy is then whether to institute priorities, i.e. promote a policy which will be opposed by strong groups protecting their own interests, or to adapt.

We believe that this brief description of what we consider to be *typical* features of our welfare institutions is more pertinent than characterizing them as promoting equality and redistributing benefits, a perspective which gives social democracy a rosier past than it deserves - provided, that is, that we like equality. The strong emphasis on equality and redistribution is rhetorical, and may lead people *away* from institutions (read: the welfare state) which both economically and with regard to use of time could be to their advantage, because not everybody considers that equality is a positive principle. At the same time, more people might have supported these same institutions if someone had attempted to show what their purpose really was and from what values they originated.

Why have so many used such an imprecise and ambiguous term as 'equality' to describe what is typical of social democracy? The most important reason is that equality, and for that matter also redistribution, have been confused with improving people's social status. Bringing the working class out of poverty and into a non-marginalized position in society, into a position where the individual himself can determine the course of his life, has been defined as supporting an ideology of equality. The term 'equality' has been used as though it were a concise description of the actual driving force in the struggle against poverty. But trying to improve people's circumstances does not presume equality as an ideology.

We do not believe that the emphasis on the collective aspect should be over-dramatized at the expenses of the individual if social democracy is to be understood as a historical phenomemon. On the other hand, the *concurrency* of the collective and the individualistic aspects should be underlined. As Mary Douglas (1982) has shown, the collective and the individualistic may well go hand in hand; they do not need to be two extremes of one and the same dimension.

Social democracy has always stressed the individual, while it is probably correct to say that the specifically collective aspects have lost some of their importance over time, indicated not least by recent developments (see next section). Social democracy has worked for fundamental changes in society, for a more efficient social system where one of the main goals is to put a stop to the fact that a large number of people were not only poor but also living in a very uncertain market position. But this does not imply equality of results as an ideological driving force or as a moral obligation - a goal in itself. A strong understanding is evolving that *equal rights* are a necessary requirement for the prevention of marginalization. This *liberal* value, which is linked closer to equality of opportunities than to equality of results (which is opposed to everything liberalism stands for), suggests equality before the law and equal *access* to public services, but can be relatively disengaged from the demand for economic, social or cultural equality.

The use of the concept of equality - without expanding on its contents - was useful as a *remedy* against poverty and in the promotion of civil rights. As we use the term today, however, it is more like a goal in itself. To an increasing degree, equality has acquired the status of a moral principle. But mobilization based on this principle is no longer easy, because the surroundings are no longer what they once were.

From a corporative representation of interests to a decentralized user-democracy?

> The Norwegian Labour Party's major difficulty in the 1980s is that it rarely represents anything more than the sum of the policies of all the interest groups (Brox 1988,83).

> The 90s must become the decade of the local level. The public sector is to be returned to the people (K.Å. Johansson, Swedish Ministrer of the Interior, *Dagens Nyheter,* 2 January 1990).

This section deals with *governmental control systems* and how these can vary yet still be in keeping with the ideological foundation of social democracy. Are we on the point of tearing down an incredibly successful social democratic structure which is in the best interests of most of us, and which in an historical and comparative perspective is virtually unparalleled? A system based on full employment, an efficient guarantee of welfare combined with full democratic rights, and small cultural and economic differences, as claimed by Brox (1988). He argues that pressure from the right is on the point making the social democratic institutions irrelevant, i.e., without decisive influence on people's fundamental concerns: work, health, care, peace and quiet, and that the consequences of the conservative wave thus may be irreversible. We may rapidly find ourselves in a situation where large parts of the population consider that their interests are best looked after by a liberal society. But that will be a system which at the same time *marginalizes* large parts of the population, i.e. leads them into a state of impotence in relation to the political system.

Something has happened to social democracy - there has been an internal dissolution (the party organization and the affiliated cultural organizations are in other words no longer what they were), but there have also been dramatic changes in the evironment that have removed social democracy from its offensive position and placed it on the defensive. It may seem as though this is the onset of ideological and institutional rigidity, without any access to new ideas or solutions to institutional problems which also safeguard the historical heritage of social democracy. However, it is not possible to adjust to every change in circumstances and yet remain unchanged; a social democratic movement. The dynamics of social democracy, like everything else, must be understood if insight is what we are seeking. This is an exceedingly difficult exercise because not only does it require us to understand what type of movement social democracy is, and thus what one may politically envisage doing, but we must also understand the role played by politics in our type of society. How autonomous is the political sphere, what limits are imposed on politics, and how do these vary over time? Few people can give satisfactory replies, and politics therefore often take turns we could not foresee.

However, any approach to the transformation process now facing social democracy cannot base itself on historical nostalgia or dreams from the past, but must take into account the consequences of the major structural changes that have taken place since the 1960s and that have made our society much less stable. The result is a weaker socializing environment, greater mobility with regard to occupation and residence, and a substantial weakening of the social and political role of the working class, along with a fundamental change in the role of women in our society. These extensive and probably radical structural changes not only result in many *more of us being subjected to influences from more sources than ever before*, but more important, *more of these influences actually concern us.* More of us are able to choose (to the extent that there is a choice) to live in such a way that the effects the various influencers are trying to expose us to actually concern us. In other words, various political directions apply to more people than earlier, because we live or can choose to live differently, and because the 'filters' around us are thinner than before, or at any rate different than before.

It is in this new landscape that social democracy must seek to find a new 'space'. The social democratic structure evolved primarily as *practical solutions* to concrete problems which private initiatives had not attempted, managed or wanted to solve (Brox 1988; Kuhnle and Selle 1990). The 'social democratic' institutions thus generally evolved out of a *vacuum* without much resistance or competition. In addition, we are (were?) a pragmatic people in whom anti-governmental attitudes are not widespread. However, not only is the ideological climate different today, it is probably also a fact that non-state institutions, primarily commercial enterprises but also voluntary organizations, have *the resources* to produce services they were previously unable to provide, if an opening is made for this in new spheres of activity. At all events, it is made to sound that way, that is to say, there has been an ideological strengthening of positions. This probably makes it more difficult than ever before for social democracy to evolve policies that *stand out* and that at the same time result in *an efficient use of resources* and *social security.*

Despite the fact that social democracy has considerable difficulty in defining such a new political *space*, social democracy need not necessarily loose its support if in future new and alternative policies cannot be produced. In all competitive democracies of this type, a large party in the centre will be needed, and it is of course not given that modern social democracy will be unable to occupy much of this space by exercising the administration of these policies and adjusting to new surroundings without the party having to be a social democracy as we have defined this term. The question raised now is therefore the *qualitative* issue: how can social democracy change and still remain social democratic? How can the historical heritage be sustained while developing a vision of society in keeping with the core philosophy of social democracy, adapted to our times, yet qualitatively different from what other political directions stand for? Is social democracy still social democracy if, during the 'modernization' of the economy and society, the value of financial growth is played down, or objections are not raised to the use of unemployment as a means of solving other problems, or if increasing marginalization is accepted, thus toning down the value of individual security and autonomy? On the basis of what has already been said, it is the author's view that using unemployment as a remedy is a less fundamental breach than 'accepting' marginalization, i.e. seeing marginalization as a modern form of *divine providence* - in other words, controlled by the environment where nothing can be done. Toning down the value of financial growth will be a major readjustment, but hardly a fundamental breach of the social democratic ideology if it takes place within overriding productive and efficient organizational forms. After all, society and therefore also the basic conditions are quite different now from what they were in the infancy of social democracy. Surely social democracy may legitimately review its attitude on the relationship between economic growth and the way in which living conditions are experienced, when the context in which this occurs has changed so fundamentally.

One may claim that the golden age of social democracy (1945-1970) was characterized by there being *coordinating institutions* where group interests and common interests were coordinated in a way not experienced today. After the post-war reconstruction ideology was dead, *because reconstruction was considered to have been completed*, the role of the coordinating institutions has become weaker, while group interests have become stronger. An increasing number of people claim that 'the concept of solidarity' has broken down, or at least is much weakened, because organizations and groups are all fighting for their own short-term interests. Because of this, the *negotiation system* does not function as envisaged. Not all who should be are in fact represented, some acquire too much power, and at the same time, the organizational control system is not always as efficient as desirable, seen from the point of view of society in general. This view coincides with dominant directions that have developed in political science and political sociology since the middle of the 1970s, where such terms as 'overload' and 'ungovernability' are used to explain why occidental political systems cannot satisfy the requirements of powerful and less powerful organized groups in society (e.g. Berger 1983). Such groups are all formally, and thus legitimately, entitled to promote their own cause because there are no rules to exclude them, thus making 'my' demands as legitimate as 'yours'. There is no reason why I should make any sacrifices to benefit for you. These changes are now creating institutional inefficiency, or at least it is felt that this is the case, and in time this will result in failing legitimacy. The institutions are being destroyed through internal dissolution, and at the same time, there is strong pressure on the institutions from the outside.

It may be argued that there used to be an organized working class which saw results from the various negotiations in terms of the consequences for the whole class, and which thus had a coordinating influence because of the long-term perspective. If we move away from class interests to group interests, we also move from a long-term to a short-term perspective. When the concept of unity or communal solidarity disappears, or at least is weakened, the long-term group perspective is no longer a rationale for those involved, because no one can predict the future, and there is no guarantee that what is not received today will be received tomorrow. It is these internal dynamics which in time have a destructive effect on the coordinating institutions. The politics of interests take over - the short-term interests of different groups where full-time employees with their loyalties to individual sectors and individual institutions over-ride the 'common interests'. Social democracy has not managed to disassociate itself from this development, but has instead been an integral part of the development itself.

More and more people underline with considerable emphasis the problems of efficiency and/or the dangers to democracy associated with the system of representation of interests which has developed via the 'corporative' channel. Lack of confidence in the *bureaucratic and centralized planning model*, seen by many as typical of social democracy, i.e. as a product primarily of the social democratic understanding of politics, has led to a sideslip towards increasing emphasis on *decentralization, user-democracy and on non-institutionalized forms of participation* also in social democracy. This is clearly reflected in public discourse, not least in a major report from SAMAK - the labour movement's Joint Nordic Committee - and in the Swedish social democrats' programme for the 1990s.[4] Above a statement by the Swedish Minister of the Interior K.Å. Johansson was quoted, and this is stated no less clearly by the leading Norwegian social democratic ideologist Reiulf Steen. The following quotation sums up in a stringent manner a social democratic 'transition' to more decentralized solutions.

I believe in de-institutionalization, decentralization which many claim will lead to greater inequality. Now it is not my experience that centralization leads to greater equality. But I believe that decentralization is a requirement for creating a balance between rights and responsibilities, between security and responsibility for welfare, a balance which in my opinion is a prerequisite for having a welfare society in the 1990s and for retaining it into the next century (Steen 1990, 26).

What this means is that the centralized control model with a strong concentration of power on the 'corporative' path has lost a great deal of its legitimacy. Social democrats are now saying that the scale for politics has become too large, that solidarity has become too remote-controlled, so that people to an increasing degree feel powerless and thus unable to take part in the political process. Society has become too institutionalized and thoroughly organized, so the distance between the governed and those governing has become too great. It is felt that this has led to a diminishing interest in politics while special interests have become stronger at the expense of 'common interests'. What is now wanted is for people to take active part in the decision-making processes that concern them through more *direct*

155

forms of participation. Not only has confidence in paramount centralized planning been reduced, but an increasing belief in collective and individual self-government has evolved. Behind this development there is a particular view of mankind, a view that has gradually become stronger. Now everybody always knows what is best for himself. This is a vigorous form of *individualism*, in which the individual is both competent and knows his own interests. In modern 'pluralism', few or no paternalistic features remain.

The centralized organization control system with strong elements of corporate structure, or which at least gives power to the organizations, but in which there are also elements of control through regulations and hierarchies, can (but does not necessarily have to) be seen as a form of government which demonstrates little confidence in the majority of the people. This applies both to the classical hierarchical state and to a more segmented state. Most people have neither overview nor insight, that is to say they are not competent. They are represented through organizations, where the inner dynamics ensure that those who become leaders are by and large 'responsible', that is to say they can interact and allow themselves to be integrated into the actual governing system. The result is both geographic and organizational centralization.

The difficulty with this system, i.e. financing, efficiency and legitimacy difficulties, have gradually become so vast that a demand and opening for alternative solutions has gradually evolved. Increasing individualization, linked to a breakdown of confidence in hierarchical forms of government, makes an approach along the lines of 'affected interests' natural. User-democracy covaries with increasing individualization, that is to say, people assume that personal autonomy is protected. At the same time, they believe in a positive relationship between closeness and responsibility. In other words, we are dealing with important changes in our views on the individual and the organization. Below, the two most important 'new' trends also influencing social democracy are discussed.

1.   The 'affected interests' view, which was also an important principle within a centralized model, is now given a broader definition. In a more decentralized structure, one assumes that one of the main objections to the centralized model with

corporative features will disappear. All interests will be heard, not only labour market organizations. There seems to be a belief that it is easier to find room for everybody on a local level.

2.   As part of this development, there is a belief that there should be an evolution away from organization towards a greater emphasis on the individual and the local community. A strengthening of the individual's rights is often envisaged through the strengthening of geographic affiliations at the expense of class or vocational identity. It is assumed that a more decentralized structure will break down the considerable power of the major organizations. A reduction in organizational power is envisaged, combined with less power to management in organizations. At the same time, the power of the professions will be reduced, and it is assumed that such a development will release new resources, both human and financial, because the distance between those making decisions and those affected by these decisions will be minimized. Less can be kept concealed, suggesting less corporate thinking and more direct democracy. Local and decentralized solutions are considered to provide better protection for civil society, i.e. local moral solidarity.

The ideological transition to decentralized solutions is a universal process that has affected the whole political landscape. Social democracy, too, is to an increasing degree being influenced by these 'new' ideas and many social democrats see increased decentralization and user-democracy as a possible solution to the serious difficulties in which the welfare state now finds itself. In addition, it is the social democratic transition to a user-democracy and decentralization that is politically most interesting, because social democracy is associated most closely with the centralized model. We also see that the political *rhetoric* behind the ideas of decentralization and the user democracy clearly corresponds to what we have defined as social democratic ideals, that is to say, that which is typical of social democracy.[5]

But by no means everybody takes it for granted that increased decentralization leads to a more efficient utilization of resources, and it is claimed that this must lead to greater inequality, both geographically and between groups of the population, thus resulting in increased marginalization. A consequence may be a strengthening of what Johan P. Olsen calls *the State as a Supermarket* transposed to the local level (Olsen 1988), a system where the authorities are more of a service institution for organized and individual interests than a superior mediator between organized interests with relatively clear objectives. If developments actually take this direction, it can hardly be said to be in line with what has been defined as social democracy, because the *intervening* and *governing* elements have disappeared along the way.

User democracy is the Left's answer to the privatization moves of the 'modern' market-oriented Right. Perhaps these are not two completely different things. In both instances we are dealing with variations on the *market idea*. In both instances a social system or government without paramount political authority is being promoted, i.e. a system without permanent hierarchies. However, in the same way that it is unlikely that everybody will have something to *buy* with in the demand model (the right-wing alternative), it is also unlikely that everybody will have the *will* or the *resources* to participate in the user model (the left-wing alternative). Both alternatives are first and foremost *demand models* where the user is sovereign. The idea of politics as an educator, the whole idea that people must be given information in order to be informed, has disappeared. In addition, both variants can be seen as antitheses to the constitutional state which is based on the ability to predict. Demand democracy, as we see it, is the actual 'gallup democracy', and user-democracy can be characterized as an understanding between the producer and the consumer in each individual activity and in each individual instance. It is a form of *'contractualism'* which depends on people's current interests, and it is a decisive break with the traditional *citizen role* in the 'popularization' of which social democracy has been an important dynamic force. We believe that a further swing in this direction will be a decisive break with the social historical heritage of social democracy.

Notes

1. This essay is not empirical in the ordinary meaning of the word. We will not discuss particular documents or political decisions which may cast light over important features of social democracy. Nor will we take up internal affairs, that is to say we will not reveal important factions and the relationship between these. Nevertheless, we believe that social democracy as a historical phenomenon must be understood as a *coalition* in which different trends have always been represented, trends which periodically have conflicted sharply with one another. Such a coalition view naturally makes it difficult to provide a universal approach to social democracy, to try and clarify what its typical features are. Perhaps there are no such 'typical' features, so that what we consider to be 'typical' in fact are really only attempts to aggregate features we vaguely assume the various factions have in common. Alternatively, this may be something we are trying to contstruct 'from above', something that is fairly universal and in which none of the factions need to recognize themselves directly. It is not possible to state how such aggregation mechanisms may have affected this essay. The problem does not become less because the article will deal with typical characteristics that must be relevant over a long historical period - even a complete century. Despite this, it is our aim to show more than just our own prejudices.

2. This is also the description given by Einar Gerhardsen, Norwegian social democratic Prime Minister for longer than anyone else. See Gudmund Hernes in *Dagbladet*, 25 September 1987.

3. This section is based on Selle (1988).

4. The SAMAK report is published in *LO-Bladet*, 23 February 1989. *90-tals programmet - en debattbok om arbetarrörelsens viktigaste frågor under 90-talet* was also published in 1989.

5. In Selle (1990) it has been questioned seriously whether decentralization will have the positive results one assumes.

From Cadres to Citizens to Clients: Toward a Theory of the Electoral Coalitions of Social Democracy

Ulf Lindström

Background

Social democracy is facing troublesome times. Its electoral support is declining; its claim to be the legitimate custodian of the welfare state is being questioned among academics or met with indifference in the public discourse; its agenda-setting momentum is lost.

Even Scandinavian social democracy has lost confidence in ever again winning fifty percent of the vote. However, this barrier has been more of an academic obsession than one of real political meaning. Absolute majority is not an unconditional prerequisite for social democracy's gaining effective control of the state. About forty percent of the vote will be enough to thrust social democracy into cabinet position. This electoral strength means that the bourgeois opposition, divided among three or more parties among whom at least one party at any given time has been willing to enter into agreements with social democracy, is too weak to offer an executive alternative of stability and durability.

The real backdrop of the issue is rather the threatening anticipation of Scandinavian social democracy's becoming a party which has difficulties in carrying more than a third of the electorate - a Denmarkization of social democracy also in the sense that, as of the autumn of 1990, the Swedish and Norwegian parties started racing each other for membership in the EC. This, no doubt, is tantamount to a substantial roll-back of the social democratic era in Scandinavia, as membership in the EC would mark at least the temporary surrender of the 'Scandinavian Model' to the less pompous all-European concept of 'Capitalism with a Human Face'.

Scope and problem

While it is true that the formation of the working class was a necessary condition for the rise of social democracy, the party's subsequent fortunes at the polls were always dependent on support also from outside the working class proper, from artisans, smallholders and lower non-manuals. It is, therefore, incomplete and unsatisfactory to see the most recent predicaments of social democracy simply as a consequence of the decline of the working-class (Przeworski 1986, 1).

Indeed, social democracy may be approached from an agnostic view on social class, emphasizing the primacy of politics. This perspective suggests that social democracy does as well as it deserves; wherever the party seizes the opportunity offered, by means of state power, to check the market forces in crucial sectors of society (education, employment, housing and health care), it is in a comparatively better position to retain political prominence (Esping-Andersen 1985, 33). By irreversibly altering the institutional structure of society, social democracy compensated in advance for the effect of changes in class structure. This approach holds a great deal of promise - were it not for the fact that at that very time when the State was in its most omnipotent position, the party began to slide at the polls (Madsen 1984).

As always, there is an elegance to macro-level syntheses, but, alas, they may be deceptive. As for the primacy-of-politics thesis, there are few reasons why people *should* repeatedly reward social democracy at the polls for giving them free or low-cost social provisions. After all, the major welfare provisions are supported by all parties, and this means that there are few straight connections between the welfare regime and personal pay-offs in northwestern Europe.

It is to that topic this paper addresses itself. Is there really a way in which social democracy can make the individual, as private citizen or as a member of a specific community, dependent on the party's electoral performance?

If social democracy is to win elections on the party's own merits, it has to do away with the intermediate bureacratic inertia that prevents partisan politics from being felt among private citizens. However, if social democracy is to win elections as a state-carrying *structure* it is well advised to further *flesh up* the bureacracy in terms of public positions as well as regulations. Ultimately, that would imply features that resemble a patron-client relationship between the welfare regime and its subjects, such as young people in job training centres or on the dole, families with many children, the not gainfully employed living off public insurance, the retired in old age homes, and, the key category, ordinary people working in both the public and private sectors whose tasks are intimately tied to maintaining precisely these functions in the welfare state.

Only in Sweden has the Social Democratic Party (so far) avoided the set-backs at the polls which its sister-parties in Denmark and Norway have suffered since the electoral debacles in 1973 (see Table 1). This paper focuses on the question whether the electoral records of Scandinavian social democracy (the SD, DNA, and SAP) may be accounted for by unravelling the mechanisms which tie citizens to the performance of the welfare state and/or the politico-cultural mentality that this regime breeds among members of specific communities.

The institutional and ideological foundations of social democracy

Social democracy is an inherently painful project. It combines the worst of two worlds: a doctrinaire legacy bestowing a class with a rightful and objective historical mission, and the Occidental belief in human intervention to change society for the better in the here and now. This dilemma has accompanied social democracy ever since its infancy.

While the working class originally provided social democracy with an all-encompassing rationale, this rationale soon evolved into a multi-faceted character which had to be reconciled with the institutional and ideological parameters that defined the party's constituency. In the final analysis, then, social democracy, and only social democracy, defines or rejects its own socialism.

163

Table 1
Social democracy at the polls: percentage of the vote in post-war Scandinavia

Year	Denmark (SD)	Norway (DNA)	Sweden (SAP)
1945	32.8	41.0	-
1946	-	-	-
1947	40.0	-	-
1948	-	-	46.1
1949	-	45.7	-
1950	39.6	-	-
1951	-	-	-
1952	-	-	46.1
1953	41.3	46.7	-
1954	-	-	-
1955	-	-	-
1956	-	-	44.6
1957	39.4	48.3	-
1958	-	-	46.2
1959	-	-	-
1960	42.1	-	47.8
1961	-	46.8	-
1962	-	-	-
1963	-	-	-
1964	41.9	-	47.3
1965	-	43.1	-
1966	38.2	-	-
1967	-	-	-
1968	34.2	-	50.1
1969	-	46.5	-
1970	-	-	45.3
1971	37.3	-	-
1972	-	-	-
1973	25.6	35.3	43.5
1974	-	-	-
1975	29.9	-	-
1976	-	-	42.8
1977	37.0	42.3	-
1978	-	-	-
1979	38.3	-	43.2
1980	-	-	-
1981	32.9	37.2	-
1982	-	-	45.9
1983	-	-	-
1984	31.6	-	-
1985	-	40.8	44.7
1986	-	-	-
1987	29.3	-	-
1988	29.8	-	43.2
1989	-	34.3	-

Source: Election statistics.

As a result of these deliberations, the electoral coalitions of social democracy have changed over time from that of comprising (i) the working class proper to (ii) the working class cum the middle class to (iii) the working class cum public employees and clients.

Social democracy led a care-free life in its early years, especially between the II International and World War I. The working class was growing in numbers and simple extrapolation told the party that it was only a question of time before the party would seize power, enabling it to realize the vision of creating a New Mankind (*Neue Mensch*). Consequently, social democracy was left to cultivate the ghetto-model, all the more so when the franchise was restricted and the parliamentary channel closed, thus barring working-man from full citizenship.

However, the instant universal suffrage was introduced social democracy could no longer remain in the ghetto. The party went for the vote also of the peripheral classes, the smallholders in the countryside and the lower salaried employees in the cities. For parliamentary majority, it seemed, was only around the corner, and any talk of the chimera of 'ministerial socialism' was irresponsible, especially at a time when fascism was about to crush organized labour throughout Europe (Lindström 1985, 7). For the remaining years before WW II this populist strategy did not divert the party's attention away from its own institutions catering to the economic and cultural maintenance of the working class, e.g. co-ops, People's Halls, and the Red Falks.

It was not until after WW II that social democracy experienced in full the conflict between maintaining separate institutions for the party's members and building welfare-state institutions for the nation's citizens. 'Before the war the political and social life of the party [the DNA] had a value in and by itself to many, and this satisfied a strongly felt desire for attachment and being together, for a sense of belonging. In more senses than one, the labour movement constituted a community of its own in society. After the war, this aspect of the organizational life decreased in importance (Berg 1987, 100). Indeed, a return to something reminiscent of the Austrian *Lager* society was effectively ruled out by the prevailing public mood as well as earlier policy commitments. First, Scandinavian social democracy had entered cabinet position on the basis of the red-green crisis agreements in response to the Great Depression (Karvonen & Lindström 1988). Second, this policy of consensus across class boundaries - it may have looked like a class alliance between two autonomous classes at the outset, but its *reception* among the public was based on the negation of class as such in favour of nationalist populism - was consummated after WW II when the concept of class was gradually replaced by those of 'people' and 'wage-earners' as the rationale for social democratic policies.

Thus, social democracy turned to the citizens. Firmly entrenched in parliament, confident in its Keynesian approach and encouraged by a steadily growing economy, social democracy set out to make the 'Provisional Utopia' come true. Provisional Utopia was an updated version of Bernstein's revisionism in the sense that it represented an attempt to read a controlled evolutionary ideology into welfare legislation. Not only did the welfare reforms benefit the working class. The provisions appealed to the middle class as well, since the bulk of the reforms were based on universalistic principles, like child allowances irrespective of household income. More important, the health-care programmes, pension schemes and extended compulsory education offered by the social democratic State - with the willing assistance of even the conservative parties save for that in Sweden (Epland 1987) - never challenged already existing arrangements administered by for instance a Catholic culture or the market and utilized by the middle class. Social democracy filled a vacuum of collective goods, also for the middle class, who, incidentally, had its socio-economic roots among the peasantry and the working class.

During the golden era of social democracy (1945-70) the main role of the cadres, apart from mobilizing the working-class constituency, was to provide manpower to occupy the administrative positions of the welfare state. (This transfer of people from the ranks of the labour movement to positions in the state, especially local government, is yet to receive close scholarly attention.) This was also the time when social democracy's policy concerning who was eligible to be considered as a client of the welfare state was straightforward. Clients, once under the tutelage of the bourgeois state, put away in poor-houses and recipients of charity, were henceforth identified, their plight diagnosed and universalistic measures for their rehabilitation worked out.

Indeed, what social democracy was all about, to speak with the late Labour Party Leader Gerhardsen, was to make it possible for 'ordinary people in ordinary circumstances to lead their own lives' (Hernes in *Dagbladet*, Sept. 25, 1987), a rationale later confirmed in the SAP's program for the ninetees: 'Politics is about trying to create the conditions under which each person is able to realize his own dreams and expectations as well as those of his nearest [family and friends]' (Olsen 1990, 102). While it is true that this is a rationale likely to be subscribed to also by contemporary neo-liberals, it nonetheless captures the essence of social democracy in its heyday. At that time (c. 1960), markets and humiliating dependence on civil networks laid restrictions on people's potentials. Politics was the liberating means. The chief instrument in severing the chains of ignorance was parliament, legislating un-ambiguous laws concerning who was eligible to receive assistance from the state, when, and under what conditions. But 'Provisional Utopia' could not do without an institutional framework to implement the welfare provisions. Once the welfare regime was put into practice, a regime that never aimed at more than serving economic efficiency and security and left to co-exist with a market alive and kicking, new problems were underway (Brox 1987; Selle 1988).

For unlike social democracy itself, the individual citizen living under the social democratic state enjoys the best of *two* worlds. The vote gives each and everyone a say in politics; the banknote gives each and everyone a say in the market. On election day the citizen may well express his wish for political regulation of housing, education, and health-care. Only the morning after, not prepared to wait for the political system to deliver, the citizen may buy a flat in the market, send his children to private schools, and have his painful knee treated at a private clinic. It is these people, the affluent middle classes who patronize and stimulate the market with money they draw as a result of public policy (above all the generous tax deductions on interest rates), who are undermining the electoral coalition that once provided social democracy with a solid and reliable constituency. Relative affluence among the middle class provokes new issues like the right of people to buy their way past the lines waiting for, e.g., advanced surgery and day-care. Social democracy is left to defend a health-care system that is basically sound, but in no position to respond to bottlenecks caused by 'the disease of the day,' or that ailment which the media at regular intervals say has stricken everybody at the same time.

The contention is, therefore, that social democracy, largely by its own hand, is outmaneuvered from the institionalized expression of citizenship, i.e., a parliament that does not permit social democracy to win the vote of the masses on the party's own merits. Instead, social democracy is tangled up in ad hoc management of the welfare state, a management drawing increasingly on inspiration from market mechanisms. As a consequence, social democracy is seldom seen in the midst of the agora pointing a finger at the visionary horizon with all its promises of a better day for everyone in the here and now. At best, the visionary horizon reaches the boundaries of the local community, for instance, as in the city of Malmö in Sweden where the local social democratic ideologue recently promised a politico-administrative revolution to do away with bureaucratic inefficiency in order to finance new *local* welfare reforms.

It almost goes without saying that the thought of social democracy returning to uncontested prominence by way of re-vitalizing its own ghetto-like institutions is unrealistic. Over recent years, despite vigorous efforts to the contrary, the DNA has registered all-time lows in party membership. Substantial branches of the working-class movement's organization are now de-activated and made to depend on government subsidies, for instnace public finance of the party, the trade unions, the press, night schools, and leisure activities. Recent data on Sweden - where, in contrast to Denmark and Norway, dormant traces of the social democratic ghetto-culture are supposed to be found - show that the potential among the grass-roots for activating the separate red *Lager* is very bleak (Petersson et al. 1989, 120).

Social democracy has been phased out of parliament, deprived of the means of making changes in public policy directly felt among those citizens the party wishes to reach. In the eyes of the citizens, nothing much emanates from parliament any more, at least compared to the days of the grand welfare legislation when parliament was unceasingly occupied in drafting and passing new reforms. True, it is not easy to invent entirely novel public provisions distributed in accordance with the universalistic principle. The principal provisions already in effect, those with a bed-rock support in public opinion transcending both party boundaries and changing *Zeitgeist*, obey by the liberal 'equality in chances' rather than 'equality in results' (cf., Selle's contribution in this volume). But this does not exclude the improvement and reformation of already existing policies. However, today's catch-words also among social democrats are 'decentralization,' 'de-

168

institutionalization,' and 'user democracy,' all liable to legitimate *inequality* in chances. In other words, parliament is about to incapacitate itself as a governing body: government is no longer predictable and held accountable in accordance with the concepts of the old *Rechtsstaat*. Politics has become a question of management.

A mixture of business management and organization sociology, this philosophy substitutes the political project for the everyday experience of people as employees and consumers of public and private benefits. In short, then, national politics is a matter of cabinet leadership more than that of offering visionary guidelines, as evidenced by the meteoric rise of the Norwegian DNA in the opinion polls after the bourgeois cabinet fell apart in disgrace in November, 1990.

Government authorities are as much engaged in introducing intra-departmental profit accountability as in implementing (vague) political guidelines. Ordinary subjects are being asked to receive a mandate from above to mind their own business, in accordance with the concept of user democracy. For instance, parents are trusted with certain responsibilities for their children's education, such as the maintenance of school buildings. Social democracy wants people to think of user democracy as an alternative to the bourgeois policy of leaving the door ajar for market mechanisms to sneak into public domains.

Is this territorial and functional decentralization of government - let the state become your friendly neighbourhood companion - coupled with a corresponding politicization of the civil sphere so as to make the welfare state a society in which the boundaries between the public and the private sectors are so blurred that only a handful of individuals still qualify to be counted as citizens whereas the vast majority of the population is best described as semi-clients of the state? Unfortunately, concepts are misleading. First, 'citizen' in its original connotation is deceptive, as no one ever floated, let alone floats, above the influence of interest links (public or private) when asked to consider matters of common concern. Second, 'client' is a derogatory word, evoking pictures of persons utterly dependant on one master. What, then, would be the appropriate theory of voter alignments in the welfare state in terms of accommodating phenomena that bear resemblance to clientelism?

Social democracy, the welfare state, and clientelism

So far only circumstantial evidence has been advanced to show that social democracy is about to enter an era in which the party will have to rely on an electoral coalition in which public employees and clients occupy a pivotal position. Because of their position, these groups will exert pressure on the party forcing it into recurrent contradictions. Social democracy will constantly be faced with a choice between responding to the so-called general opinion and adapting to demands voiced by narrow interests. The latter have the advantage provided by an extensive network of functionaries tied directly to the labour movement or considered subsidiaries of the labour movement.

There are three reasons why it is assumed that today's social democratic leadership feels the push to go forward. First, the proportion of the industrial working class, the 'core proletariat,' fell from about 40 to less than 30 per cent of the total work force between 1970 and 1985 (Oskarson 1990; Overrein 1988). Second, the petty bourgeoisie and salaried employees in the private sector are affluent enough to stimulate the supply of services that until recently were provided by state monopolies as part of the welfare regime, monopolies now under heavy ideological barrage for being akin to the defunct East European regimes. Third, social democracy is hard put to convince the electorate that the bourgeois parties are liable to dismantle the main pillars of the welfare state, widely accepted by the public at large, when assuming cabinet position. The record simply does not corroborate hints to that effect since, in Norway, the bourgeois parties were cofounders of the grand welfare programs, and, as is brought out by the case of Denmark which has been governed by bourgeois cabinets for more than a decade, 'the bourgeois reaction has yet to show its real face,' as the argument would go among social democrats who entertain a black version of wishful thinking.

This is not to say that all that remains is to pity social democracy for living in such an ungrateful world and wish it all the best for its sunset years. Nothing prevents the party from making an attempt to check or even reverse at least some of the consequences of the most recent development of the welfare state, consequences believed to harm social democracy. Indeed, the SAP together with the Liberals recently introduced a major revision of the tax system which, in effect, will withhold at least part of the generous subsidies on interests rates that enable the middle class to afford services previously not known to be offered by the market. Ironically enough, the immediate response from the party's *working-class* constituency has been one of fierce protests! Theoretically, social democracy might return to its natural habitat, parliament (Petersson, et al. 1990, 278), with the intention of outfoxing the opposition on a new welfare reform. Such a policy could refer to the new Europe and scrap 75 per cent of both military spendings and agricultural subsidies in favour of care for the very young and very old. But no, to the Swedish SAP the new Europe meant a call for full membership in the EC in order to stop capital from fleeing the country and, to fight decreasing productivity, a reduction of sickness pay to 75 per cent of the wage for the first three days of absence.

Social democracy epitomizes political pragmatism, it is a 'project of survival' in its own right. One is therefore well advised not to interpret the golden era of social democracy as one during which the party was rewarded solely for a coherent and far-sighted policy. Even in those days politics had an erratic element to them, among parties as well as constituents. Yet, it will always be the rightful mission of the analyst never to surrender to 'garbage-can' approaches to social democracy. And, indeed, there are few if any aspects of the party's relationship to the working class that have not been (allegedly) accounted for and (carelessly) extrapolated from. It now remains for us to focus on the category of public employees and clients to find the rationales for their sympathy for or antipathy to social democracy.

Why it makes (no) sense for public employees and clients to vote for social democracy

Social democracy itself wants everyone to believe that he or she is worse off without the party in power. To find out if there is any substance to this assertion it is imperative that evidence is collected at the very level to which the promises were adressed: among the constituents. Juxtapositioning of, on one hand, party programmes, cabinet propositions, overbidding among the opposition, and, on the other, costs and benefits incurred among large aggregates of voters is to be avoided.

Substituting the top-down for the down-up perspective, it is possible to paint composite micro-sociological portraits of the most likely and least likely voters of today's social democracy: (i) Most likely: woman, 30 years old, single, with pre-school children, holding a diploma in public administration, occupying a non-tenured position with the state labour exchange; (ii) Least likely: male, 28 years old, single, no children, holding a diploma in business management, occupying a position with a finance broker.

If the balance of what she receives from and pays to the welfare state turns out to her disadvantage when compared to the balance of the man - not a far-fetched assumption - not only the legitimacy of the welfare regime must be questioned. It would also put social democracy in an embarrasing spot in as much as this provides conclusive evidence that the cumulative effect of the welfare regime enacted by parliament is counterproductive to the original intention behind each piece of tax cum welfare legislation.

Why is it that, in this example, the woman, unlike the man, has a *legitimate* claim to the provisions of the welfare state and is right in holding *social democracy* responsible for the unjust system? There are three immediately relevant aspects (disregarding gender and generation): she is a single bread-winner with children who need attention during office hours; she is a professional but her job is not safe; she partakes in a function that for both ideological and legal reasons is not open to market competition, yet is never fully a government monopoly. It is in the woman's, but not the man's, interests that fees to day-care centers are publicly subsidized; that her professional capacity is recognized, preferably extended; and that her agency is given protection from market alternatives.

Now, what kind of motives remain for the woman to vote for social democracy and why does the man not switch to social democracy? It is worth recalling that the issue at stake does not allow for external motives, such as international solidarity and environment protection, to help rationalize the way the two persons vote. Moreover, it would not make much sense to muddle the issue by throwing in qualifications about who, the man or the woman, is better off in the very long run with social democracy at the helm.

Are there well-founded reasons for suspecting that the woman's loyalty to social democracy, despite being disfavoured by the net provisions provided by the party's policies, means she is dependent on the welfare *state* and, ultimately, a client of social democracy? Put differently, is she living in the worst of one world, the political world in which the patron rules the client, whereas the man is living in the best of two worlds, in which the patron (government) is but the last resort to turn to in case the stock market were to crash?

The woman is dependent on the state and social democracy if, and only if, her professional status is completely worthless outside the labour exchange, and all other parties except the Social Democratic Party promise not only to close the state labour exchange but also to ban labour exchanges altogether. In short, then, the original maximalist connotation of the concept of 'clientelism' is not applicable to the study of voter alignment in the welfare state (either). Very few people are in such a situation that they would be deprived of the means of existence the instant social democracy was ousted from government. In addition, if the woman in this example should, of her own free will, quit her job with the state to become a personnel manager with a private company - and yet remained a loyal social democrat - would she still count as a client of the welfare state and social democracy?

A less niggardly but more realistic perspective on social democracy's appeal to public employees and clients is that which acknowledges the complex world of marginalities. Individual interests and public policy do occasionally harmonize so as to produce results that comply not only with the original intentions of the welfare reforms but also with what people in general view as fair. But, equally true, there are numerous instances when individuals see rightfully earned gains depleted by personal sacrifices felt to be unjust also among the public at large. This is not to say that it is time to revisit rational-choice models, to calculate marginal costs and benefits for each voter. 'Marginalities,' as understood here, is the grand sum of very different and incompatible units: pay, professional satisfaction, affective ties to local community, etc.

Ordinary people, such as public employees, may well draw up balance sheets on their own marginalities. However, such home-made cost-benefit analyses are never made in a vacuum of objectivity. Structures and institutions breed personal interests as well as social norms that repeatedly distort people's ability to process information in a way which would be agreeable to the scholar's perception of what is 'really' rational (Elster 1990).

It is a worthwhile task to identify these structures and institutions; to find out whether there is a political-cultural mentality in the welfare state that *prevents* public employees and clients from arriving at unprejudiced views on who - social democracy, the bourgeois parties or none of them - offers the most favorable marginalities in the welfare state.

Social democracy at work

Outside parliament's plenary hall, social democracy has just one arena left in which it can fight for the means for its political position: the work-place. Elsewhere the party is losing ground. Multi-class residential areas do not uphold political boundaries in people's everyday-life, do not breed those mental one-party cultures in which individuals were stigmatized if they went against the crowd. New communication technology is changing the pattern of leisure activities and consumption of culture, robbing social democracy of its initiative as the prime agenda-setting party in a public debate largely restricted to the national scene.

This emphasis on the work-place is not to be confused with the traditional reference to the corporate channel in Scandinavian politics. This supplementary setting designed for the redistribution of wealth is being undermined primarily by the rapidly increasing internationalization of capital and the concomitant adaptation of national institutions as the state responds to this challenge. The corporate channel has been deprived of its mandate, substance as well as priciples guiding its redistributive task. The immediate evidence for this devaluation of the corporate channel is the recently adopted policy of the Employers' Federations to resign from the public committees, and the difficulties of the trade unions to reconcile labour militantism at shop floor level with the cabinet's call for wage-freezing 'social contracts'.

Time and again the labour-free society has been prophecized, but the records say otherwise. Never before have so many sold their labour for a living. And never was class identity as low as it is today among the labouring masses. Whether this is caused by women flooding the labour market, or the shortening of working hours, or less alienation in the work process cannot be determined here. It is sufficient to realize that work - being employed, being given responsibility and coming up to expectations, getting acquainted with colleagues, being rewarded or punished - is the only common denominator in a society growing increasingly complex. At 9 p.m., for instance, people are engaged in a wide variety of different activities, but at 9 a.m. the following morning, millions will be engaged in the same activity: they will be at work. It is at the work-place that parties have the only remaining permanent scene on which they can stimulate a public discourse in which ordinary people take part. While the family may be a permanent institution it is not a public agora, and while politics may be discussed in cafes and on subway trains, this is not a context to which people have to return to the next morning to continue the discourse.

It is therefore in the interests of social democracy that there are as many public employees as possible, yet that they are employed at a limited number of work-places. The logic behind the argument is borrowed from Tingsten's 'law of the social centre of gravity,' only the territorial context (working-class neighbourhoods) is substituted for the functional context (public sector work-places) (Tingsten 1937). For a work-place milieu to exert biased political pressure on the employees, the number of staff must be fairly large. Only then is the workplace characterized by a formalized hierarchy fostering anonymous relations and collective identities. These identities, congenial also to unionization and other collective projects, manifest themselves in responses both to internal and external challenges, like demands from management about introducing new routines and calls from elected assemblies for reduced appropriations.

By way of example, a university hospital serving a popula-tion of one million people is more likely to evolve a distinct in-house politically biased culture compared to a health-care center offering emergency-care for the local community. In-house political culture at small health-care centers, if it exists at all, is probably indistinguishable from that of the surrounding community.

This is elementary sociology blended with timeless psychological mechanisms such as pressure toward conformity. It is just as easy to understand why the worker living in a working-class neighbourhood in the fifties was afraid to reveal that his sympathies were with the Conservative party as it is to understand why a civil servant working at the labor exchange bureau feels uncomfortable being a neo-liberal or Conservative. But what, more precisely, is it about this modern version of Tingsten's theory that once again favors social democracy at the polls?

Figure 1 illustrates the rational as well as the theoretical caveats of extending Tingsten's idea to the work-place context. What, if anything, is lost as territorial context is substituted for the functional context (1), and what kind of sociological forces are at hand at the public work-place that did not bear on working-class residential areas? What kind of political sociology did heavy industrial work-places have that is not to be found at the work-place concerned with public administration and services, and what is unique to the latter (2)? What was the combined impact of workers being under the homogeneous influence of the proletarian milieu, the day-and-night context (3)? Finally, what - in terms of political sociology - is the end product of people not being exposed to any uniform pressure (4)?

Figure 1: Moving Tingsten's 'law of the social center of gravity' from the territorial to the functional context.

Year	Territory Residential area			Function Work-place
	(original context)			
c. 1950	Working-class neighbourhood	<--- 3 --->		Heavy industry
		1	2	
			(new context)	
c. 1990	Multi-class neighbourhood	<--- 4 --->		Public administration and services

Among the many positions in the public sector - too many of too different a nature to make it meaningful to speak of a *class* of public employees - some go back a long time whereas most others are offspring of the welfare state. Positions with a formalized threshold for entering the career and setting standards for promotion, like those in the military and judicial branches of government, are the least vulnerable to politics. In fact, these positions, typically occupied by the sons and daughters of the bourgeoisie, after they have earned their laurels in fair competition with others, have survived despite social democracy's promise that one day they would all be obsolete.

In-house political disposition at defense headquarters, customs controls, fire stations, police stations, courts and penitentiaries is, at best, lukewarm towards social democracy as the party is suspected of wanting to make these positions expendable by replacing them with professions whose task it is to prevent even the occurrence of war, smuggling, fire and crime.

Maintenance and utility personnel responsible for public infrastructure provided social democracy with its original cadres. Municipal workers were among the first to unionize. Municipal tool depots and workshops are social democratic territory. If there ever was such a thing as patronage in Scandinavia, this is where it was (is) to be found. Positions were often filled by friends telling friends of vacancies.

These two examples of in-house political cultures at public work-places contain the essence of what is supposed to favour social democracy at the polls: internal tradition and continuous exposure to external forces. Some public work-places, like the municipal tool depots, are just as reliable a social democratic stronghold as any one-party territorial unit. Other work-places, like the army officers' club, continuously exposed as it was to what it believed to be social democratic cutbaks in military appropriations, never became anything but a conservative oasis. (Whenever the social democratic government has boosted their budgets, officers have felt that they would have received even more from a bourgeois cabinet).

These are archetypes of public work-places. The work-places that epitomize the modern welfare state, in terms of both historical affinity to and budgetary dependence on social democracy, fulfil the role of physical, mental and social correction. However, it would be a rash conclusion to expect all these work-places to foster socialist leanings among the staff. Conservatism of the traditional cut is just as feasible as radicalism among teachers, librarians, and museum clerks, professional positions which transcend both regime types and party politics. Left-wing politics have the edge at work-places dealing with citizens as individual persons, especially if the civil servant is required to use his/her own discretion when interpreting the rules and regulations guiding public provisions. Such situations are anathema to the conservative *Rechtsstaat* whereas they acknowledge social democracy's old belief in sociology as an indispensable tool in forging the great society (Rothstein 1988; Hirdman 1990).

Indicative of Swedish social democracy's long-standing (and mutual) trust in public employees is that: 'The administrative credo under which neutral - yet concerned - civil servants ruled according to the letter or a firm universalistic collection of statutes, was finally replaced on 1 January 1987 by a new credo under which the civil servant is not only allowed but is *required* to use his/her personal discretion. According to the country's Minister of Justice at that time, the new exercise of governmental authority must be founded on 'empathy' (Nybom 1988, 35). This administrative credo (and the right of Swedish civil servant trade unions to attend meetings of local government boards) fits in well with social democracy's praise of decentralization and user democracy as the new meta ideology of the welfare regime.

In this day of unabated criticism of civil servants for doing more harm than good, this downward transfer of power from the legislature to the administration may be appreciated among the public employees as an act of trust from the master. It does not, however, guarantee a durable in-house political aura sympathetic to social democracy. No matter how often public employees are reminded of which party founded and fed their bureau in its infancy and which party provides additional tasks as the bureau's original assignments are succesively completed and who protects the bureau from attacks by evil forces, loyalty is also a question of money. If decentralization is offered as a substitute for appropriations including pay (which, in fact, is the case as more and more public agencies are called to introduce internal accountability and charge fees for part of their services), social democracy will soon find itself on the defensive, trying to convince public employees that the party is a *more* reliable alternative than the bourgeois parties and the radical left.

This is an issue which one would expect not to be an issue at all at public work-places. At the municipal tool depot and in the staff canteen of the Central Bureau of Statistics common wisdom says that social democracy, with the help of the radical left, is the natural choice when it comes to next year's budget. Yet, perhaps as many as forty percent of those who have to endure such arguments day in and day out cast their ballots for the bourgeois parties. Why?

First of all because of the secret ballot vote that protects everyone from being harassed by the majority, be they colleagues or friends. The rationale for voting bourgeois would include the following responses to the budget argument:

-not true; the bourgeois parties have no previous record of being tight with, let alone cutting back, appropriations. And even if the election manifestos of the bourgeois parties call for reductions in the public sector, a bourgeois cabinet will not be able to accomplish this because of inertia in the governmental process.

-true; but that would only serve many of my fellow public employees right, some of whose jobs, I feel, are to produce nothing but red-tape. And if the money saved was then transferred to my department or spent someplace else where it was much needed (on cardiology, for example), so much the better.

-so what?; I can always manage, even if the cutbacks mean lay-offs at my work. There is always a demand for my professional skills in the market.

-I don't care; politics is an unintelligible business when it comes to the implementation of vague principles, and rather than worrying about the day when something might happen to my work-place, I prefer to spend my alotted time on the family, recreational activities, and to be concerned about global problems, problems that are being overlooked by social democracy.

Returning to the Tingstenian typology above, this rationale for questioning and ultimately deserting social democracy would never had been considered among the workers at heavy industrial plants, let alone among workers living in the so-called day-and-night milieus. In such contexts it was simply beyond doubt that a bourgeois cabinet would reduce appropriations that would benefit the working class; it was never believed that lay-offs at other plants owned by one's own company would mean higher pay to those remaining; and unemployment was certainly not viewed as an excellent opportunity to consider a new exciting career.

Social democracy cannot set the clocks back to prevent public employees from entertaining doubts as to who their partisan ally is: it would be absurd to re-segregate multi-class residential areas in order to create a day-and-night context for civil servants similar to the microcosm in which military officers lived before WW II (and similar to social democracy's contemporary stronghold par excellence, the old-age home).

No longer helped by two-tier structures that evolve norms so strong that the mere thought of social democratic followers doing private rational calculi on their choice of party is just a joke, social democracy is left to cultivate a congenial atmosphere in the remaining structure. Workplaces still breed political single-mindedness. Danish bank employees, restaurant waiters and coiffeurs return more than eighty per cent of their vote to the bourgeois parties, whereas 77 per cent of day-care staff vote left socialist. However, 63 per cent of the members of the Women Workers' Union (*KAD*, organizing personnel employed by local government to provide domestic help for the elderly and disabled) cast their vote for the social democratic party (Andersen 1989, 184f).

Initially at least, social democracy has in a comparatively better standing with public employees than the conservatives and neo-liberals. The dilemma of the right-wing parties is that they have to reassure public employees and clients over and over again that precisely their agency and the provisions for which they are responsible will be exempt from the cutbacks in the public sector that these parties propose. However, social democracy's recently acquired policy conviction, that both the served and the servants are better off if *all* public institutions add a touch of market mechanism and/or user democracy to their operations, may just erase what remains of differences between social democracy and the bourgeois parties, as perceived by the public employees and those they serve.

As for individual marginalities, then, it makes as much sense for public employees to vote bourgeois as socialist, provided that two conditions are met: in-house political culture is lax or pluralistic, making it possible for the employees to voice counter-arguments without paying the price in terms of friendship, promotion and, ultimately, resignation with all the ensuing consequences for the employee's private life. Second, in-house political culture is only moderately sensitive to signals from the outside on the possible effects of changes in party policy, strength and cabinet composition.

Testable proposition

Scandinavian experience suggests a pathology of social democracy in decline. The Swedish SAP, polling close to 45 per cent of the vote, mobilizes almost 70 per cent of the working-class vote; the Norwegian DNA, polling about 40 per cent of the vote, mobilizes almost 60 per cent of the working-class vote; the Danish SD, polling about 30 per cent of the vote, mobilizes about 40 per cent of the working-class vote. (Borre 1987; Todal Jenssen 1988; Holmberg & Gilljam 1987) Defection among the working classes is accompanied by an exodus of the middle class, whereupon - as is brought out by the tragedy of the SD - the public employees desert social democracy for the radical left (see Table 2).

The data also reveal that the relative success of the SAP is not primarily a result of the party's appeal to public employees as it (37 per cent) was only marginally above that of the DNA (31 per cent) in the parliamentary elections of 1985 and 1989 respectively. (The net effect increased the SAP vote because of a higher number of public employees in Sweden.) It seems as though the class crucial to social democracy is still the salaried employees in the *private* sector. The SAP upholds its position among these voters, whereas in Norway they have been mobilized en masse by the right-wing (47 per cent compared to only 29 per cent in Sweden). Again, however, the overall development in Scandinavia is far from comfortable from the point of view of the SAP.

The special position of the Swedish Conservative Party, stigmatized by its historical relationship to the welfare state, is brought out by Table 2. Only 19 per cent of the public employees vote for the conservatives, whereas the corresponding figure in Norway (conservatives cum neo-liberal party) is 28 per cent. Swedish social democracy is thus left to fight with the centre-liberal parties for the vote of the public employees.

Table 2
Party preference among non-manual employees, by sector,
in Scandinavia c.1988.
Percentages. (Share of the vote in brackets).
< -- Polarization -->

Party:	Soc. Dem.	Soc. Dem. +	Rad.Left	Conserv. + Neo-Lib.
Denmark 1987	(29)	(48)		(All bourgeois p., 52)
Private	17	39		61
Public	26	60		40
Differ- ence	+9	+21		-21
Norway 1989	(34)	(44)		(35)
Private	25	34	< -- 81 -->	47
Public	31	52	< -- 80 -->	28
Differ- ence	+6	+18		-19
Sweden 1985	(45)	(50)		(21)
Private	33	36	< -- 65 -->	29
Public	37	45	< -- 64 -->	19
Differ- ence	+4	+9		-10

Sources: Andersen 1989, 180; Valen, Aardal & Vogt 1989, 70; Holmberg & Gilljam 1987, 197.

The growth of the welfare state covaries with a massive influx of women into the labour market to fill positions in, above all, the public sector (see Table 3). Two gender-related aspects may be added.

Table 3
Labour force in Scandinavia 1970-1985, by sector and sex.
Percentages

Country Sector & Sex	1970(a)	1975	1980(b)	1985(c)
Denmark				
Private Sector Male:	51.1		46.3	42.2
Priv. Sector Female:	25.7		23.2	20.7
Public Sector Male:	8.7		11.3	14.0
Publ. Sector Female:	14.5		19.2	23.1
Total:	100.0		100.0	100.0
Norway				
Private Sector Male:	49.9	49.1	45.2	42.6
Priv. Sector Female:	23.6	23.1	23.1	22.7
Public Sector Male:	13.5	13.3	13.8	14.5
Publ. Sector Female:	13.0	14.5	17.9	20.2
Total:	100.0	100.0	100.0	100.0
Sweden				
Private Sector Male:	49.5	45.9	42.6	40.5
Priv. Sector Female:	24.2	23.2	21.5	21.3
Public Sector Male:	11.1	11.7	12.3	12.5
Publ. Sector Female:	15.2	19.2	23.6	25.7
Total:	100.0	100.0	100.0	100.0

(a) Denmark 1972, Norway 1973; (b) Denmark 1979; (c) Norway 1984.

Source: Alestalo 1989, Tab.5.

The end of the golden era of social democracy coincided with women entering the labour market in great numbers, and the prediction was that conservative values among women would boost the bourgeois constituency now that the woman had freed herself from her husband, at least in his capacity as sole bread-winner with the self-proclaimed right to impose his own political will on the entire household, *the* day-and-night milieu. But an equally plausible theory was that social democracy had nothing to fear since the working woman would know whom to thank for slackening her bonds to the house and, later, for helping her to unfetter the chains of hard and underpaid labour. The third point in this contention holds a bleak future for social democracy as the party is solidly anchored in the patriarchy of the industrial society, unwilling and unable to adjust to the full range of the emancipation and politicization of women.

A substantial number of the women working in the public sector are still to be regarded as first generation employees (mother not a wage-earner) and as such of special interest much in the same way as other first generation categories, for which there is a specific political sociology. In addition to this, controls must be applied for the timing and political context prevalent at the time of women entering the labour market. If this first generation of women public employees was largely recruited before 1970, its collective political memory may well be marked by the idea that, if politics had anything at all to do with it, social democracy opened up a new world to women. Conversely, if the majority of women public employees entered the labour market piecemeal from the seventies onwards, social democracy is collectively felt to deserve little or no credit for this. As a consequence, the party may have lost the 'second-generation women working-class' which was left on its own to pursue the myth of the 'open frontier.'

People tend to forget, so whether there exists a viable 'first-generation political culture' among women public employees grateful or at least susceptible to social democracy is also contingent on structures and institutions endogenous to the work-places, some of which are more or less unique to women: part-time employment which is counterproductive to the cultivation of in-house political culture, cutbacks in appropriations that hit the low-status productive positions occupied by women long before the adminstrative positions dominated by men are affected.

Table 4 shows a uniform pattern for gender in Norway and Sweden (comparable Danish data are not available, but other sources confirm the conclusion, Andersen 1986).

Social democracy has the edge among women in general, surpassing men's support for the party with four or five percentage points. The gap is even wider for the conservative and neo-liberal parties, women depriving them of about seven to eight percentage points.

The structures, institutions and the resultant norms that constitute the in-house political culture in public work-places and which finally determine the prospects of social democracy are summarized below in the form of testable propositions, see Chart 1.

184

Table 4
Party preference among men and women in
Norway and Sweden (1985). Percentages

Party:	Soc.Dem.	Soc.Dem.+	Rad.Left	Conserv.+ Neo-Lib.
Norway				
Men	35	40		36
Women	39	45		28
Difference	+4	+5		-8
Sweden				
Men	41	47		23
Women	46	51		16
Difference	+5	+4		-7

Sources: (N) *Storting Elections 1985*, Vol. II, Central Bureau of Statistics of Norway, p. 28. (S) Holmberg & Gilljam, *op. cit.*, p. 174.

The design uses the work-place as the unit of analysis, and since surveys of party preference among specific work-places are liable to violate personal integrity, the empirical testing of the propositions runs into difficulties. Re-analysis of data deposits has its limits as the ordinary election surveys contain too few cases to allow for aggregation of individuals into relevant contexts. For the time being, the only economical option is to select only those individuals in surveys whose occupational status is self-explanatory as to the character of their work-place. Admittedly, this solution excludes all public employees from the ordinary surveys except those whose profession is recorded as, e.g., 'director general', 'lighthouse attendant' and 'national park guard.'

Conclusions

Social democracy cannot make people personally dependent on the welfare state and, ultimately, on the party itself via the parliamentary channel. The main welfare provisions that people are entitled to, those

Chart 1. Social democracy and public employees and clients: testable propositions.

_____ Macro level _____

1. 'The cabinet issue' (socialist vs bourgeois) in national political discourse, as perceived by the electorate, is an asset to social democracy.
2. The stigmatization of conservative and neo-liberal parties in national political memory as threats to the provisions of the welfare state, as perceived by the electorate, is an asset to social democracy.
3. Sustained conflict over legitimate right to the foundation of the welfare state, as perceived by the electorate, is crucial to social democracy (Madsen, 1984).
4. Women public employees of first generation carry collective memory favorably to social democracy.

_____ Meso level _____

1. Exposure to in-house political culture at the work-place affects the employee's party preference.
2. In-house political culture requires a large workplace.
3. Large work-places foster a collective identity distinguishable from the surroundings, and covaries with unionization and other collective activities.
4. Professions drawing legitimacy from traditional state functions, and requiring a formal diploma, are less vulnerable to partisan politics than professions associated with continuously evolving socio-technology.
5. Positions filled by informal recruitment preserve the established in-house political culture.
6. Part-time work detrimental to in-house political culture at the work-place, erodes collective memory, and hampers unionization and other collective activities.

they could not afford over-night if put on a private basis, are backed by consensus across the party spectrum. Second, social democracy cannot win elections on the party's own merits because of extensive inertia in the governmental process, chiefly caused by bureaucracy and the non-intended consequences of additional reforms as they come to interact with already existing legislation on provisions and taxes.

To be concrete, out of one extra billion kroner in appropriations to the elderly a substantial portion is likely to be siphoned off by an insatiable bureaucracy or otherwise tampered with. As the rest is credited to the retired it may cause some total household incomes to surpass the upper limit for, e.g., local government housing allowances and subsidized domestic help.

While private citizens are out of the reach of social democracy's alleged attempt to establish a direct link of gratitude between the people and the welfare state, public employees are part of the welfare regime. To what extent are public employees themselves clients of the welfare state and, ultimately, the *Staatstragende* social democracy? Theory alone helps to realize that not even the public employee administering subsidies of theater tickets - perhaps *the* honorary position in the social democratic state - is in such a dependant situation that she deserves to be smeared as 'client' of the welfare state and social democracy. Without too much inconvenience, she could be put to *market* theater tickets for a private company.

Nonetheless, there are mechanisms in the institutional arrangements of the welfare regime known to exert an oblique impact on the position of public employees vis-à-vis the Social Democratic Party.

It was suggested that the strength and policy of social democracy is as linked to the sphere of work as ever before - probably even more than before now that the party is no longer in control of the day-and-night contexts. But work means more than both class identity, which is losing its importance as a source of party affiliation, and appointed representatives in one of the many committees in the corporate channel of government.

Work influences people's party preferences through the composite character of the work-place, its in-house political predispositions. Transferring Tingsten's socio-territorial theory to the functional context - the public work-place - means emphasizing the importance of boundaries creating norms that check the employee's movements and perceptions, distorts her mind as to what she feels she can and cannot think, say and do without inflicting pain onto herself. In essence, then, a working class neighbourhood of the fifties and a public work-place of the ninetees are comparable contexts in terms of maintaining boundaries that have a bearing on people's political behavior.

However, the viable in-house political cultures at certain public work-places that are known to favour social democracy, a political sociology which begs for extensive empirical documentation, are being jeopardized, not least by social democracy itself with its recently acquired conviction that public services are best served by adding market mechanisms and other decentralization measures to their operations. Only twenty years ago, social democracy polled about the same proportion of the non-manual public employees' vote as the Conservative Party; today the Swedish SAP polls twice as many votes as the conservatives from among this category.

Thus, the reason why the Swedish Social Democratic Party has maintained its position as a 'forty-plus-party' into the ninetees is only partly explained by its own strength among the public employees (whose absolute number exceeds those of Denmark and Norway) relative to that among private employees. What sets the SAP apart from the SD and DNA is, first, its grip on the community of *private* non-manuals and, second, the aversion among Swedish public employees to voting for the right-wing parties.

A definite chance to dismiss the concept of a social democratic coalition of workers cum public employees as wishful thinking or Leninist phantoms is rapidly approaching. Swedish opinion pollsters do not leave much room for doubt (e.g. *Dagens Nyheter*, 17 November 1990); in September 1991 the electorate will inflict a historic vote of no confidence onto the SAP, reducing its strength to about a third of the valid vote. If the forecast is accurate, it will soon afterwards be proved that it was the private non-manuals and other 'extra-coalition' categories who were deserting the party in disproportionate numbers.

The Electoral Decline of Social Democracy: Is There a Geographical Factor?

Ingemar Wörlund

Introduction

Less than a year before the parliamentary elections of September 1991, *Statistics Sweden* confirm that the Social Democratic Party is losing ground to the conservatives. The two parties are expected to poll 32 and 30 per cent of the vote respectively. This in itself would qualify as a historical watershed in Swedish politics. An extraordinary feature of this swing to the right is its socio-geography. In the metropolitan Stockholm area, the Social Democratic Party will slide to about 27 per cent, whereas the conservatives are predicted to win almost 40 per cent of the vote. In less affluent northern Sweden, however, social democracy retains its dominant position and is predicted to receive close to 50 per cent of the votes, whereas the conservatives may score 15 per cent.

This pattern, incidentally, recurs in several other West European countries such as the United Kingdom, where Labour remains particularly strong in the north which was industrialized in the early stages of the industrial revolution more than a century ago. The southern parts of the country, whose industrial base is that of contemporary high technology, are solidly conservative. The Norwegian Labour Party is yet another case in point. It is currently in the process of losing ground to the Conservative Party in urban areas, while gaining support in the less developed, peripheral regions.

This raises a number of important questions. Are the party arena events a function of the changing socioeconomic structure? Are we witnessing the emergence of a new kind of party regionalism which is about to break the prevailing trend of inter-regional equalization of the past two decades? Or is it simply that political parties are facing a crisis because they are at odds with traditional class interests?

It has recently been suggested that the traditional political regions lost their *raison d'etre* during the 1980s (Holmberg and Gilljam 1987; Bjørklund 1989; Gidlund and Gidlund 1989; Listhaug and Aardal 1989). In the 1985 election study, Sweden is divided into three types of regions - Problem Sweden, Twilight Sweden and Urban Sweden. The partial correlation between regional and party preferences, controlled for occupation, turns out to be significant, and this the authors take as an indication that region does indeed play an independent role in the mobilization of the partisan vote. The conservative and liberal parties were found to perform at their very best in urban Sweden, where they were pushing the social democrats back. Problem Sweden provides a mirror image, with a strong Social Democratic Party on - what seems to be - an uninterruptedly favourable trend (Holmberg and Gilljam 1987, 201-203).

The Norwegian party system also seems to be moving towards increased polarization with the Conservative and Progressive Parties strengthening their positions in the urban environment and with the Labour Party gaining ground in the sparsely populated rural periphery. The way Bjørklund (1989) sees it, this is a by-product of a high rate of unemployment and continued migration from the periphery which is in the process of losing its subsidies from central government. As a consequence, the periphery has developed into somewhat of a hotbed of resistance against the new Right with its commitment to reducing the public sector. The Social Democrats and the small regional parties such as the 'Finnmark List' have benefitted from this trend in the Norwegian rural periphery (Bjørklund 1989; 20-22; Valen, Aardal and Vogt 1990, 100).

Data and method

The regionalization of Norway and Finland draws on the same logic as the partitioning of Sweden into different regions. The terms C-, M- and B-regions were introduced by Jan-Erik and Gullan Gidlund in a report on 'Urban Parties and Participation 1948-1988' (Storstadsutredningens rapport: 'Storstadens partier och valdeltagande 1948-1988'). The C for C-regions refers to expansive areas which rank high on culture and creativity, for instance the urban university and educational centres. The B in B-regions represents basic regions which are characterized by the socioeconomic structure of the rural periphery. In this typology, the M-regions are a residual category.[1] This is where we find the localities which are neither urban nor rural.

The three regions of Finland, Norway and Sweden never evolve in such a way as to satisfy the strict proximity criteria of the geographer.[2] The careful scholar is also well advised to keep the time factor in mind. Appearances may be deceiving and the C-regions of today may not be representative of the urban centre some ten, fifteen or twenty years ago.

The problem must not be blown up out of proportion. The data testify to a great deal of underlying geographic stability throughout northern Scandinavia, whose rural periphery has undergone only minor changes since the end of WWII; it may indeed be worthwhile studying electoral mobilization and party strength from such a regional perspective.[3]

The regional profiles of the social democratic parties 1945-1989

The Social Democratic Parties of Norway and Sweden follow with the same trend. Electoral support hovered around the 40% mark until the early 1970s, when both parties suffered a decline which became particularly sharp in the 1980s. Finland deviates on two counts. The Finnish Social Democratic Party has never been as close to an electoral majority in its own right as have the Social Democratic Parties of Norway and Sweden; and with the exception of 1962, when there was an open split within the party (see figures 1 - 3), the Finnish Social Democratic Party has always had a more stable

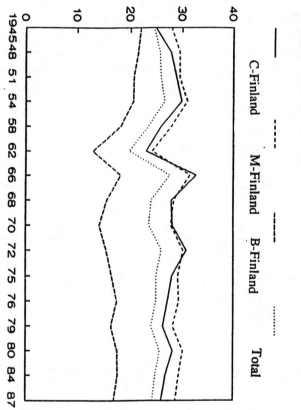

Figure 1: The regional profile of the Social Democratic Party in Finland 1945-1987 (per cent)

C-Finland   M-Finland   B-Finland   Total

192

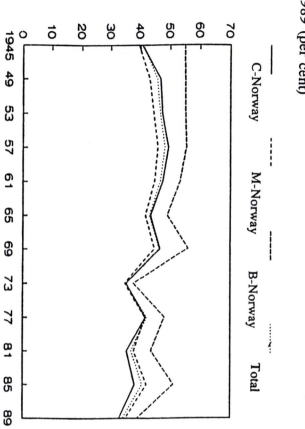

Figure 2: The regional profile of the Norwegian Labour Party 1945-1989 (per cent)

C-Norway   M-Norway   B-Norway   Total

193

Figure 3: The regional profile of the Social Democratic Party in Sweden 1948-1988 (per cent)

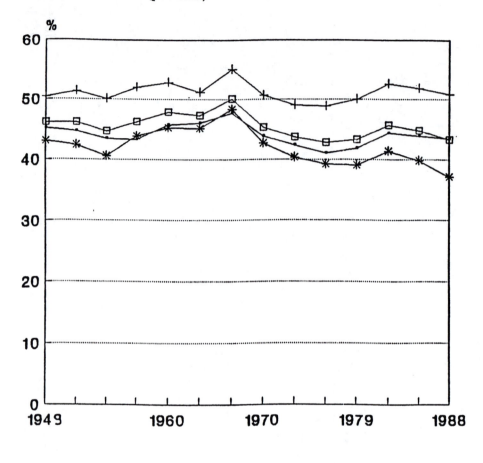

M-Sweden   B-Sweden
C-Sweden   Total

Source· SOU 1989:68

electoral backing than the Social Democratic Parties of Norway and Sweden.

The Social Democratic Parties of Finland, Norway and Sweden do not comply with the same underlying model. The clear-cut differences between the stagnant periphery (the B-regions) and the expansive centre in Sweden are much more blurred in Norway and hardly visible at all in Finland (see figures 1-3). The Finnish data testify to the urban character of the Social Democratic Party which in a sense has lost the countryside to the Communist and Centre parties. The differences between the Finnish C- and M-regions on the one hand and the B-regions on the other have in fact increased since 1970. In Norway the Social Democratic Party has its stable strongholds in the B-regions, but the inter-regional differences have been gradually washed out ever since the 1960s and hardly make themselves felt at all today. In this respect, the Swedish experience differs from the Norwegian pattern. In Sweden the gap between the C-regions and the B-regions almost doubled between 1970 and 1988 (from 8 per cent in 1970 to 14 per cent in 1988).

The regional profiles of the conservative parties 1945-1989

The electoral support of the conservative parties does not lend itself to interpretations in terms of one underlying pattern. In Finland the Conservative Party had an electoral backing of a stable 15 per cent until the 1970s, when the party embarked on a slow upward trend. In 1987 the Finnish Conservative Party polled a little more than 20 per cent of the votes (see figure 4). The conservative Parties of Norway and Sweden also enjoyed a period of relative stability (with 18 and 15 per cent of the votes respectively behind them), and this lasted until the early 1970s. They then embarked on a ten year period with a strongly positive electoral trend, interrupted - at least temporarily - by the two most recent elections when both parties suffered setbacks of around 5 per cent (see figures 5 - 6).

The electoral profiles of the conservative parties are in a sense mirror images of the patterns characterizing the social democratic parties. They have consistently strengthened their hold on the urban and metropolitan centres (see figures 4-6). The gap between the C-

195

Figure 4: The regional profile of the National Coalition Party in Finland 1945-1987 (per cent)

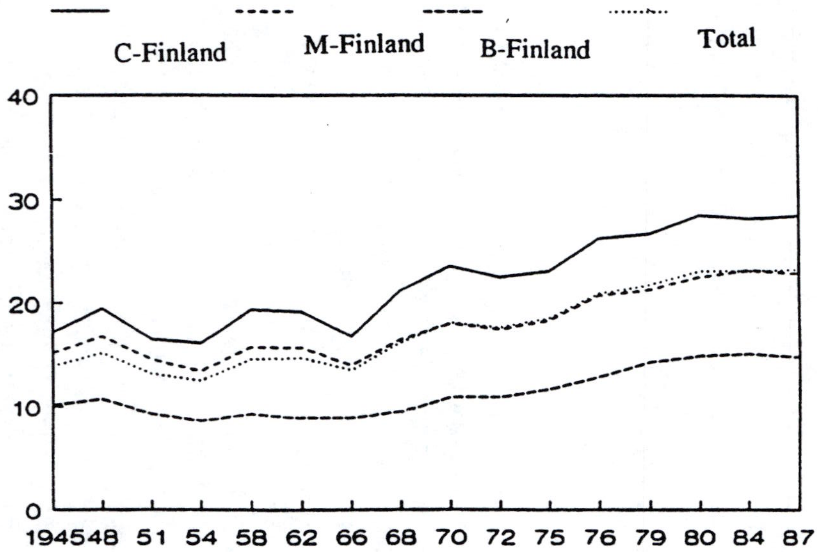

C-Finland   M-Finland   B-Finland   Total

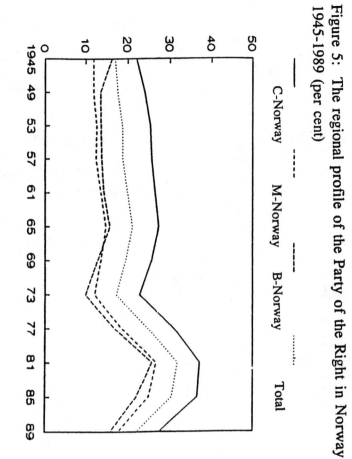

Figure 5: The regional profile of the Party of the Right in Norway 1945-1989 (per cent)

C-Norway ———   M-Norway ----   B-Norway ----   Total ·········

Figure 6: The regional profile of the Right/Moderate Coalition Party in Sweden 1948-1988 (per cent)

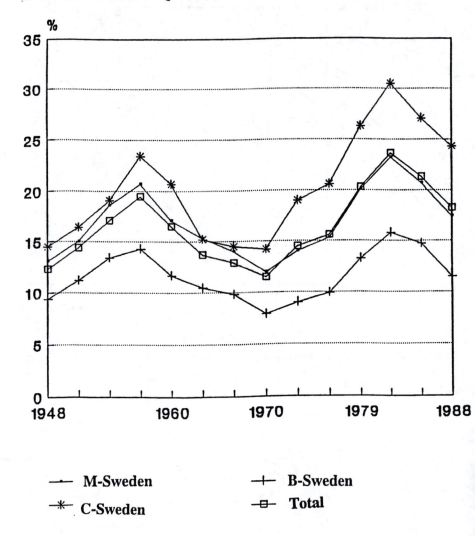

- M-Sweden
- C-Sweden
- B-Sweden
- Total

Source· SOU 1989·68

regions, where the conservatives are strong, and the B- and M-regions, where they are relatively weak, has more than doubled since the 1940s. The turning-point occurred in the early 1970s, when the conservative parties enjoyed some spectacular victories at the polls throughout northern Europe.

Some general trends deserve to be elaborated upon a little further. There is evidence of a geographic realignment revolving around the social democratic and conservative Parties of Finland, Norway and Sweden. The conservative parties have gained considerable ground in the expansive C-regions. In Norway and Sweden this has been achieved at the expense of the social democratic parties who have compensated for the loss of the urban centre by further penetrating the rural periphery (the B-regions). The Finnish social democrats never managed to penetrate the countryside. The Finnish Social Democratic Party has always had a distinctly urban profile which sets it apart from the social democratic parties of Norway and Sweden and with which it is not strictly comparable. On the whole, the three conservative parties display many more underlying similarities. There is the rapid expansion in the growth areas over the last twenty years and the loss of influence in the periphereal B-regions. Of the three social democratic parties, it is the Swedish party that is marked by the most pronounced regional 'polarization'. There is a similar trend in Norway, but not in Finland.

The emergence of new patterns of regional support?

What accounts for the different regional bases of the major political parties of Finland, Norway and Sweden? This question may be approached from a number of theoretical perspectives. They differ in terms of emphasis, but they do have one common denominator. They all suggest that we are in the midst of a transition period with a number of minor or major indications as to where we are heading. According to a popular theory, we are in the process of moving from one kind of society to another, from the traditional industrial society to the modern information society, with all that entails for the socio-economic structure and for the political parties (Glimell and Lindgren 1988; Pettersson 1988).

199

Electoral trends are often accounted for in terms of structural changes (see Gidlund and Gidlund 1989; Aardal and Valen 1989). The implication is that the social democrats owe their decline in the urban environment to structural changes that have reduced the importance of the secondary sector to the advantage of the service related tertiary sector. The social democratic core - the industrial workers - is withering away, while the non-socialist parties benefit from an influx of new voters from within the expanding tertiary sector. Whether this is so or not is readily seen by analyzing the socioeconomic development in terms of the same regional categories (Maktutredningen: Medborgarundersökningen 1989, 5-37).

The Swedish data from 1950-1983 do *not* lend support to this hypothesis (see figures 7-9). The data do testify to the decline of the primary and secondary sectors and to the expansion of the tertiary sector, but the main impression conveyed by the regional data is, nevertheless, one of remarkable stability over time. The socio-economic groups have defended their numerical positions surprisingly well within the regional context. If socioeconomic structure were all there was to it, the Conservative and Liberal Parties would have gained the upper hand in urban Sweden long before their actual breakthrough. If socioeconomic structure were the decisive determinant of voting behaviour, we would be hard put to account for the regional profile of the Social Democratic Party which is up against a continuous attrition of its socioeconomic core throughout the country. The process of attrition is somewhat more rapid in the urban environment, but not by much and definitely not by enough to uphold the tentative hypothesis on class and party.

Generally speaking, the patterns which have been found to characterize Sweden apply to Norway and Finland as well. The primary sector has been subject to a dramatic decrease, particularly during the last twenty years and particularly in the M- and B-regions. The significant decline of the secondary sector, which is readily apparent in the Swedish case, is not of the same magnitude in Finland and Norway.

The socioeconomic development of Finland differs from that of Norway and Sweden in two important respects. It has been more rapid and more uniform in the sense that there are only few traces of regional differences (figures 10 - 13). On a nationwide basis, the size

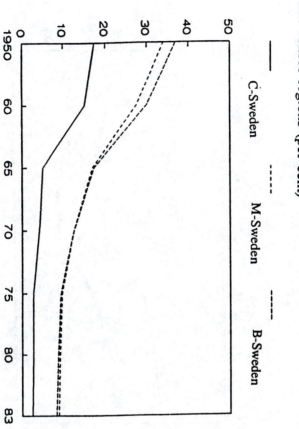

Figure 7: The development of the primary sector in Sweden 1950-1983. Three regions (per cent)

C-Sweden ——

M-Sweden - - - -

B-Sweden - - - -

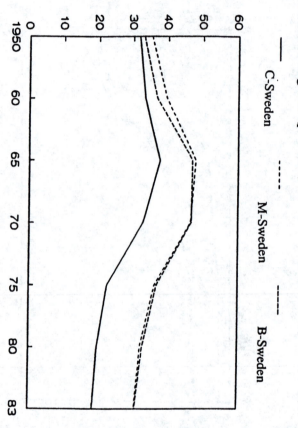

Figure 8: The development of the secondary sector in Sweden 1950-1983. Three regions (per cent)

C-Sweden

M-Sweden

B-Sweden

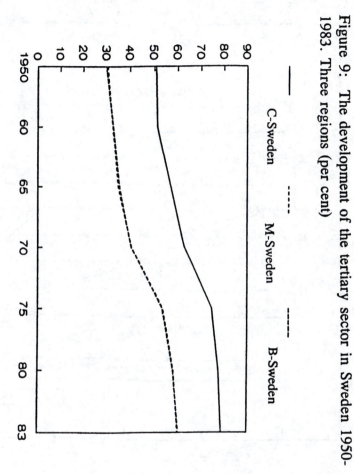

Figure 9: The development of the tertiary sector in Sweden 1950-1983. Three regions (per cent)

C-Sweden   M-Sweden   B-Sweden

203

Figure 10: The development of the primary sector in Norway 1950-1980. Three regions (per cent)

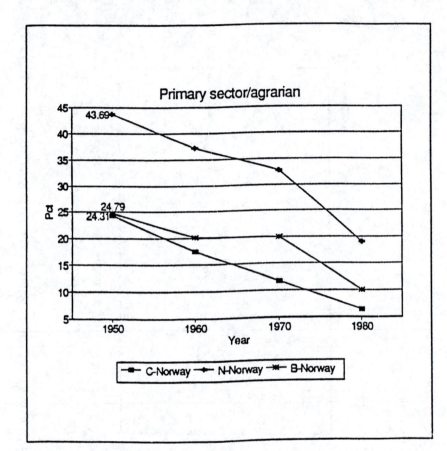

Figure 11: The development of the primary sector/fishing in Norway 1950-1980. Three regions (per cent)

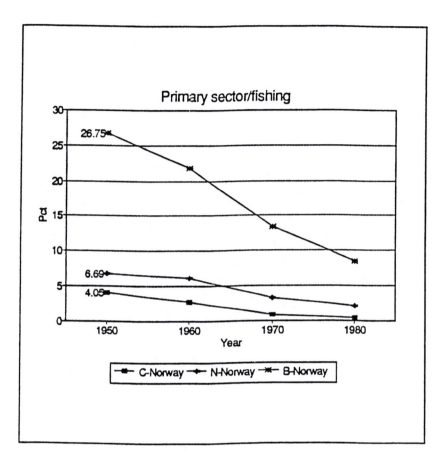

Figure 12: The development of the secondary sector in Norway 1950-1980. Three regions (per cent)

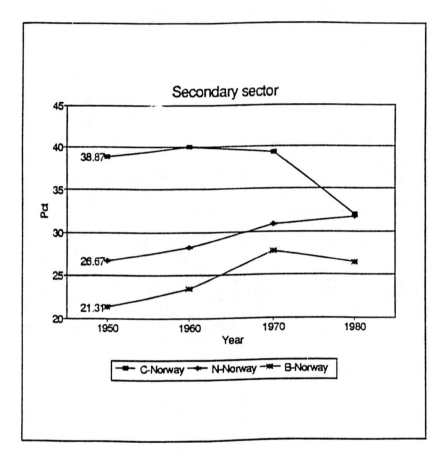

Figure 13: The development of the tertiary sector in Norway 1950-1980. Three regions (per cent)

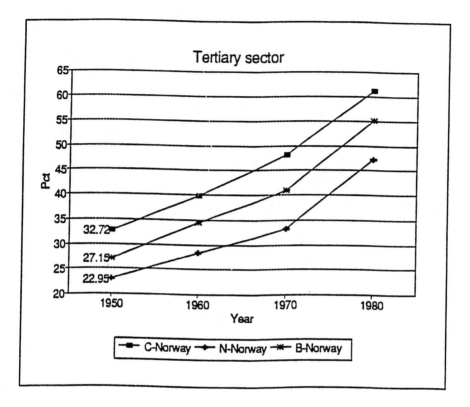

of the secondary sector may be seen to grow by a couple of percentage points between 1950 and 1970, just to plummet to the pre-1950 level (27.5 per cent) by 1980.[4] In Norway, the secondary sector develops in a way that is almost identical with that of Finland (see figures 14 - 17).

Similar comments apply to the growth of the tertiary sector. The three countries are clearly moving in the same direction, but Finland and Norway are lagging behind. The socioeconomic and political data from the regional arenas of three countries actually lend themselves to the tentative conclusion that the Finnish and Norwegian party systems are more sensitive to socioeconomic change than the Swedish party system. But the conclusion is tentative and comes with the same provisos attached to it as the socioeconomic model we tried on Sweden. If the socioecomic structure were all there was to it, the conquest of the centre by the conservatives and the loss of the centre by the social democrats should have materialized considerably earlier than it did (cf Bjørklund 1989).

The traditional centre/periphery cleavage is re-activated by those who would attribute the recent developments in the party arena to the rapid economic growth in the urban and metropolitan areas during the last ten or twenty years. With the influx of new city dwellers, this has contributed to a political rootlessness which is unique to the urban environment. In a similar vein, it may be argued that we are facing a new set of political values (post-materialistic values) which make themselves felt with particular strength in the expansive urban centres (Gidlund and Gidlund 1989). But this kind of logic is not entirely flawless. The reader is entitled to know what causes what. Do the changing values result in behaviour modification; does the changing political behaviour carry over into the domain of values or are the two processes interrelated?

We have some adequate data for these kinds of questions for Sweden. The data were generated within the framework of the recent Swedish study on the distribution of power and influence in Swedish society and politics. They are presented in terms of the same kind of regions with which we operate, and it is readily seen that there is indeed a gap between the offensive C-regions on the one hand and the defensive B-regions on the other (see appendix 2). Though signifi-

Figure 14: The development of the primary sector in Finland 1950-1980. Three regions (per cent)

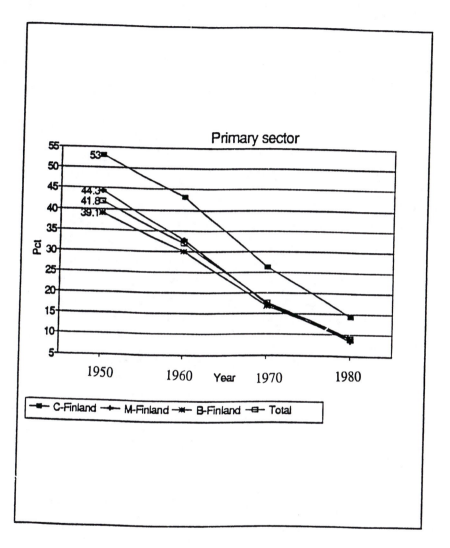

Figure 15: The development of the secondary sector in Finland 1950-1980. Three regions (per cent)

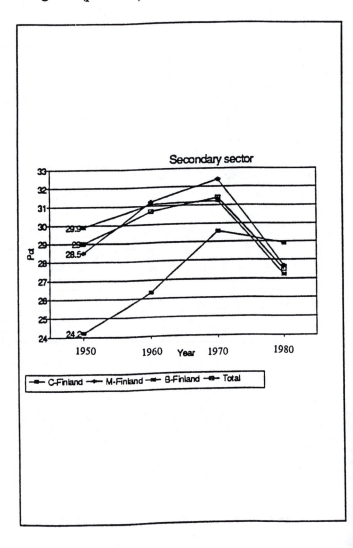

Figure 16: The development of the tertiary sector in Finland 1950-1980. Three regions (per cent)

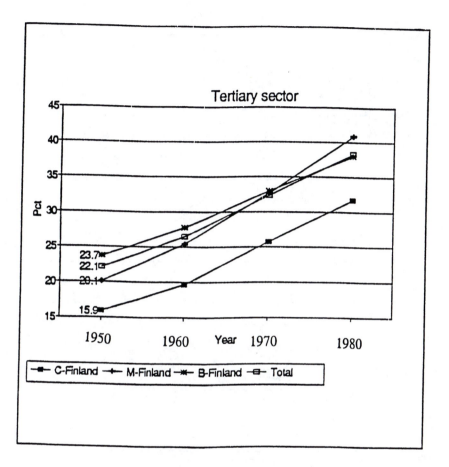

Figure 17: The development of the tertiary/others sector in Finland 1950-1980. Three regions (per cent)

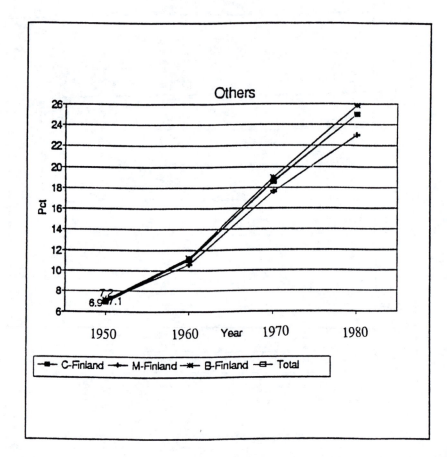

cant, the differences between the regions should not be exaggerated. It is after all only a matter of a few percentage points.

The data derive from a 1987 survey. They provide clues to the attitudes and values which are prevalent in the different parts of the country, but understandably they do not contribute towards our knowledge of the value changes which may have occurred.

Those who live in the urban and metropolitan areas are particularly prone to distrust political parties and political authorities, whether national, regional or local. But this does not prevent them from being more active than others in promoting change, even though the instruments (petitions, appeals and outright protests rallies) they use tend to bypass the political parties.[5]

Concluding discussion

We set out to describe and analyze the social democratic party profiles in Finland, Norway and Sweden. This study has confirmed some widely spread conceptions of political behavior in northern Europe.

There have been important regional changes since the end of WWII. The conservative parties have carved out a niche for themselves as the largest parties in the electorally promising urban environment, where the social democratic parties have experienced one electoral setback after the other. Finland represents a somewhat deviating case, *not* because the Conservative Party failed to win the big cities but because the Social Democratic Party failed to carry the rural periphery.

The changing conservative and social democratic regional profiles date back to the early 1970s. They coincide with an equalization of the regional support for the centre and liberal parties of Norway and Sweden during the 1980s. In this respect, Finland stands out as a deviating case by virtue of the fact that the regional differences were marginal to begin with. The parties of the Left have scattered strongholds in the dynamic centre (the C-regions) and in the rural periphery (the B-regions), but not in the localities which represent the middle of our geographic spectrum by being neither urban nor rural (the M-regions), where they have a long-standing history of electoral weakness. In Norway and Sweden the penetration of the centre occurred during the 1970s and the 1980s.

The regional differences between conservatives and social democrats in the urban and rural areas (the C- and B-regions) of Sweden are part and parcel of general trend in northern Europe, with Sweden in the lead and with the two other countries lagging behind. In Finland and Norway there is a line of demarcation which sets the urban centre (the C-regions) apart from the rest of the country. The changes which have occurred have almost exclusively affected the urban arena but not the rural periphery, which has remained a stronghold for the same parties ever since the end of WWII.

How are these changes to be understood? There are at least three separate interpretations or lines of inquiry, of which the last two are complementary rather than mutually exclusive. The development may thus be attributed to:

1   random variations in electoral support
2   the changing socioeconomic structure over time
3   changing social values over time

The trends have been identified on the basis of small but significant shifts in party support mainly over the last ten years. It would be risky to suggest that they are irreversible and they may in fact be a product of random variations over time. There is probably much more to it than the random factor. Over the last two decades, the social democratic and conservative parties of Finland, Norway and Sweden have experienced a variety of variations in electoral support, but the long term regional trend has remained the same. The conservative parties have improved their position in the expansive C-regions at the expense of the social democratic parties which have been pushed back into the rural periphery.

The other interpretation has it that the electoral swing in favour of the conservative parties is a by-product of the changing socioeconomic structure. There is a drastic scenario on this theme which interprets the swing to the right as the beginning of a permanent partitioning of the Nordic countries into a 'rich South' (the urban areas) dominated by the conservative parties and a 'deprived North' (the periphery) represented by the social democratic parties. But this

214

interpretation is not borne out by our data on socioeconomic change. The 'new' regional cleavage is not solely a function of the changing socioeconomic structure at regional level.

The third line of argumentation implies that the Nordic countries are in the midst of a transition period from industrial to post-industrial society. The data from the recent official investigation of Sweden's power structure would seem to suggest that there are values, attitudes and potential for action in the dynamic C-regions which do not make themselves felt in the stagnant B-regions, but the differences are not particularly impressive and do not lend themselves to far-reaching conclusions. It is an entirely open matter whether - and to what extent - the changing regional party profiles are by-products of changing social values. And if that turns out to be the most plausible explanation of the structural changes over the last two decades, it remains to be seen what will happen in the long run. What looks like regional polarization today may be something completely different tomorrow, if the electoral wind keeps blowing in the same direction for a few more years. We may very well be at the beginning of a gradual partisan shift against social democracy and in favour of the conservative parties which started out by conquering the expansive urban areas and which are on their way to making permanent inroads into the rural periphery.

Appendix 1:

Norway: Social Democracy is equated with:
The Norwegian Labour Party: 1945-1989.
The Conservative Party is identical to:
The Party of the Right: 1945-1989.

Sweden: The Conservative Party is identical to:
The Right/Moderate Coalition Party: 1948-1988
Social Democracy is equated with:
The Social Democratic Workers' Party (SAP): 1948-1988

Finland: The Conservative Party is identical to:
The National Coalition Party: 1945-1987.
Social Democracy is equated with:
The Social Democratic Party (SDP): 1945-1987.

Appendix 2: Have tried to exert political influence

	Type of Region		
	B	M	C
have approached politicians	8	9	8
have approached an association and/or interest org.	14	19	23
have approached an official representative of central or local government	18	22	22
have taken part in a demonstration (excl. the May Day demonstrations)	4	4	7
have contributed towards a boycot	13	13	18
have signed a petition	36	33	41
have worked in political action group	2	2	2
have worked in political party	2	2	4

How much do you trust:
(on a scale from 0 for 'no trust at all' to 10 for 'a great deal of trust')

	B	M	C
the local authorities	4.8	5.2	4.8
the national authorities	5.1	5.2	4.9
the courts	6.2	6.4	6.3
parliament	5.9	6.0	5.8
the news coverage of the mass media	5.1	5.2	5.0
the political parties	4.5	4.8	4.4
the large interest organizations	5.2	5.4	5.1
the large private companies	4.6	4.7	4.5

Source: Blomberg, G. et al 1989, 28, 34.

Notes

1. The same kind of regionalization as that in the national inquiry of 1989 (SOU 1989: 68). B-areas: characterized by a socioeconomic structure based on basic industry like forestry, mining, power production (mainly from water), 122 localities in Northern Sweden (excl. the greater Umeå and Östersund areas), Central Sweden (excluding the cities of Karlstad and Örebro) and the South East (excl. the cities of Växjö and Alvesta). M-areas: 109 localities in the central and southern parts of Sweden. C-areas: 53 urban communities dominated by the tertiary sector and characterized by high levels of technology, creativity, communication and culture.

2. From a political science point of view, it may make sense to think of localities which are hundreds of miles apart as belonging to the same region, on the basis of some kind of similarity requirement. But from a geographic point of view, it would not make sense make to accept other regions than those where the localities fulfil the proximity requirement by being geographically adjacent to one another (Berglund et al., 1979 and Moring 1990).

3. Finland: B-area: 271 communities.
            M-area: 122 communities.
            C-area: 52 communities.
   Norway: B-area: 83 communities.
            M-area: 296 communities.
            C-area: 75 communities.

4. The branchwise socioeconomic statistics for Finland are divided into four categories, including a residual category (others) which counts unemployed as well as economically inactive independents. If these groups were to be included in the tertiary sector, it would produce a highly misleading picture. This is also why we chose to report fishing separately in the Norwegian case.

5. Sweden was divided into another set of regions by the official inquiry into the power structure. The categories were periphery (sparsely populated areas), community, city and metropolis. The differences between the C-regions and the city and metropolitan areas turned out to be minor.

PART III
BEYOND SCANDINAVIA

Democratic Socialism in Spain, Portugal, and Greece

Einar Berntzen

By way of introduction: Social democracy - the nordic and southern European countries[1] compared

Just as the economic crisis began to erode the social democratic dominance in northern Europe, the southern socialist parties experienced a historic sweep into power. Unlike northern Europe, where the social democrats shared, and often dominated, power during the postwar period, the southern European socialists were virtually excluded from power until the late 1970s and early 1980s. By 1983 there were socialist parties in government in Greece, Spain, Portugal and Italy. There were high hopes that in the 1980s the southern European social democrats would 'show the way' for their frustrated northern counterparts, but these hopes have been dashed.

In terms of theory, this chapter will parallel discussion on why is there no socialism in the United States (Sombart 1976). Similarly, we are going to suggest possible answers to the question 'why is there no social democracy in southern Europe?' In the Nordic countries social democracy was the historical product of an economic and political conjuncture of the 1930s. The fight for the vote and the right to organize were perceived in terms of opposition to hierarchical class rule, as part of a broad struggle for equality. The early access to the franchise of the working class and the availability of bourgeois parties with which to collaborate led to cooperation in Parliament to attain various economic and welfare measures. Even though some southern European countries *de jure* introduced

219

universal male suffrage relatively early (e.g. Spain in 1890), the governments *de facto* continued to manage elections as they pleased through the control of *caciques*, or local bosses, in rural areas. Similarly, the business classes in southern Europe continually resisted coming to terms with the trade union movement. Although unions had *de jure* recognition, the history of labour in these countries was characterized by constant warfare. Particularly in Spain anarchism grew in response to alternate periods of legal toleration and savage repression. This pattern culminated in the triumph of right wing dictatorships in Spain (1939), Portugal (1926) and Greece (1936 and 1967) and the establishment of regimes that were primarily oriented towards maintaining the *status quo* in terms of economic conditions and class structure. When these authoritarian regimes broke down in the mid-1970s, the historical, political and economic conditions in Southern Europe were totally different from those on which the Nordic social democratic experience is based. It is to these differences that we now turn.

In addition to having long experiences of executive power, the Nordic social democratic parties differ from their southern counterparts in two main respects:

1) They enjoy the backing of united trade union movements.
2) They played a prominent role in the struggle for political democracy.

In northern Europe, the social democratic parties became *worker* parties. In southern Europe (with the possible exception of Spain) it is the communist parties that represent the workers. The most influential trade unions are dominated by communists in Portugal, Italy, and Greece. In Spain the balance of forces is more equal. Hence, the newly founded (or reestablished) social democratic parties in southern Europe formulated their ideologies in the absence of effective pressures for social democratic policies from trade unions which were weak and divided. Because unions were weak, the conditions for the emergence of a genuine working-class leadership were absent. Or in Gramsci's words, no organic elites were formed. Consequently, intellectuals or other upper-class radicals came to dominate the labour movement (Lipset 1983, 11). The parties 'created' in southern Europe in the mid-1970s were all led by elites of middle or upper-class origin (e.g. Papandreou; Soares).

The democratic breakdowns in southern Europe followed by long periods of right wing authoritarian regimes created another important difference in relation to the Nordic experience: the role played by the social democratic parties in the struggle for political democracy. In the Nordic countries, the social democratic parties pursued policies of welfare and economic redistribution as a continuation of the struggle for political participation and democracy. In southern Europe this struggle ended at first in civil wars, breakdowns of democracy and the establishment of dictatorships.

Much of the ideological luggage of the southern European socialist parties had accumulated during the long years of opposition against authoritarian regimes. The environment of clandestine struggle in which the Greek, Spanish and Portuguese left existed contributed a great deal to these parties' revolutionary and maximalist images.[2] The longevity of authoritarian regimes (two of them in NATO, and all closely allied to the United States) formed the basis for a strong anti-imperialist and *tercermundista* emphasis in the foreign policy of Greek, Spanish and Portuguese socialism. The persistence of pockets of extreme inequality in all of the southern countries gave a more traditionally socialist edge to the programmes and platforms of the southern parties. The presence of strong communist parties also pulled these parties toward the left.

The sudden democratic transitions of Greece, Portugal and Spain caught the socialist parties unprepared for their rise to power. The initiative in the democratic transitions in southern Europe in the 1970s was in the hands of the centre-right (Spain, Greece) or the radical military and the communists (Portugal). Hence, the ideological legacy from the years of dictatorship entailing the policy of mobilizing for a complete break with the old regimes was soon abandoned. There was an absence of a large, nation-wide democratic task for the socialist parties in southern Europe to face once the democratic transitions from above were in place. Then the task of the southern European socialist parties in this respect became one of adapting to the system (laid down by the centre-right) in order to gain executive power. Once in power the primary task became that of defending the democratic system.

221

The end of authoritarian rule in Portugal (1974), Greece (1974) and Spain (1975) produced precarious democracies that were initially threatened by the possibility of military coups. The priority of southern European socialists in power was thus to make democracy work rather than to implement traditional socialist aims, given the special requirements of regime consolidation following the end of authoritarianism.

Economic factors were crucial in the breakdown of authoritarianism in southern Europe. Democratic transitions were 'necessary' in order for these countries to become accepted as members of the EC. Executive power therefore also entailed another primary task: that of integrating the southern economies into the European and global economy. Against a background of weak trade unions and the absence of a genuine working-class leadership, both tasks tended to change the southern European socialist parties into centre parties. In actual fact, the southern European socialist parties moved towards a version of orthodox liberal market economics that would surprise even the most right-wing of northern European social democrats (Petras 1984). The southern European socialist parties actively sought to 'restructure capitalism' in order better to integrate their economies with European and world capitalism, even at the cost of abandoning the construction of a social democratic welfare state.

The road to power of the southern European socialist parties was in many respects smoothed by the phenomenon of Eurocommunism. Let us therefore briefly consider this development:

In the mid-1960s, when the Nordic social democratic parties were enjoying their heyday, the southern European working classes were all led by communist parties. But these parties either lived in a ghetto as the Italian PCI, or in illegality as the Spanish PCE, the Portuguese PCP and the Greek KKE. But from the late 1950s the southern European countries experienced rapid economic development and social change. Peasants left their villages and moved into the cities, and the industrial and service sectors expanded heavily. A new middle class emerged. These processes changed the living standards and expectations of the masses. In the early 1970s it was clear that political changes were needed to adapt to these new social realities caused by the capitalist modernization. The phenomenon of Eurocommunism must be viewed in terms of this social transformation. The communist parties of southern Europe adapted strategic perspectives similar to those taken by the Nordic social democratic parties in the 1930s. But the Eurocommunist parties' attempt to adapt ideologically to the new situation was hampered by their organizational structures which dated back to the Stalinist epoch. The result was that they paved the way for the emergence of new or resurrected real social democratic parties. These parties emerged suddenly from marginal positions to occupy the forefront of the political scene at the expense of the communist parties. This seems perfectly logical: if the masses in a developed capitalist society have to choose between two parties that both profess to promote social democratic policies, there is probably every reason for them to choose the most coherent version, namely the one which is also based on social democratic *organizational models* and corresponding international contacts.

This logic applied with varying strength in the different countries, and most dramatically in Spain. The Spanish Socialist Workers' Party, the PSOE, consisted of only a handful of members at the time of Franco's death. The Spanish Communist Party was a mass organization whose cadres had led the resistance against Franco's dictatorship for decades. Still, it took only a couple of years to turn the whole situation upside-down. The PCE sacrificed its entire militant past in favour of the Bourbon monarchy, national unity and capitalist constitutionalism. In 1982 the PSOE won an absolute electoral majority, whereas the PCE had been reduced to a shadow of itself, obtaining only 4.1 percent of the vote.

In Italy the PCI went even further trying to engineer a *compromesso storico* with the DC while eagerly supporting NATO. Exploited and dumped when the 'historical compromise' no longer interested the DC, the PCI has had to witness how the PSI succeeded where the PCI had failed: increasing its power and influence by cooperating with the DC to the point of occupying the post of Prime Minister from 1983 to 1987.

The developments in Portugal and Greece were quite different.The demise of the authoritarian regimes occurred not as a consequence of internal developments but as an effect of external circumstances: the Portuguese colonial war in Africa and the Cyprus invasion respectively. The local communist parties showed no inclination to move in a Eurocommunist direction. Greece and Portugal are the two Western countries that have been closest to a social revolution in the postwar era: Greece in 1944-48, and Portugal in 1974-75. The communist parties played prominent parts in both crises, and not only the ruling classes but also the urban middle classes and the peasants have traumatic memories with regard to the role of the communist party. When the authoritarian regimes were overthrown there was a *vacuum in the centre* which could be filled by the emerging social democratic parties. The Greek PASOK was in fact a direct continuation of the Centre Union of the 1960s (Mavrogordatos 1983b). But since the Greek civil war had taken place that long ago the Greek party was more radical than Mario Soareas' PSP, which in the late 1970s was performing the role of a counter-revolutionary buffer against the legacy of the 1974 revolution.

Socialism in Spain: the Sevillian Duo

The PSOE won consecutive absolute majorities (the first two in Spanish history) in the 1982 and 1986 general elections, and dominated local and regional politics during that period. Share (1988) argues that the remarkable political success of the PSOE in the 1980s and the party's equally rapid abandonment of social democratic policies once in government are closely related to each other. The PSOE's ability to bury its democratic socialist agenda was a crucial precondition for its rise to power in 1982, but the rejection of much of its social democratic programme once in power was not required by political and economic constraints.

How can one understand the PSOE's behaviour in government after 1982? Let us briefly survey the record of the Spanish socialists in economic and foreign policy arenas: The PSOE came to power with a promise to create 800,000 new jobs and to use state investment to promote economic growth (Nash 1983, 60). But upon taking power, rather than implementing the expansion-oriented, job-creating political economic policies called for in the 1982 party programme, the Spanish socialists immediately implemented a set of neo-liberal economic measures, including economic austerity and a plan for the economic streamlining of industry. Social security costs were attacked by cutting pensions, tightening up the rules for pension recipients, and increasing worker and business contributions to the scheme. This controversial policy was openly opposed by Nicolas Redondo, leader of the socialist General Confederation of Workers (UGT). The industrial streamlining programme entailed a huge increase in unemployment, which during the PSOE's first term jumped from 16 per cent to an alarming 20 per cent. Working-class opposition has been constant and increasingly violent. Police repression and the weakness of the Spanish trade union movement explain why mass opposition has not deterred the PSOE from implementing its neo-liberal economic policies. The PSOE electoral platform also supported the removal of Spain from NATO, as well as a nonaligned foreign policy. As was the case in the economic sphere, the socialists abandoned their 1982 pledges. In late 1983 and early 1984 Gonzalez began to vacillate on the NATO question, ultimately siding with the pro-NATO forces. Gonzalez submitted a 'compromise' plan to a referendum in March 1986, calling for continued membership in NATO (but not in its military command), a reduction of US troops based in Spain, and a ban on nuclear weaponry on Spanish soil.

The PSOE's history before and during the transition to democracy (1975-78) set the stage for its conservative behaviour in government. The PSOE entered this transition with two contradictory historical legacies. One was the disastrous experience of the Second Republic (1931-36), when the PSOE played a leading role in the ill-fated democratic experiment. Given the repression suffered by many PSOE militants during the Francoist regime (1939-75), it is not surprising that socialist leaders would later come to regard the preservation of democratic politics as their first priority, displacing other programme goals. During most of the Franco regime, the PSOE had become stagnant and largely inoperative within Spain, while the PCE became the principal leftist force. By the mid-1960s a group of young, middle-class professionals, including Felipe Gonzalez and Alfonso Guerra, both from Sevilla ('The Sevillian Duo'), were rebuilding the PSOE and were increasingly at odds with the party leadership in exile. By 1974 the younger members of the interior had wrested power away from the *históricos*, and had gained the support of the Socialist International. The ascent of Gonzalez and the younger generation within the PSOE also marked a dramatic radicalization of socialist ideology. At the 27th PSOE congress (1977) the party defined itself as 'mass, Marxist and democratic'. With respect to the transition to democracy, the PSOE insisted on *ruptura*, an abrupt break with Francoist authoritarianism.

The PSOE's radicalism and insistence on a democratic break were questioned by socialist leaders as it became apparent that Suarez's strategy could indeed produce a democratic regime from within authoritarian political structures (Share 1985, 98-102). By 1978 Gonzalez had decided that a substantial ideological overhaul was necessary. The first and most important reason why Gonzalez sought moderation of party ideology was the logic of elections. Party leaders interpreted the lack of electoral progress in March 1979 as evidence that the PSOE must broaden its appeal to encompass the vast 'middle classes' and to incorporate traditionally ostracized sectors of the electorate (e.g. the Church, small farmers, and entrepreneurs).

Socialist leaders were also motivated to moderate the party ideology because they were concerned about threats against the new democratic regime. Socialist leaders increasingly harboured real fears about the fragility of democratic politics, concerns that were compounded by persistent terrorism and by Lieutenant-Colonel Antonio Tejero's attempted coup of 23 February 1981 (the so-called *Tejerazo*).

Moreover, the protracted disintegration of Suarez's governing centrist party, UCD, created the potentiality for a dangerous political polarization between an anachronistic and questionably democratic neo-Francoist right, and the PSOE left. For much of the party leadership this scenario was too reminiscent of the disastrous Second Republic. The PSOE was not willing to initiate the types of reforms contemplated in the 1977 party platform if it entailed any risk to democratic stability. Finally, the socialists were in no position in society to carry out a radical democratic socialist platform. In 1982 the PSOE had only 100,000 members, and one of the lowest ratios of members to voters of any major West European political party. While the PSOE enjoyed close links with the UGT, the UGT was only one of several competing unions within an extremely weak

226

trade union movement. At the 28th PSOE Congress (May 1979), Gonzalez proposed an end to the Marxist definition of the party. The move was defeated by the delegates, and for four months Gonzalez stood down as leader of the PSOE. But at an extraordinary congress in September 1979 the *sector crítico* was finally defeated by Gonzalez and his supporters. A change in the method of delegate selection from local branch elections to the formation of delegations at provincial or regional level ensured that loyalists drowned out dissenters. By the 29th Party Congress (October 1981), the social democratization of the party ideology and programme was complete.

The 1982 electoral programme, like the 1979 version, proposed a moderate but still ambitious set of social democratic policies. However, whereas in 1979 the PSOE was still widely viewed as a potentially revolutionary party, by 1982 the socialists had effectively created an image of ideological moderation. The rapidity with which the PSOE exchanged its democratic socialist ideology for social democracy cannot by itself explain the socialists' abandonment of social democratic policies in favour of neo-liberalism once in office. However, it did create a political momentum for further ideological moderation.

Which factors limited the costs of such a policy shift? In 1982 the PSOE not only won an absolute majority but the party's two major competitors (the centrist UCD and the communist PCE) were virtually destroyed in the election. Moreover, both parties further self-destructed after their respective electoral *debâcles*, with the UCD disappearing altogether (1983), and the PCE splitting in two (the Eurocommunist PCE and the Stalinist PCPE). The major consequence of the destruction of the PCE and the UCD was to provide the PSOE with an electorally inexpensive opportunity to occupy *centre ground* in the party system. The PSOE was free to pursue neo-liberal economic policies without fearing punishment by a communist left. The PSOE was confident that, barring the unlikely rebirth of the centre, it could compensate for the small loss of votes on their left with the mass of 'party-less' voters in the centre. In effect, the PSOE had encroached on the terrain of the modern right, creating an awkward situation for the fragmented *grupúsculos* of the centre and the main conservative party, the Alianza Popular (1989: Partido Popular).

If the electoral costs of the PSOE's moderation were thus reduced, what about the potential for internal party rebellion? Two interrelated features of the PSOE are the key to understanding how the Gonzalez leadership imposed its revised policies on the Socialist Party: first, Gonzalez's charisma and power within the party, and second, the maintenance of a centralized and often authoritarian party structure.

The PSOE leaders have come to view capitalist democracy as the only feasible and desirable political economic arrangement for Spain. Spanish socialists no longer seek to alter capitalism fundamentally in the name of equality and economic democracy. Having rejected democratic socialism as unfeasible and undesirable, the PSOE has adopted a new image, based on its technocratic-administrative capacity and the charisma of Gonzalez, and it is rapidly shedding its social democratic skin. The PSOE lost its absolute parliamentary majority in the October 1989 election. The practice of 'socialist clientelism' has also occurred under PSOE governments in Spain. According to Gallagher: 'The Spanish political spoils system has allowed the PSOE to hand out thousands of jobs in the public sector and the administration. The result is a well-disciplined party. Up to 80% of the delegates attending the Socialist party congress in December (1984) are reckoned to have benefited from PSOE Government patronage' (Gallagher 1989, 149).

Socialism in Portugal: the unmaking of the Carnation Revolution

Within two years of its foundation in April 1973, the PSP had become the leading force in Portuguese politics. Amongst its promoters were Marxists, progressive Catholics, Freemasons, republican liberals, and former members of the PCP. A distinguishing feature of the PSP that was evident from the outset was the lack of a strong base in the working class. Members of the middle and upper-middle classes dominated the upper echelons of the party, with representatives of the liberal professions, especially lawyers and academics, being particularly prominent. Even the party functionaries and intellectuals, who in other European socialist parties can trace their working-class origins despite their middle-class attributes, were not to be found in the PSP hierarchy. During the revolution, the PSP established for itself a solid reputation for anticommunism and opposition to radical forms of socialism. By firmly establishing its identity vis-à-vis the PCP, it won support from the bourgeoisie. But it also became the prisoner of this strategic choice, since it cannot now form even a tactical coalition with the PCP for fear of losing its credibility and a large part of its electorate. This has effectively prevented any opening of Portuguese politics on the left. In contrast to Spain and Greece, there was much more intense competition for the centre of the electoral space in Portugal between the PSP and the PSD. This tended to draw the PSP increasingly to the centre so as to out-manoeuvre the PSD.

So far the PSP strategy to conquer the political centre has assumed three forms. After its victory in the 25 April 1976 elections, the PSP decided to form a minority government without contracting any alliance either on its left or right. In December 1977 Soares's government was forced to resign. Soares then formed an unlikely coalition with the small CDS, the most right-wing of the parties represented in the Assembly. This revealed a desire to cling to power for power's own sake. For reasons of expediency, a number of socialist economic policies were quietly dropped while decollectivization of farm land was speeded up. In 1978 Mário Soares was dismissed as Prime Minister by President Eanes on the grounds that the PS-CDS coalition was no longer viable and that it was impossible to find a new party-based government within the Assembly. Mário Soares never forgave Eanes for taking such action.[3] In late 1978 Soares realized that the PSP was badly in need of a new image. At the 3rd congress in 1979 the PSP threw overboard the strategy of homogeneous minority socialist governments. Soares now proposed to widen the PSP's sphere of influence on the left and the right. In 1980 the party thus tried to copy the success of the Democratic Alliance (AD), an electoral coalition between the CDS and the PSD, by creating its own broad electoral coalition, the Republican Socialist Front (FRS). The strategy proved a complete fiasco. The defeat of the FRS heralded another change in PSP strategy.

The only viable alternative then became that of a coalition with its nearest partner on the right, the PSD. With the breakup of the AD in 1982 after the death of its founder, Sá Carneiro, and the election results of 25 April 1983, the PS-PSD alliance became a reality. The PS-PSD coalition governed until 1985 and was known as the *bloco central*, an indication of the extent to which the PSP had moved to the centre in its latest phase. For two years Soares presided over the 'most drastic austerity programme to be implemented by any western socialist leader' (Giner 1984, 149). The *bloco central* broke up due to a leadership change in the PSD: years of confusing internecine warfare ended when Aníbal Cavaco Silva seized the helm and proclaimed the need for the party to rediscover its identity independent of the socialists. The effective collapse of the *bloco central* paved the way for fresh elections in October 1985. The October 1985 election was a veritable *debâcle* for the PSP, who reached an all time low of only 20.4 per cent of the vote (compared to 36.3 per cent in 1983), the biggest single fall in support any European socialist party has yet had to suffer (Gallagher 1989, 24). The heavy socialist loss was mainly due to the appearance on the electoral scene of former president Eanes' Party of Democratic Renewal (PRD), which won an impressive 17 per cent of the vote. The PSD won 29.9 per cent of the vote and formed a minority government. It fell to a censure motion in April 1987. New elections on 19 July 1987 resulted in an absolute majority for the PSD (50.2 per cent of the vote), the first majority government in democratic Portugal.

In 1987 the PSD captured most of the votes of the Democratic Renewal party (votes which had been largely taken from the PSP in the 1985 election). The Democratic Renewalists lost more than two-thirds of their support, whereas the PSP modestly reinforced their 1985 strength (See table 1).

These rapidly shifting strategies to form a single party majority government had a deep effect on the party's programme. Like all southern European Socialist parties, the PSP developed a radical language which hardly corresponded to its practice. By the time the party had taken over the government in 1976, it had shifted decisively to the right and implemented very few policies that could be called socialist or even social democratic. This was acknowledged indirectly at its 3rd Congress in March 1979, when the PSP adopted a new party programme with the title *Dez anos para mudar Portugal* (Ten years to change Portugal). With this programme the PSP abandoned all official reference to Marxism. This ambitious

document took the mixed economy as its base model for development and accepted that redistribution of wealth should occur not
through any further alteration in property rights or the means of
production but by means of social reform. The document marked a
further step in the deradicalization of the PSP. The theme of Europe
was very important for the PSP. In the 1976 election the party's
slogan was 'Europa esta connosco' (Europe is with us), and in 1977
the socialist government applied for membership in the Common
Market. Mário Soares's rule over the party was based on the
relationship with the parties of the Socialist International. It was
through Soares and his European contacts that the PSP received
outside finance. In fact, his control of the PSP's external finances
was undoubtedly a key element in his absolute control over the

Table 1

Social Democracy in Southern Europe at the Polls:
Percentage of the Vote

Year	Portugal (PSP)	Spain (PSOE)	Greece (PASOK)
1915	1.6	-	-
1933	-	19.7	-
1936	-	(48.1)[4]	-
1974	-	-	13.6
1975	40.7	-	-
1976	36.7	-	-
1977	-	30.3	25.3
1979	28.2	30.5	-
1980	28.7	-	-
1981	-	-	48.1
1982	-	46.5	-
1983	36.3	-	-
1985	20.4	-	46.0
1986	-	44.1	-
1987	21.0	-	-
1989 (18/6)	-	-	39.1
1989 (29/10)	-	39.6	-
1989 (5/11)	-	-	40.7
1990 (8/4)	-	-	38.6

party. The policy of the PSP was fundamentally the policy of Mário Soares, who belongs much more to the democratic, republican tradition in Portugal than to that of socialism. His personality and tendency to impose his interpretation of the party's policies created deep divisions within the party.

Geographically the PSP enjoys, more than any other party in Portugal, an even spread of support throughout the country. Likewise, more than any other party, the PSP can claim to be representative of every social class. It may be true that the social basis of the party is above all an alliance between the moderate working class from the north and the urban petty bourgeoisie coming mainly from the Lisbon metropolitan area, but a survey shows that in the 1983 elections, the PSP received the votes of 27 per cent of the upper class, 31 per cent of the upper-middle class, 36 per cent of the lower-middle class and 33 per cent of the lower class. Fortyone per cent of PSP's support came from the lower-middle class (Bruneau 1986,75). Another survey shows the PSP to be one of the parties that can depend least on the fidelity of its electorate. Unlike the PCP and the PSD, the PSP has been unable to establish a real network of social contacts or institutions that would allow it to put down firm roots in Portuguese society. Until 1978 the PSP was more or less excluded from the organized working class due to the almost total communist control over the CGTP. In 1978 the PSP and PSD were finally able to establish their own union federation, the UGT. As yet the unions affiliated to the UGT are primarily active in the service industries, and the PSP's hold over industrial workers is still fairly weak. Like its southern European counterparts, oligarchical and centralizing tendencies have dominated the evolution of the PSP's organizational structure. Power within the PSP is concentrated in the hands of the Secretary-General, especially since the 4th Party Congress in 1981.

This concentration of power in the hands of the Secretary-General is underlined by the fact that the party's group in Parliament must submit to the party executive. Thus, in 1981, when Soares was having difficulty with the majority of the party's deputies, he simply decided to depose the party's parliamentary leader, Francisco Salgado Zenha.[5] On the other hand, the leadership does not expect the party executive to exercise any control over its actions in government. One of the greatest mysteries of the PSP is its membership figures. During the revolution it claimed to have some 80,000 members and by May 1983 announced a rise to 130,181. These figures are completely fictional. Most informed guesses put the party membership nearer 30,000 (Bruneau 1986, 69). New members of the PSP often obtained a party card in order to secure state promotion or state jobs and the conditional nature of their support often proved to be a doubtful asset to the party.

To prepare for the presidential contest, Soares stepped down from the leadership of the PSP which was inherited by his protégé Almeida Santos, a wealthy lawyer who made his fortune in Mozambique in colonial times. The elevation of such a figure was received badly in the country.

At the 6th congress of the PSP on 28-30 June 1986, Vítor Constâncio was chosen as the new Secretary-General of the party in place of the discredited Almeida Santos. His first promise was to restore the PSP's fortunes after its 1985 electoral defeat, by creating a more decentralized and democratized party. The PSP now tried to refashion its identity. In 1985 a leading party member had admitted that apart from its commitment to democracy and Portugal's entry into the EC, the main motivation inside the PSP was the exercise of power for its own sake (Gallagher 1989, 27). Constâncio had been governor of the central bank, the Bank of Portugal, since March 1985, resigning this post to contest the PSP leadership. He had also served as Finance Minister under Soares in 1978, when he was responsible for implementing the government's austerity programme, and had been president of the commission which negotiated Portugal's entry into the EC in January 1986. The June 1986 congress also agreed to strike out remaining references to Marxism from PSP statutes. Other measures included moves to decentralize power within the party by making the leaders accountable to the congress rather than to the party's national executive and by giving local branches a greater say in the running of party affairs.

The PSP has had a sense of disorientation since July 1987, when Mr. Cavaco Silva's PSD won the first parliamentary majority since Portugal returned to democracy in 1974. The battle for the centre of the electoral space between PSP and PSD thus ended with victory for the latter. However, at the 7th congress of the PSP in February 1988, billed as *El Congreso de la Convergencia*, which re-elected Vítor Constâncio as Secretary-General with a 94 per cent majority, some signs of progress in revitalizing the PSP were becoming evident. For instance, a quota of 25 per cent of all elected party offices was to be reserved for women, a decision insisted upon by the party leader.

On 27 October 1988, Vítor Constâncio unexpectedly resigned. According to his own statement, divisions within the party regarding its policy direction and the continuing influence of Soares had prompted his resignation. Thus it seems that the Portuguese socialists still have to emerge from the shadow of Mário Soares, who formally abandoned party politics when he was elected National President in 1986. At a meeting on 14-15 January 1989, the party elected Jorge Sampaio (49), a lawyer, as his successor. His nearest rival, Jaime Gama, regarded as a protégé of Soares (under whom he had held various cabinet posts) had also stood against Constâncio when the latter was elected in June 1986.

Socialism in Greece: the rise and eclipse of the Green Sun

The October Revolution in Russia created the split between socialists and communists. In Greece, however, there was no split at all, due to the fact that the first socialist party was founded only *after* the Russian Revolution. Hence, there existed no previous socialist party that the communists could split from. The Workers' Socialist Party, founded in November 1918, became the The Communist Party of Greece (KKE). There existed no 'socialist' party in Greece before the formation of PASOK in 1974. On 3 September 1974, Andreas Papandreou announced the establishment of the *Panellinio Sosialistiko Kinima* (the Panhellenic Socialist Movement) which was to become the first mass socialist party in modern Greek history.

In both its origins and its formation, PASOK differs markedly from its sister parties in southern Europe, which can all trace their history, however broken, back to the heyday of the Second International (e.g., the PSOE was founded in 1879 and the PSI in 1892).[6] In Greece, bourgeois liberalism (the Venizelists) and communism

234

formed the opposition to the authoritarian right (the royalist anti-Venizelists), and when the hour of southern socialism dawned in the 1970s, it here took the form of a disintegration of the liberal centre. In fact this even found personalized expression in the generational renewal of the Papandreous: father George aged and declined with the Centre Union and left behind no obvious successor upon his death in 1968. His son Andreas took over the charismatic mantle and adapted it to the changed circumstances of the 1970s. The colonels' coup in 1967 then drove him into exile, where he organized the Panhellenic Liberation Movement (PAK) whose actions against the dictatorship made it the most widely known, though not the most solidly founded of the resistance groups. Once the junta had fallen, Papandreou rallied militants from PAK and a number of smaller groups (the most important of which was Democratic Defence) launching the explicitly socialist PASOK.

PASOK entered the arena of Greek politics in a dramatically radical and dynamic fashion. The party contained 'something' for everyone but not 'everything' for everyone. PASOK consisted of three wings of thought: the socialist (PAK); the technocratic; and the *palaiokommatikoi*,[7] which claimed most of the popular support from the farmers and the petty-bourgeoisie.

According to Spourdalakis (1988), the logic of early elections in November 1974 gave an advantage to the organization's more astute political forces which were the *palaiokommatikoi* and Papandreou. PASOK's eventual 'conservative' development was favoured by social and political factors external to the Movement. The lack of a long industrial working class tradition gives an overwhelming petty-bourgeois flavour to Greek politics. This factor assisted those tendencies which eventually gained the upper hand in the organization: the *palaiokommatikoi* and the technocrats. *Palaiokommatikoi* preferred a loose organization around a charismatic leader, geared to running successful electoral campaigns. An organization like this would in turn be more amenable to their clientelistic practices.

Thus, by 1977 PASOK had dramatically changed its image from a movement of protest to a viable alternative to the ND government. The political, social and economic developments of the first post-*metapolitefse*[8] years were conducive to PASOK's movement away from its original radicalism in several ways. On the one hand, the presence in Government of a moderate right-wing party (*Nea Demokratia*) was forcing PASOK to respond programmatically not with the vague radicalism of 1974, but rather in a concrete, 'serious' and technocratic fashion which would address the solution to the country's problems. This fact entailed ostracizing the militants of the former PAK in 1976. PASOK's new moderate image paid off handsomely in the 1977 election: it nearly doubled its 1974 14 per cent share of the vote to 25 per cent (see table 1).

On 18 October 1981 PASOK obtained 48 percent of the vote after its electoral campaign of *allaghi* (change), and the first socialist government which Greece had ever experienced was formed. An attempt to 'stimulate the economy' by manipulating the demand side failed. This Keynesian interval (1981-82) indicates the Government's response to the pressure exerted by the politically influential *palaiokommatikoi*. The cost-free social reforms (abolition of the institution of dowry, change of the legal framework regarding the position of women, divorce by consent, civil marriage and equal rights for children born out of wedlock) can be seen as the Government's response to the admittedly much less influential radical tendency. The market forced the 'Keynesian hopes' into the background and gave rise to the monetarist policies of austerity which in effect brought the technocrats to the fore. From the summer of 1983, when the controversial anti-labour legislation concerning state-owned enterprises was introduced until the autumn of 1985, when the severe economic measures of austerity were introduced, the Government not only demonstrated a determination to go ahead with its economic strategy but also indicated that the technocrats had almost completely taken over. This meant the end of the internal pluralism in PASOK. According to Spourdalakis (1988), this homogenization will inevitably lead to PASOK's own demise. PASOK's political support is to a great extent based on the strata which the technocrats are trying to undermine. PASOK has had to face the harsh reality of power before making its political orientation clear. PASOK has thus been forced to undermine the very basis of its strength: the tacit articulation of a tri-polar pluralism. The timing and outcome of this scenario is going to be determined by Papandreou himself. After all, without Papandreou there is no PASOK. PASOK existed for over 9 years without a congress. Also on this score PASOK can claim to be internationally unique. At the 1st congress on 10-13 May 1984, the equation PASOK = Papandreou, established by practice up to that point, was not only tacitly recognized but also institutionalized. The congress consolidated the degeneration of PASOK into a monolithic organization. The movement, in its short march to power, has destroyed the organizational structures which might have allowed for the possibility of a radical revitalization of PASOK.

With PASOK at the helm there has been an unprecedented centralization of state power. There is a continued exclusion of certain sectors of the governmental apparatus from democratic control in the name of efficiency: the military, diplomacy and justice. The phenomenon of 'green guards' has taken on immense dimensions. These patronage appointments (based on party membership) may very well be understood as a continuation of the long tradition of clientelism.[9] What is new is the political discourse which accompanies the state's actions under the new socialist rule. There was co-optation of PASOK's organization through massive recruitment into the state apparatus. It was consequently during this period that the Greek state experienced possibly the most extensive patronage recruitment in its history. Of PASOK's members in 1984, 70 per cent had joined the party after 1981 (Spourdalakis 1988, 249). Against this background it hardly comes as a surprise that the PASOK government is bedevilled with corruption scandals and power abuse (the Koskotas-affair). Despite this and his sexual extravaganzas with his curvaceous mistress, the seductive Dimitra Liani, whose nude photos appeared on the front pages of opposition newspapers, Papandreou still entertained hopes of winning the 18 June 1989 elections. PASOK lost its absolute majority but still obtained 39.1 per cent of the vote (from 46.0 per cent in 1985) in spite of the scandals and in spite of eight years at the helm and many unfulfilled promises. On the other hand, ND failed to win an absolute majority in spite of PASOK's weakened position. PASOK tried unsuccessfully to establish a coalition with the communist Left Alliance but that proved impossible as long as Papandreou was party leader. ND therefore formed a unique Black-Red coalition government with the communist Left Alliance, thus bringing the communists into a Greek government for the first time since 1944. The communists were given the Ministries of Justice and the Interior. The communists had just one condition for participating in the government: ND leader Konstantin Mitsotakis should not become Prime Minister. The government was thus headed by the former naval officer Tzannis Tzannetakis whose sole purpose was to clean up in the scandals surrounding PASOK and Papandreou. The Tzannetakis government resigned after the decision of the Greek Parliament to bring Papandreou and other PASOK politicians to trial.

In the election campaign preceding the 5 November election, PASOK had abandoned the rethoric of the great 'change' (*allaghi*) and instead exploited the man in the street's fear that a conservative government majority would conduct tough Thatcherite policies. These elections, too, failed to produce an absolute majority for any of the parties. An interim all-party coalition government headed by Xenofon Zolotas was formed, consisting of all the three major parties: ND (6 members), PASOK (5 members) and the communist Left Alliance (2 members), with the remaining members being non-party technocrats. For the third time in ten months the Greeks went to the polls on 8 April 1990. This time ND was just one mandate short of getting an absolute majority. ND achieved this mandate by signing an agreement with Kostas Stephanopoulos' centre-right Democratic Renewal Party (DIANA) whose single Member of Parliament was willing to vote with the 150 conservative ND representatives.

By way of conclusion: why no social democracy in southern Europe?

The southern European socialist governments that have come to power in the 1980s are of a substantially different character from those headed by post-war welfare state social democrats. After the crisis conciliation pacts of the 1930s, the Nordic social democrats replaced the notion of socialist transformation with that of the welfare state: their efforts were henceforth directed at increasing the wage workers' share of the economic pie and at improving the standard of living of the toiling masses. Contemporary southern European socialists, in stark contrast to their recent radical image, have not only rejected social democratic goals outright, but have proceeded to undermine trade-union rights and institutions in the name of the market, private enterprise and capital. Business, not labour, has become the key target group for southern European socialist support. Southern European socialists have supported the employers' efforts to promote greater 'labour flexibility' (i.e. wage cuts), attacks on collective and social security, more rapid mobility between jobs, and less regulation of employer power to hire and fire. The contrast between the programmes implemented by past 'reformist social democrats' and contemporary neo-liberal southern European socialists is clearly demonstrated by the latter's total disregard for the issue of unemployment. In every single country where the southern European socialists have held executive power, the number of unemployed has increased during their periods in office.

There are two fundamental reasons for this difference, and both have to do with the overall relationship between capital and labour that has characterized the southern European experience. The contrast between contemporary southern European socialists and the Nordic welfare social democrats can partly be explained by the *timing* of their coming to power and the place they occupy in the capitalist division of labour. The Nordic social democrats reaped their successes during the postwar economic boom. The class compromises that became institutionalized were the fruit of high economic growth rates and solid labour organization. None of these conditions prevailed when the southern European socialists received their turn at the helm. World capitalism had entered a phase of depression and had become far more internationalized than in the immediate postwar period. Embedded in the iron logic of the market, fearful of being uncompetitive for capital location, the southern European socialists saw the extension of workers' power or even welfare programmes as an obstacle to 'modernization' and as an invitation to a flight of capital. The vertical ascent of the technocrats schooled in neo-liberal economics within the southern parties was accompanied by the horizontal transfer of 'free-market' ideology from the hegemonic northern European countries. This ideological transfer had particularly damaging effects because, unlike in northern Europe, it was not preceded by the construction of a dense social welfare network. Hence, when the social cuts took place in the south, they affected classes that were already living under precarious circumstance. The political consequences of this rupture with the welfare tradition are likely to be particularly damaging to the southern European socialist parties.

Equally important is the position of labour unions in southern Europe. Southern European social democracy emerged in surroundings marked by extremely weak labour movements compared to Nordic standards. For instance, the level of unionization is 80-90 per cent in Sweden, whereas it is closer to 15 per cent in Spain (Anderson 1988). The southern European socialists have been downright hostile towards the trade unions. It is precisely within the trade unions that the communists have been able to maintain their last strongholds, even if they have lost their political positions to the socialists.

The southern European parties are mainly electoral machines, at the parliamentary and administrative level completely dominated by teachers, lawyers, civil servants, economists, in short by layers of the upwardly mobile professions out of touch with or without any roots in the real life of the working classes. PSOE, PSP or PASOK have in this way primarily functioned as channels for the new middle classes' climb up the social ladder.

The authoritarian regimes that preceeded the southern European democracies created an objective space for the socialist parties: the bourgeois-democratic tasks were not completed. Cultural, legal, family political and administrative reforms that long since had been introduced in northern Europe were placed on the agenda.

The rise of the southern European socialist parties was as sudden and dramatic as their subsequent shift away from social welfare policies. The most damaging consequence is the devaluation of socialist ideology. In lieu of the promise of social change (*cambio, allaghi*), the electorates will associate socialism with austerity, unemployment, and the regrouping of the old centres of power. The results are already visible: an even more cynical and depoliticized electorate, the resurrection of patronage and corruption as the only worthwhile goals of political participation.

Notes

1. Attention will be focused on Spain, Portugal and Greece because of the similarities in the context in which socialist parties have been operating. Within a period of merely two years, they all witnessed the demise of authoritarian regimes. Moreover, as soon as democratic elections could be held, socialist parties became predominant on the left in Spain and Portugal, as well as in Greece.

2. Are the southern European so-called 'socialist' parties basically different from the Nordic 'social democratic' parties? Duverger, for example, operates with the concept of a 'troisième voie' between what he terms 'le socialisme totalitaire' and 'le socialisme reformiste' or 'la social-democtratie' (Duverger 1980). In southern Europe the term 'social democracy has traditionally (i.e., until the late 1970s) been a word of abuse. The parties so called, namely the Portuguese PSD and the Italian PSDI, are generally considered to be bourgeois parties, although it is a fact that both the PSI and the PSDI are members of the Socialist International. The PSD wanted to be accepted as the Portuguese representative in the International but was ultimately turned down.

3. Still smarting from his abrupt dismissal by Eanes in 1978, Soares refused to accept the PSP decision to back Eanes for a second presidental term in 1980.

4. The percentage refers to the Popular Front consisting of the PSOE, the PCE and various bourgeois republican parties.

5. In the 1986 presidental election Zenha hit back by resigning from the PSP to run for president for the Democratic Renewal Party (PRD), created by the followers of President Eanes.

6. The particularity of PASOK is further underlined by the somewhat mystifying PASOK symbol of the Green Sun instead of the usual Red Rose.

7. The name given to the politicians or political activists who were associated with the clientelistic politics of the prejunta period.

8.   The period following the fall of the junta in the summer of 1974.

9.   The phenomenon of PASOK's 'Green Guards' of the 1980s is thus not completely distinct from the phenomenon of *kommatarches*, the local representatives of the parties, a characteristic of Greek political life since the 19th century. The same can be said of the role of Papandreou in the party. The role which party leaders traditionally have held in the Greek party system from Venizelos to Karamanlis has to be considered if one wishes to put Papandreou's role in PASOK into perspective.

Italian Socialism:
A Century of Trial and Error

Ann-Cathrine Jungar

Introduction

The Italian version of reformist socialism makes rather a sad story. The PSI (*Partito Socialista Italiano*) was the first modern party to be founded in the unified Italian state; soon it was also first in political strength. Its ties with the emerging industrial classes were close, and before the First World War the PSI controlled the trade union movement with about two million members. Of the European socialist parties, only the German Social Democratic Party was stronger in 1919. After the Second World War, however, the Italian socialists started on a downward trend which seems difficult to reverse. Inconsistencies in policy and alliance formations have undermined its credibility among the electorate throughout the postwar period. Roughly equal to the Communist Party (PCI) in the first post-fascist parliamentary election, the PSI was soon outdistanced by its revolutionary rival. In the 1950s the PCI was twice as strong as the PSI, and in the 1970s the PCI polled three times the vote of the PSI. Today, however, with worldwide communism on its last legs, the PSI bears hopes for the future and has in fact reduced the PCI lead to a certain extent.

One of the most puzzling questions in Italian politics is in fact why a reformist socialist party has not succeeded in Italy. Forty per cent of the Italian electorate vote socialist, but a majority prefers the PCI which has come to resemble the Scandinavian social democratic parties more and more in terms of policy formulations. This fact has led many people to regard the PCI as the social democratic party of Italy. From a historical point of view, however, it has been a revolutionary party par excellence; a social democratic label would not do the PCI justice.

This study highlights the history of the PSI throughout the century that has passed since its foundation. In an attempt to explain the limited success of democratic socialism in Italy, it is argued that the PSI's organizational weakness, its feeble hold on the working class and its organizations, and the ambiguity of its coalition politics have been the main factors which have prevented it from developing into a strong political force.

The question of participation

What separated the parties belonging to the socialist family at the turn of the century was their attitude towards participation. They differed concerning what degree of participation was optimal for the creation of a socialist society. This has continued to be a dilemma for the PSI, as the party has not developed into a 'state-bearing' party like its Scandinavian counterparts. The attainment of socialism has not only depended upon the PSI, but also on finding the optimal partner. Whether the PSI should participate in coalitions and governments, when, and especially with whom, have been the major questions for the Italian Socialist Party from the very beginning. The question of participation has been at the core of the party's history ever since its foundation in 1892; therefore, it will be a central focus for this study. Especially alliances with other parties have been centres around which the party's other activities have revolved and by which they have been conditioned.

Adam Przeworski uses the concept of participation as a point of departure when examining social democracy as a historical phenomenon. Here, his framework is enlarged insofar as the concept of participation not only includes involvement in Parliament but also collaboration with other parties in the political institutions, above all in government (Przeworski 1987, 7-46).

The socialists were the ones who decided to use political action instead of direct action as a means of changing society. In Italy this line of demarcation coincides with the foundation of the PSI. The first General Workers' Congress assembled anarchists, syndicalists and socialists in Genoa in 1892; the question of participation was the main theme. Already on its second day, the congress was divided into two; the socialists founded the PSI with the objective of taking part in the political institutions and elections, while the anarchists chose the anti-parliamentary direction (Galli 1983, 56; Arfé 1977, 9). In the First International, the abstentionist current lost its support after 1893, and the division of the socialist movement was soon a fact all over Europe.

Anarchism: the first organized protest movement

The anarchist movement in Italy was one of the largest in Europe and socialism's main competitor before industrialization. The take-off phase of the Italian economy coincided with the foundation of the PSI, and so did the take-off phase of the modern political system and the social mobilization of the masses. Anarchism was the first organized protest movement in Italy and the first one to have a distinct ideological framework (Galli 1983, 54 ff.). Anarchism represents a symbiosis of protest and passion; these worshippers of the precapitalist utopia attacked the new Italian state primarily because of the various regulations imposed by the state authorities. Taxation and the criminalization of old traditions like *usi civici* and *vendettas* belonged to their targets.

Among the anarchists, on the one hand, were artisans and petit bourgeois who defended their traditional rights, and on the other hand, radical intellectuals opposing the State. Especially the intellectuals were inspired by Bakunin, who lived in Naples, the anarchist capital, in 1865-67. His emphasis of the revolutionary role of peasants and students held a strong appeal for the Italian anarchist movement. Strikes, riots and brigandage were traditional forms of protest in the agricultural milieu; consequently, the anarchists found response in these environments. The golden age of anarchism was 1870-1880 and as the the twentieth century drew closer their methods became increasingly spectacular; in 1900, King Umberto was assasinated by an anarchist. Many others came to share his fate.

This lack of belief in political rights implied a total rejection of any form of purely political action. Errico Malatesta describes the method of the anarchists in an almost religious language: 'Anarchists have always kept themselves pure, and remain the revolutionary party par excellence, the party of the future, because they have been able to resist the siren song of elections' (quoted in Przeworski 1987, 8). Electoralism paralyzed revolutionary action.

The first mass party

The split between the PSI and the anarchist movement can be described in terms of a disengagement; the more radical elements of the revolutionary movement simply remained outside the PSI. Consequently, the leadership of the party came to have a strong reformist orientation. At the level of the electorate, however, there was considerable support for a more radical line and widespread distrust in the idea of cooperation with conservative forces. This discrepancy was to manifest itself later in many ways.

There were socialist deputies in Parliament before the foundation of the PSI. Ironically enough, the first socialist deputy elected into Parliament in 1882, Andrea Costa, was a former anarchist leader. He founded the first reformist socialist party in Italy, *Partito Socialista Rivoluzionario Romagnolo*, which contrary to its name propagated socialism through parliamentary means. This party also presented the first 'socialist' demands upon the State - the right to strike, land reform, abolition of indirect taxes, support to women and children, improved industrial working conditions etc.

The involvement in the state apparatus and even the cooperation with the conservative parties did not raise much internal criticism in the party, in fact almost none at all. This led the leadership to believe that the anarchist and revolutionary component had been eradicated for good with the scission of 1892 (Galli 1983, 80).

The PSI was the first modern party on the Italian Peninsula, the first mass party to be organized on a social basis. The liberal and conservative parties were reminiscences of the *Risorgimento* Movement of the days of Italian unification, representing an almost feudal model of politics. Modern society clashed with the old one representing hierarchy and tradition; *Italia reale* versus *Italia legale* (Blinkhorn 1984, 2; Arfé 1977, 22). The PSI represented the former, and the election results proved that a new social force had found political expression. Although the general male franchise was not fully extended until 1912, the PSI grew steadily in terms of electoral support and soon developed into the largest political party in the country.

A hybrid of workers and intellectuals

The PSI was founded before industrialization and indeed before the emergence of a 'proletariat'. It was the most dynamic parts of the bourgoisie who constituted the vanguard of the first Italian mass party. Former members of the radical and republican parties provided an intellectual leadership for a party that was basically supposed to represent the working class (Galli 1983, 78). Seventy-two per cent of the members were manual workers in 1903. Still, the party was dominated by middle class socialists; 'the party of the teachers' is a label which has often been used to describe the young PSI. In the country a vital socialist subculture flourished, impregnated with the older risorgimental ideals of local cooperatives and self-help, of laicism and mutual aid (Clark 1982, 142). From your first scream to your last sigh socialism would accompany you - socialist christenings, confirmations, marriages and funerals were provided as a substitute for the Catholic rituals. The impact of localism was strong; it had produced a culture and a political class used to disobediance and programmatic minimalism. (Clark 1983, 42). This *Lagermentalität* constituted an anticulture to the Catholic subculture and bourgeois paternalist societies. The activists in the socialist societies were also self-sufficient in relation to the party that claimed to represent them. They became an intertwined group of public bodies, supported by and supporting the hordes of landless labourers. This was to give the emerging socialist labour movement a peculiar characteristic - a substantial number of the agricultural labourers were socialists, and the *Federterra* was the first national union that was founded. In 1901, one-third of the members of the socialist trade union CGL (*Confederazione Generale del Lavoro*) belonged to Federterra. Ten years later, the members of Federterra constituted half of the CGL membership (Arfé 1977, 68-70).

This dialectical relationship within the socialist camp between the independent socialist organizations and the party was to become a weakness, as the PSI did not bother to integrate these elements into the party apparatus despite the fact that this spontaneous organization enjoyed rapid growth and presented a great potential to the party. Or as Clark puts it:

> At local level party branches came and went, largely run by the secretaries. A socialist subculture was slowly spread by skilled workers and artisans, via Chambers of Labour, cooperatives, etc. At national level efforts centered on propaganda and journalism and around struggle for victory at the next party congress. The deputies went their own way, as much as they dared. And the unions grouped together in the CGL, pursued their own interests independently of the party and each other (Clark 1982, 143).

The counterstrategy of absorption

How did the PSI make the most of its talents? Were social reforms implemented and was a socialist society within reach? The beginning of the twentieth century was a period of economic prosperity and indeed of social reforms. The development of the backward southern parts of Italy, public works and social legislation were some projects undertaken. But these reforms were not realized so much thanks to the socialist parliamentarians, but to the Giolittian strategy of reconciliation of the people to the regime (rather than vice versa). Giolitti was the liberal Prime Minister, who like Bismarck was aware of the emerging social forces - catholic, socialist and radical subversives - and their threat to the existing structures. The paternalistic attitude towards the working classes was highly respected by radical and some socialist deputies. The independent socialist organizations were the main targets of the Giolittian strategy; the CGL negotiated directly with the government and did not use the PSI as a parliamentary mediator; the economic organizations and cooperatives also often acted above the local party branches. The gap between the party leadership and the grassroots was widening.

The main element in this strategy of absorption was neutrality in the conflicts between capital and labour. Independent conciliatory courts in which the unions, the employers as well as the State were represented were set up to resolve conflicts in the labour market. It implied a recognition of the labour movement and gave it an institutional role of its own. This deprived the Socialist Party of the possibility of using labour dissatisfaction to improve its position.

This method of disarming the opposition has been a frequent feature of Italian politics - from Cavour to *Democrazia Cristiania*. Count Camillo Cavour, Prime Minister during the days of the unification of Italy, is the father of *trasformismo* - 'the practice of remaking cabinets in order to include dissenting elements and to evade dangerous parliamentary criticism' (Clark 1982, 24; Blinkhorn 1984, 3; Pridham 1981, 3).

During the age of the Depretis governments (1876-1887) *trasformismo* in the form of a systematic conversion to the centre prevented the formation of any kind of opposition and increased the distance between the political elites and the emerging electorate at a time when suffrage was being extended. The Giolittian version of *trasformismo* that developed between 1892 and 1914 entailed the separate cooptation of different elements of the socialist movement, thus preventing the formation of a homogeneous and united socialist force (Galli 1983, 46-47, 78).

The *connubio cavouriana* not only gave Cavour considerable freedom to manoeuvre, but blocked the growth of a multi-party system; instead, Italian politics came to revolve around single leaders like Cavour, Giolitti and ultimately Mussolini.

For a while, Giolitti's strategy seemed succesful. He had, however, 'swallowed the head, but not the backbone'; he had managed to buy off the socialist leadership, but not the Socialist Party, in the country (Clark 1982, 140).

The radicalization of the party

In 1903, party leader Turati was invited by Giolitti to take part in the government, but he had to refuse because of the internal, subcultural criticism against the socialist deputies' silent agreement to government oppression. Socialist institutions such as the trade unions and the Chambers of Labour were bought off, but this was partial and temporary. A leftist wing was taking shape, and the party congresses of the beginning of the century were ravaged by endless conflicts between left and right wingers.

In 1904, Italy experienced the first general strike, and the revolutionary line gained a temporary majority in the PSI. In 1908, however, the moderate elements regained their majority. In 1912, the left wing finally took over the party, twenty years after its establishment and after the PSI had supported the government in 1910-1911. That same year, suffrage was extended to all men over thirty. The lateness of this extension was due to the resistance of the liberal and conservative parties. After the 1911-1912 war against Turkey, however, they could not defy the opinion that those who had fought for the country should also have the right to vote. Thus far, the PSI had been pursuing reformist policies with moderate demands; with the economic recession and diminishing government benevolence, this social harmony was crumbling. At the 1912 Party Congress, the left wing regained a majority of the electorate. A report presented by the group of parliamentary deputies was criticized for being 'feeble and skeletal'; moreover, the left wing held that 'the lack of political activity by the group... has helped to demoralize the masses' (Clark 1982, 143).

The whole Italian society was moving towards a polarization and the socialist party was a microcosm of this development. The economic recession and the ongoing war in Libya that helped Italian industry but not its workers were factors that influenced the leftist wave (Galli 1983, 93). The party was increasingly divided into three factions. The left wing criticized the ministerialism of the socialist deputies and their lack of real opposition to the government. The right wing wanted the workers (i.e., their associations - the aim was a corporatist state) to be fully integrated into the State; this group wholly approved the autonomy of the parliamentarians. Between these bitterly opposed groups stood the former party leader Turati whose only mission seemed to be mediation and compromise between the blocks. Once again, the question of participation was on the agenda.

During *Biennio Rosso*, the 'red years' of 1918-1920, the conflicts reached a climax. The following eighteen months witnessed the creation of two new parties with a socialist ideology; the Communist Party and the United Socialist Party. There was an explosion of both the socialist vote and socialist party membership - in 1919, the PSI won 32.3 per cent of the vote, and the number of members increased sevenfold from 1917 to 1929: 30,000 members in 1917, 87,000 in 1919 and 216,000 in 1920 (Galli 1983, 209).

The collapse of the liberal state

Nearly three decades after the foundation of the PSI a massive physical and mental mobilization of the working class took place. Most of these workers were not prepared to support gradualist policies. In the elections of 1919, the PSI and the Catholic *Popolari* became the largest parties, whereas the fascists were not yet succeeding in mobilizing the electorate. The sudden rise of the *Partito Popolare* was due to the Pope's withdrawal of the *'Non expedit'*, an encyclical given in 1867 to announce that the Pope would have no dealings with the Italian state. In connection with the unification of Italy the Pope was deprived of the Papal states and Rome; as a consequense of this the Catholics were instructed to boycott the democratic parliamentary system. They were forbidden to vote and to take part in political actions, except for through a number of socio-political organizations and mutual-aid societies. In 1919, however, when socialism constituted a real threat to the existing structures, the Pope withdrew the encyclical and the Catholics were given bene-diction to participate in the elections in order to prevent the socia-lists from gaining power. This offered the possibility of organizing the Catholics in a party of their own (Irving 1979, 1-4; Galli 1978, 10-12).

The rise of fascism took place in 1920-22, and in the 1921 general elections thirty-five fascists were elected into Parliament. With the fascists knocking at the door, an electorate wanting fundamental change and with the PSI internally divided - what course did the socialists choose?

At the 1921 Party Congress the question of cooperation with bourgeois forces was the main theme. The representatives of the moderate wing advocated cooperation in an antifascist front in order to save the country from chaos and to promote developments towards a modern democracy. They showed an interest in promoting the whole society and suggested an inter-class strategy. The leftist forces were prepared for revolution, and the fascist uprisings were seen as preludes to the total collapse of bourgeois democracy. The method of a revolutionary party was to exclude every form of collaboration. In 1921-22 the PSI was split into three different socialist forces - the Communist Party PCI, the United Socialist Party (*Partito socialista unitario*) and the original PSI.

The inability to present a united antifascist strategy paved the way for fascism as a political vacuum arose between the 'old' forces which had lost the confidence of the electoral majority and the new forces that were not prepared to shoulder governmental responsibilities. Together with an unbalanced economy, this favoured fascism (Blinkhorn 1984, 2).

The incapacity of the socialist parties to unite around a common strategy of participation led to political immobility on the part of the working class. Instead fascism moved, but that can not only be seen as a consequence of the unwillingness of the socialist parties to take part in an antifascist front. Fascism was a protest against the incapability of the liberal regime to enhance state legitimacy among the masses. The polarization to the left and to the right were reactions to the amoeba-like politics practiced hitherto. The contempt of political action and the rise of Italian nationalism gained ground among all segments of society. Among the cultural élites an admiration of force, speed and technology was given artistic expression - the futurists were the protagonists of Italian modernity. The writer Gabriele d'Annunzio channeled this popular discontent into political action. In 1919 he and a privaty army seized Trieste, the eastern part of Italy that had not been included in the unification in 1861 - they claimed it was the second phase of the *Risorgimento*, but above all it was a spectacular demonstration of the weakness and incapacity of the liberal regime. The d'Annunzian army stayed in

Trieste for over a year, from September 1919 to December 1920 when they were expelled. The language of power proved to be stronger than the zig-zagging in Parliament by the liberal and conservative forces who were now attacked on two fronts - by nationalists as well as by socialists. The removal of political action from the institutions out into the streets was the common denominator for the challengers for power.

Fascist persecution and terror reduced the socialist and communist parties on the national as well as the local level; in 1924 only 20.000 members were registered in the files of the PSI. Party Secretary Matteotti was assasinated by the fascists, and many of the leaders fled to France after the victory of the fascists in the 1924 general elections; their communist colleagues had Moscow as their place of refuge. In 1925 Mussolini announced his dictatorship.

How was this strange death of socialism, if only 'partial', possible? The obvious answer is because the socialists could not stop the fascists by themselves and would not participate in an antifascist front including the bourgeois parties. The polarization of the socialist party was a reaction to the collaborationist strategy the party had formerly pursued. The working class issues had been 'compromised away', and the time was not right for further cooperation as revolutionary tendencies were spreading all over Europe. There were moderate elements propagating cooperation with the aim of saving democracy, but these groups were marginalized as the nonintegrationist strategy of the Communist Party had a radicalizing impact upon the left-wingers of the PSI.

In terms of the Przeworski scheme, the issue of participation came to a head with the rise of fascism. As a matter of fact, it had never been resolved within the party; until 1910, the party leadership had not faced any 'revolutionary' criticism (Arfé 1977, 356). The discussion had been dismissed after the split with the anarchists, but as the vision of a socialist society seemed to vanish behind the strategy of 'social harmony' or appeared to be absorbed by the 'old regime', criticism increased. The radicalization of the party was connected with the development of socialism into a mass movement. As the PSI developed into a genuine mass party, the support for the moderate collaborationist strategy diminished.

A communist front

In the first elections after the war in 1946, the two postwar political forces appeared clearly - the Christian Democratic Party on the one hand and the PSI and the PCI on the other. More than seventy per cent of the electorate voted for these parties, and the prewar political parties were marginalized.

The question was no longer whether or not one should participate; all parties joined an antifascist governmental front in order to secure the democratization of Italy institutionally as well as mentally. The PCI had temporarily abandoned its revolutionary program. In a reassuring manner, the communist leaders emphasized the consolidation of democracy as the overshadowing concern.

The PSI followed a similar course. The party had been reconstituted by Pietro Nenni in France; in 1935, the two parties in exile had signed a Unity Pact of Action. In 1943, both parties had recognized the Soviet Union as their common leader and inspiration, and soon the PSI professed itself an adherent Marxism-Leninism. In the first postwar parliamentary elections, the party presented a joint ticket with the PCI. Thus far, the PSI had been the electorally more successful party. For instance, in 1946, when the Constituting Assembly was elected, the PSI had polled almost twice the vote of the PCI. In 1953, however, this relationship was reversed.

The symbiosis with the PCI watered down whatever there was of a social democratic heritage. In 1949 the PSI broke its contacts with trade unions in western countries, and at the beginning of the 1950s the party was no longer recognized by the Socialist International (Spotts and Wieser 1986, 70ff.; Galli 1983, 361). As a reaction against subordination to the PCI, the right wing of the PSI broke away and founded the Social Democratic Party of Italy (PSDI) in 1947. The party was reduced by about one-third of its membership; the bulk of the youth organization and the intellectuals joined the reformist party. Between 1947 and 1950, the party lost about 400,000 members. As the cold war broke out and Christian democratic forces were consolidated, the PCI was no longer desired in government. The PSI joined the opposition along with the PCI.

Why did the PSI subordinate itself to the PCI and adopt a Marxist-Leninist program? The reasons were both ideological and strategic;

the Soviet Union was regarded as the prime conqueror of German nazism and the communist troops in the *Resistenza* Movement (the resistance against the Germans in Italy) had been among the most active and heroic, while the socialist impact had been very weak. The PSI nurtured a belief that wherever socialists and communists were divided, the working class had been defeated. The cooperation with the PCI was strategically dependent on a belief that parts of the communist nimbus would accrue to the PSI. Alas, these calculations proved to be wrong. The voters chose 'the real thing', the PCI instead of the PSI, and in the 1953 elections the PCI grew twice as large as the PSI. The communists started to take over the rank and file of the PSI after the fall of fascism; before the end of the war, the communists had undermined the twin pillars of socialist strength; the trade unions and the agricultural cooperatives. By 1946, half of the socialist electorate in the North had switched to the communists; by 1948 the control of the trade unions had passed over to them (Spotts and Wieser 1986, 71).

With the onset of the cold war, communism was depicted as the main threat to democracy in the world, and after the invasion of Hungary 1956 and the Twentieth Congress of the Soviet Communist Party, the PSI Party Secretary Nenni realized that further cooperation with the PCI would cause the party gradually to whither away.

The Centro-Sinistra

With the recognition of Italy's economic and military cooperation with the western world, the drift of the PSI towards the centre of the party spectrum started. The aim was to become a party that would be politically credible as a government coalition partner. In 1960, the PSI supported the governments externally, and in December 1963 the first government of the historic *centro-sinistra* formula took office. In 1964 the left wing of the party broke away and formed the PSLI (*Partito Socialista dei Lavoratori Italiani*) as a reaction against the moderation of the PSI. Whatever had remained of the trade union activists left the party with this split.

The PSI was not only politically 'house-trained' for the DC, but above all necessary for the formation of a majority government as the

Liberal Party (PLI) was no longer interested in participating in government having had its electoral strength reduced. The PSI had become a pivotal party and believed it would be able to use this position to implement socialist issues. The merger with the PSDI between 1966 and 1969 was an attempt to make social democracy a strong political force.

The change of partner from the PCI to the DC proved, however, to be like jumping out of the frying pan into the fire. The electoral results of the PSI continued to display a downward trend as its socialist projects were gradually replaced by the rough and tumble of day-to-day politics. Instead of attempting to reach ideological goals, the PSI soon learned the art of political patronage and the method of *sottogoverno* - the establishment of clientelist relationships and the infiltration of parallel semipolitical bodies as a means of control and compensation.

A political animal

The PSI developed chameleonic qualities in relation to its partners. When in alliance with the communists, the party adopted communist features; in government the PSI came increasingly to resemble the DC. When the PSI developed its party organization towards the end of the 1940s, the PCI served as a model; an Executive Committee with 30 members, a Central Committee with 225 members and a National Congress consisting of 1,000 delegates were established. The traditional communist symbols, the hammer and the sickle, were also used by the PSI until 1978. In spite of the centralized party organization, factionalism flourished. Initially, the tendencies could be differentiated on an ideological basis, but when the PSI entered government the factions developed into party machines competing for power over the party and for the spoils of the *sottogoverno*. The geographic and social composition of PSI membership changed; from a party that had attracted members from the northeastern industrialized parts of Italy, the PSI turned into a party with half of its membership in the South. The South is an area in which party membership is traditionally based upon clientelist methods of enrolment (Hine 1977, 75).

In 1972 the PSI vote fell to below ten per cent and the party was in a state of paralysis. Whether in government or in opposition, the PSI continued to lose votes. Thus far, the PSI had participated in three types of alliances: the postwar conciliatory alliance including all antifascist parties, the socialist alternative, and the centro-sinistra. For the formation of a majority alternative the DC and the PCI were necessary; on the other hand, the PSI was pivotal in relation to both major parties.

Whether in cooperation with the PCI or with the DC, the PSI had not succeeded in retaining a clear identity of its own. It had been dominated by its greater allies, and the electorate apparently did not look upon the party as a credible alternative to these two. In fact, the party had not yet proposed any real programmatic alternatives; when in symbiosis with the PCI it was no more than a communist front and the sharing of governmental spoils was given priority over policy formulation when the PSI was in government with the DC.

At the beginning of the 1970s, a process of secularization became clearly discernible in Italy. Questions like women's rights, abortion and divorce were brought to the fore in the political debate. The PSI made an attempt to capitalize on these questions, hoping that this would bring a new, modern, secularized group of voters to the party ranks. But the leftist wave favoured the PCI, which grew from 27 per cent to 34 per cent between 1972 and 1976, while the PSI had to content itself with less than ten per cent at both elections.

The new direction chosen by the PCI - the *via italiana al socialismo* which envisaged a socialist society within the framework of parliamentary democracy - had proven to be a source of electoral strength. As it was impossible to remove the DC from its governmental hegemony, the *compromesso storico* was the only way by which the PCI could enter into government. The alliance of all major political forces had been tried once before in 1945-1947. In 1973 the formula was relaunched under the banner of 'saving the state' in the face of a deteriorating economic situation, mounting terrorism, and increasing unemployment.

The scenario of the PCI being in government was anything but encouraging for the PSI which found itself in a rather schizophrenic situation. The PSI had held the role of mediator between the two 'churches' (an expression coined by the sociologist Francesco Alberoni) of Italy -christian democracy and communism - but as they approached one another, the risk that the PSI was becoming superfluous increased. This was indeed a strategic dilemma. If the PCI was included in the government, the communists would no longer be able to use their position of opposition and would become as compromised as the PSI in the eyes of the electorate; at the same time, the risk of the PSI becoming a *quantité negligeable* was obvious.

During 1976-79 a new governmental formula was tried as a consequence of the communist advances. The governments were formally DC minority governments but enjoyed external support from all major parliamentary parties except the neofascist MSI (*Movimento Sociale Italiano*). In fact, the DC negotiated with the supporting parties before taking major decisions. According to the sophisticated political vocabulary used in Italy, the PCI was *'nella maggioranza'* - in the majority - and the future prospects for the PCI's being included in government were brighter than ever. The PCI had succeeded in breaking its political isolation and was closer to government than ever before since the party was expelled from government in 1947.

Strategic considerations predominated when the PSI in 1978 launched a 'Socialist Plan for A Left Alternative'. The alternative consisted of the proposition that the two parties on the left form a government coalition in the same way that Mitterrand had entered into an alliance with the French Communist Party. Simultaneously the PSI rejected communist participation in a centre-left government front. The ideological content of the alternative consisted of a critique of the anticompetitive politics of consensus that would ensue from a PCI government together with the DC. What the PSI urged on was a democracy based on conflict, an alternative to the 'Historic Compromise' that in fact was an affirmation of the DC hegemony in government. The PSI called for moderation with regard to economic policy and welfare distribution. The distributive restraints imposed on the budget should, however, be balanced by an expanded worker-participation and self-management in the industries (Hine 1980, 137ff; Pasquino 1986, 121ff).

The two front-war was came to a head during these years. The PSI tried to place itself to the left of the PCI in order to gain from the leftist wave; simultaneously, it criticized the DC's position as a gatekeeper for participation in government. In the 1979 elections the electorate said no to PCI entrance into government and the Left-Wing Alternative was no longer politically relevant. The PSI could continue to count on its pivotal position. In fact, the strategical lesson for the 1980s was increased PSI independence from both the DC and the PCI.

The reorganization of the party

The 1980s were a golden age for socialism in southern Europe. Mitterrand had managed to gain power by allying himself with the communists. In Spain, Portugal and Greece socialism was reviving. This was the point of departure for Bettino Craxi, who was elected Party Secretary in 1976, when reformulating the role of the PSI. The PSI was to become the party of modern Italy; the DC and the PCI were depicted as dinousaurs, creatures that had outgrown their function in the emerging society. The line of demarcation between old and new politics was one between 'devastating practice of mediation, brokerage among various the competing and sometimes conflicting interests, the outcome being a slow, incoherent, unproductive, erratic decision-making process' (Pasquino 1986, 130) and a modern, efficient, market-oriented style with visible results.

Mitterrand's success consisted of three elements: 1) renewal of the party organization, 2) creation of flexible but productive ties with the trade unions 3) utilization of the Fifth Republic institutions to provide the environment for an expanded role for the *Parti Socialiste* (Pasquino 1986, 122). Craxi, eager to be seen as the equal of the French socialist leader and anxious to share Mitterrand's popularity, started by reshuffling the party. The great variety of factions, 'parties in the party', prevented the PSI from designing any coherent strategy. The mobilization of voters depended on the factions; as a consequence of this, turnout was always higher in local than national elections. The solution from Craxi's point of view was a centralized party with a strong party leader at the helm. He succeeded in uniting the party and strengtheneing his own position by playing off competing factions against one another. Later he also succeeded in placing himself above the factions by moving the election of the Party

Secretary from the Central Committee to the National Congress, thus reducing their impact. He met with little resistance and was soon elected unanimously. He was in fact perceived to be so powerful that political cartoonists started to depict Craxi in Mussolini's uniform.

In 1984, the Central Committee was replaced by a new type of body, a 473-member National Assembly comprising a cross-section of Italian life - 200 representatives of local party organizations, 100 deputies and 100 prominent figures from the world of culture, science, economics, entertainment and sports who were party members and symphatetic to socialist causes (Spotts and Wieser 1986, 77ff; Pasquino 1986, 124). This is a good illustration of the development of the PSI into a modern market-style party oriented towards mass media. Craxi established links to different segments of Italian society, for instance with the President of FIAT, Agnelli, who was the symbol of the economic miracle of Italy in the 1980s. Craxi hoped to become the political miracle of the decade. What in fact happened was a development of the PSI into a catch-all party par exellence and a parallel cutback in the party apparatus. The decision-making structures in the party became highly concentrated and the role of the party organization in policy formulation diminished (Massari 1989, 579).

Unlike Mitterrand, Craxi did not establish links with the trade unions; that would indeed have been a difficult task as they were almost totally dominated by the PCI. Craxi wanted to attract the new urban technocrats, the personifications of the new efficient Italy; efficiency was what the PSI wanted to transmit to the political institutions. The recipe for a more efficient political system was the same formula that Craxi had prescribed for the PSI; a strengthening of the executive and a corresponding weakening of Parliament. The vote of confidence should not be given to the government as a whole, only to the Prime Minister and his program. Thus, the Prime Minister would not have to strike a balance between the different factions of different parties in front of Parliament. Other institutional reforms suggested were the ban on using the vote of no confidence if one could not propose another governmental formula; this would reduce the possibilities of toppling governments. Moreover, direct presidential elections (instead of indirect ones through Parliament), a reduction in the number of deputies and senators, etc. were proposed

(Nilsson 1987, 84) The PSI would not itself profit from these reforms if they were realized unless the electoral strength of the party was to increase dramatically.

In August, 1983, Italy experienced the first socialist Prime Minister ever. The main reason was not any major increase in the electoral strength of the PSI, but rather the weakening of the DC. The installation of Craxi in government coincided with a wave of economic prosperity, and his government soon gained popularity outside the party ranks. But the socialists still had difficulty in convincing the voters that there was a socialist alternative distinct from both the communists and the christian democrats.

Governmental acrobatics

During the premiership of Bettino Craxi the *pentapartito* formula was institutionalized. This five-party formula contains all major parties except the PCI, the fascist party MSI and the Radical Party. The rationale offered for the formula lies in the phrase *equilibri più avanzata* - 'the most advanced equilibrium' - an act of balancing between all parties. This is the cul-de-sac of the Italian party system, where there is no alternative to the DC hegemony. The postwar governments have without exception revolved around the DC; no other west European party has had such a dominant role in government. The DC has participated in all postwar governments and the Prime Ministers were until the beginning of the 1980s always DC leaders. Moreover, the party has dominated ministries that have been of crucial importance for maintaining the party's position in the *sotto-governo*. For the control of the political arena at large this has been of paramount importance even though the governmental base has been widened. The DC has institutionalized itself in government and the other parties have defined themselves in relation to the DC. The DC has successfully performed the function as an indispensable gate-keeper for government entrance and has been able to disarm the opposition. There has never really been any alternative to the DC in government - the governments have only been expanded to the left as the PSI and the PCI have gained credibility. From the right, the DC has not faced any serious competition. The postwar governmental politics have entailed a drift towards the centre of the party spectrum, a tendency that was heightened in the 1970s and 1980s.

For Craxi an alliance with the liberal, radical and social democratic parties was a precondition for a reduction of the DC position and an alternative to a leftist alignment. But such a governmental formula remains wishful thinking, since it is extremely unlikely to produce a majority. The resulting strategy was a mixture of facts and aspirations; the lay parties (except for the Radical Party) were included in government as a counterweight to the DC, but the DC was still indispensable for a majority.

Electoral successes

In the parliamentary elections in 1987 the PSI vote increased from eleven to fourteen per cent. The PSI was thus rewarded for being in government and holding the premiership - the downward trend since the 1970s had apparently been broken. The party had increased its support with almost five percentage points in five years. Until the beginning of the 1980s alliances and coalitions had been disastrous from the point of view of electoral support, but the sharpened profile of the PSI had clearly attracted new voters. The PSI seemed able at last to profit from its pivotal position and thus exert an influence that far outweighed is electoral support. How was this possible, or rather, why did the DC tolerate this? The DC suffered from a multitude of problems typical of a party which has been too long in the middle of the game. Scandals, the inefficiency of government and the paralysis of political life were closely connected with the DC and its dominance over the last forty years. By giving the premiership to the PSI, the leadership of the DC hoped to be able to gain strength; maybe it was time the PSI got its fair share of the dissatisfaction. If this was the idea, the DC was taken by surprise. The PSI held the premiership during a time when Italy rose to the rank of one the wealthiest countries in Europe and the labelling of Italy as a tourist-economy finally became outdated. The people, who came to have more money in their wallets than ever before, rewarded the PSI; moreover, Bettino Craxi was a politician whose popularity extended far beyond the PSI rank and file. However, the PSI had an agreement with the

DC on sharing the premiership, and in 1987 it was again turned over to the DC.

A Socialist Unity?

Despite the increased influence of the PSI, the basic political structure seemed more or less unaltered as the 1980s drew to a close. Once again, however, history favoured the PSI and once again international events came to have a great impact on the fundamentals of Italian politics, not unlike when the cold war broke out and the PCI was thrown out of government in 1947. The fall of the Berlin Wall in November 1989 and the bankruptcy of the eastern European version of socialism have shaken the PCI. Internal conflicts and factions have been exposed as the discussion of the post-wall *'via italiana al socialismo'* has proceeded. The questions of participation in government and a rapprochement with the PSI are once again on the agenda (*L'Espresso* 1.7.1990). During the Party Congress in Bologna in the spring of 1990, the PCI discussed a change of the party name and decided to apply for membership in the Socialist International. One thing was clear; a majority of the party no longer wished to be identified with the bankrupt version of socialism.

Craxi was not slow in seeing the opportunities this development offered. He declared that he was convinced that this was the right direction for political change since the rationale for the postwar antagonism no longer existed. Craxi saw the development as a great opportunity both for himself and for the PSI. When the congress was held, Craxi presented a proposal for socialist unity, a deal that would respect the differences, the divergent experiences and traditions of the two parties (*L'Espresso* 18.3.1990). This was, of course, political rhetoric on a high level of abstraction. At a more concrete strategic level, the PSI and Craxi opposed PCI participation in the Socialist International (when a party wants to join the International, other parties from the same country already members in the International must agree). Moreover, Craxi put forward a change in the name of the PSI - *Unità Socialista* - in order to prevent the PCI from taking this name (*Panorama* 14.10.1990). The dialogue was to become less cordial as time passed, because the PSI feared it would become inferior in this competiton for tomorrow's socialism in Italy.

The regional elections of the spring of 1990 showed a decrease in PCI support; the party polled about 22 per cent of the vote which corresponds to a four per cent decrease since the parliamentary elections of 1987 and five per cent less than in the elections to the European Parliament in the spring of 1989. Although these figures are not directly comparable, they indicate a downward trend for the PCI. Interestingly enough, the PSI has not clearly managed to capitalize on communist dissatisfaction; its share of the vote in the regional elections remained around 15 per cent. What in fact has happened is a decrease in the socialist vote as a whole, a trend that has been registered all over Europe.

Conclusions

The PSI is in many respects a negation of its northern colleagues in the Socialist International, although the parties at times have faced similar possibilities. The failure of the PSI to develop into a strong socialist force is a mix of both strategic and structural components, but the party's inability to respond to and formulate political alternatives has been the decisive reason for its weakness. Especially the choices made in the prefascist period have had a crucial impact on the failure of the PSI to develop into a strong political force - history is not easily reversed. In these concluding remarks the ideological and strategic choices of the PSI will be contrasted with those of the Scandinavian parties. A special focus will be the question why the PSI failed where the Scandinavian social democratic parties have succeeded.

1. The Scandinavian social democratic parties have had a strong and well-disciplined party organization on both national and local levels. They were successful in mobilizing and involving the subcultural milieus in the rank and file of the party, which the PSI failed to do efficiently enough. Why was this the case? As we have seen, the subcultural settings were strong and general especially in the red northern regions of Italy, including the agrarian milieus. The socialist subcultures in Italy consisted of different elements that were more or

264

less offshoots of the Chambers of Labour (local labour organizations); housing co-operatives, co-operative shops and educational organizations were among their main fields of activity. These organizations stood in total contrast to the Catholic and lay associations, infiltrated both the public and private sectors and formulated the economic and moral ideals for 'true socialists'. The motion picture '1900' by Bernardo Bertolucci gives an excellent illustration of this socialist subculture at the beginning of the 20th century. The socialist church was the 'House of the People', ecclesiastical education was replaced by scientific socialism; these activities were supposed to nurture a new, modern generation, and they were widespread both in Scandinavia and in Italy.

Why, then, did the Italian socialists not succeed in tying these local activists to the party? In the Italian case is it crucial to underline the concept 'local', as an opposite of both 'central' and 'national'. The local activists and party branches were in many respects self-sufficient. On the other hand, if they were weak - which they often were - there was no system of central support for local branches which could have fostered a loyal party hierarchy. Instead, a kind of mutual disinterest came to prevail. Secondly, it is important to bear in mind that Italy was a young nation - being Italian was secondary to being Roman, Piemontese, Lombardian etc. The geographic identifications naturally coincided with diverging social classes, and the gap between parliamentarians and grassroots was wide geographically as well as ideologically. National identification was weak, especially as the unification of Italy had affected the lower segments of society severely through taxes and other restrictions.

The lack of a well-coordinated and well-defined organization proved to be crucial after the red biennium of 1918-1920 when the socialist vote increased. Instead of using the confidence expressed by the electorate as an instrument of parliamentary action, the PSI stood by as the center of political activity moved out into the streets. Organizational weakness was to strike the PSI severely once more. In the post-fascist period, it was instrumental in strengthening the PCI. In 1946-48, the PCI took over major parts of the socialist trade unions and succeeded in attracting former PSI members thanks to its superior organizational capacity.

The party organization has remained fragmented during the postwar period and party cohesion has been low. During the *centrosinistra* governments factionalization increased as a consequence of competition over the spoils of *sottogoverno*. New alliance strategies have almost invariably been weakened by party splits; in 1947 the PSDI was founded as a reaction to the cooperation with the PCI, and in 1964 the PSLI split as a consequence of the participation in *centrosinistra*. Today the party seems to have united around Bettino Craxi; factionalization has decreased and internal disputes have been played down. Still, this is hardly a matter of coordination between local and central levels; rather it is a question of non-interference in one another's affairs. The local branches make their own choices, for instance in choosing partners for local governments; what importance the centralization of the party around Craxi will have in the future is still quite unclear.

2. The Scandinavian social democratic parties succeeded in monopolizing the working class electorally and ideologically. The prefascist PSI was mainly a workers' party in the sense that major parts of the working population voted for the PSI. When the male franchise was extended in 1912, the electoral support of the PSI increased rapidly, a trend that was strengthened in 1919. The PSI had in fact attracted large segments of the working population, but why did they not succeed in maintaining this trust? The failure was due to the fact that the PSI did not monopolize the workers' issues in Parliament. The party was more inclined towards gradualist politics than the grassroots. As a consequence of this half-heartedness and the practice of *trasformismo*, the labour unions often negotiated directly with the government or other bodies concerned. The PSI was mainly a parliamentary party, not a general working class organization. The independent organizations and their members, mainly the labour unions, were the main actors as political action was radicalized; also, the PSI was negatively affected by their subordination to and silent acceptance of the old regime.

The main problem of the PSI has been the lack of a distinct subcultural supporting group. The average socialist is a professional belonging to the middle class and living in the north of Italy. In the 1980s, the PSI tried to attract the young urban professionals in the cities with some success. Here, the PSI in fact compares favourably to its Scandinavian counterparts. The social democrats in Scandinavia are loosing support in urban centres and have difficulty in attracting voters among the young professionals (cf. Wörlund's study in this volume). In this respect, the PSI profits by the changing structure and increased volatility of the electorate.

A party official once lamented that 'the Communists stand for the working class and social change; the Christian Democrats for the mother of the family and the Pope; we are just a party' (quoted in Spotts and Wieser 1987, 84). This weak identification may not be as much of a disadvantage in the future as it has been in the past.

3. The Scandinavian social democratic parties have succeeded in forming and establishing strong and durable coalitions. The alliances with the agrarian parties in the 1930s constituted the spring-board to social democratic dominance in government in the years to come. The main problem of the PSI has been the coalitions; the party has so far, except for the last years, never profited from alliances with other parties either in opposition or in government. Its various attempts at coalitions can rather be associated with ensuing electoral losses, party splits and an undermined credibility.

The PSI has been severely struck by the immobility of the Italian party structure. The party has been jammed between the two main parties and has not been able to move them in either direction in order to gain more space for itself. On the other hand, the PSI has been able to profit from its pivotal position and has functioned as a mediator between the DC and the PCI. But as the PSI succeeded in creating a distinct image as a party independent of both the PCI and DC, it was rewarded electorally. The centre of the party spectrum is likely to become even more crowded, with the PCI disposing itself of the last remains of its communist past. The crucial question is where the lines of demarcation between the parties will be drawn and what new constellations of alliance options will be given in the future.

Appendix. Election results in Italy, 1948-1990 (percentages)

A. Chamber of Deputies, 1948-1987

Party	1948	1953	1958	1963	1968	1972	1976	1979	1983	1987
DC	48.5	40.1	42.4	38.3	39.1	38.8	38.7	38.3	32.9	34.3
PCI	31.0	22.6	22.7	25.3	26.9	27.2	34.3	30.4	29.9	26.6
PSI		12.8	14.2	13.8	14.5	9.6	9.6	9.8	11.4	14.3
PSDI	7.3	4.5	4.5	6.1		5.1	3.4	3.8	4.1	2.9
PRI	2.5	1.6	1.4	1.4	2.0	2.9	3.1	3.0	5.1	3.7
PLI	3.8	3.0	3.5	7.0	5.0	3.9	1.3	1.9	2.9	2.1
PR	-	-	-	-	-	-	1.1	3.5	2.2	2.6
MSI	2.0	5.8	4.8	5.1	4.4	8.7	6.1	5.3	6.8	5.9
Others	4.9	9.6	6.5	3.0	8.1	3.8	2.4	4.0	4.7	8.2

B. Elections to the European Parliament (1989) and regional elections (1990)

Party	1989	1990
DC	32.9	36.7
PCI	27.6	22.7
PSI	14.8	14.9
PSDI	2.7	3.0
PRI	4.4	3.0
PLI		1.7
Greens	6.7	3.4
MSI	5.5	4.3
Others	5.4	10.3

Parties: DC (Democrazia cristiana), PCI (Partito comunista italiano), PSI (Partito socialista italiano), PSDI (Partitio socialista democratico italiano), PRI (Partito republicano), PLI (Partito liberale italiano), PR (Partito radicale), MSI (Movimento sociale italiano), Greens (Liste verdi).

East European Social Democracy: Reborn to be Rejected

Ulf Lindström

The problem

On March 25, 1990, the Hungarian Social Democratic Party (MSzDP) earned itself a pitiful entry in the annals of international labour. Probably never before in the history of free and fair elections did a social democratic party score such a low percentage of the vote. Eleven weeks later, the Czechoslovak Social Democratic Party (CSD) confirmed the predicaments that the social democratic parties were facing in the first free post-war elections in Central Europe.

What looked like a success story in the making after the transitions to democracy in 1989 - pollsters and informed commentators were apportioning somewhere between 30 and 40 per cent of the popular support to a non-descript 'social democracy' - proved to be a resounding fiasco at the polls as the MSzDP and CSD gained less than four per cent of the vote. Why? After all, we had been told that people in Central Europe were anxious not to lose their welfare provisions and looked for cues to a future solidly planted in the centre lane between a command economy and a cut-throat market?

This essay addresses itself to the results of the first free Central European (the GDR, Hungary, and Czechoslovakia) elections with key emphasis on the social democratic vote. While the primary purpose is to find correlates that may help explain the modest showings of the parties, the paper will also offer a theoretical framework for understanding the predicaments of a social democracy reborn into a world in which the very word 'socialism' is stigmatized;

269

in which both industry and the working class, as well as the nation-state, are said to be obsolete; in which public employees incarnate a system held in (self-)contempt by the body politic; and in which - in the eyes of the people of Eastern Europe -the West European market economy never was the Darwinist market spectre raised by Western left-wing radicals and Eastern officialdom.

The elections in the GDR, Hungary, and Czechoslovakia

The first three democratic elections in Central Europe produced three seeming exceptional as far as both turnout and party distribution of the vote is concerned, see Table 1.

With much of the agenda and format set in Bonn, the election in the GDR was a quasi-referendum on German reunification. Indeed, the results came to look like the prologue to the West German two-and-a-half party system. And primarily on account of the ongoing proceedings on reunification the *Volkskammer* approved a grand coalition cabinet, in which the SPD was generously accommodated.

The election in Hungary stands out for its extravaganza in political centrism. At times it was, and still is, difficult to make sense of the differences between the centre-left Free Democrats (SzDSz) and the centre-right Democratic Forum (MDF). In addition, the mind boggles at the Agrarian Party (FKgP) in so far as it is pro EC and calls for a rapid and extensive deregulation of the banking system, but argues for a solution pitting the family against the market when it comes to the privatization of farming. The cabinet that was subsequently formed included the Forum, the FKgP and the Christian Democrats with the Free Democrats serving as the principal opposition party.

The election in Czechoslovakia is exceptional for the way in which it thrust power onto the original heroes of the revolution, the Civic Forum, which in the process dwarfed and atomized the opposition. The parliamentary arena was subsequently so thoroughly conquered by the Forum and the Christian Democrats that Czechoslovakia will have to do without a real opposition for the duration of the two-year parliamentary term.

Table 1
Parliamentary elections in the GDR, Hungary (1st), and Czechoslovakia. Percentages and (Seats).*

	GDR	Hungary	Czechoslovakia
Turnout	93.2	65.1	96.0
Minor left-wing parties			
United Left (VL)	.2 (1)		
Communist Party (KPD)	.1		
Kadarite Communists (MSzMP)		3.7	
Socialist Party (CSS)			1.9
Reformed communists	16.3 (65)	10.9 (33)	13.6 (24)
Social democratic parties	21.8 (87)	3.6	3.3
Liberal parties			
Liberal Party (LDP+FDP+Forum)	5.3 (21)		
Democratic Rise (DA)	.9 (4)		
National Democrats (NDPD)	.4 (2)		
Free Democrats (SzDSz)		21.4 (92)	
Young Democrats (FIDESz)		8.9 (21)	
Democratic Party			1.3
Forum parties	2.9 (12)	24.7 (164)	46.3 (87)
Green parties	2.0 (8)		3.2
Agrarian parties			
Peasant Party (DBD)	2.2 (9)		
Indep. Smallhold. Party (FKgP)		11.8 (43)	
Agrarian & Rurals			3.4
National, ethnic, regional p.			
Moravian & Silesian Party			5.8 (9)
Slovak People's Party			3.6
Coexistence Minority (Magyar)			2.7
Christian democratic p.	6.3 (25)	6.5 (21)	11.6 (20)
Center-right parties			
Christian Democrats (CDU)	40.9 (164)		
Magyar People's Party		.8	
Sectarian parties			
Alternative Youth List	.1 (1)		
Democratic Women League	.3 (1)		
ASZ (Agrotechnocrats)		3.2 (1)	
VP (Employer's party)		1.9	
HVK (local dignitaries)		1.9	
Independent and other MP:s		(10)	

*As distributed in Hungary after the final round.

As for parallels, the first to come to mind is of course the debacle of social democracy. Second - and part of the explanation for the social democratic dilemma - is the relatively good showing of the reform-communists, who seem to have been drawing on similar rationales across the borders. The PDS, the KSC, and the MSzP polled about 13-18 per cent.[1] Third, the compartmentalization of the non-centre-forum vote into small sectarian parties with little or no potential for shouldering the responsibility accompanying cabinet status is a feature shared by all three countries.

Transition, political space, and social democracy as a late-comer

The electorates of Central Europe were fed up with a bankrupt system and voted with their stomachs for a future in carefree affluence. This is about as informative an account of the results as to say that in West European elections, the electorates have been happy with a sound system and voted with their brains for a future voice in a discourse devoid of timid material concerns.

The East European command-economy was done for, even the communist parties recognized that. Yet the Germans, Hungarians, and Czechs differed greatly among themselves in expressing this conclusion. For one thing, the Berliners, the constituents of Somogy in south-central Hungary, and those of Roznava in south-eastern Czechoslovakia, returning well above the average of the national vote to the reformed communists, did not share in the urge to sweep away everything and everyone associated with the past. So, merely a comparative *tour de horizont* across and within the three countries is enough to expose the unlikely as well as incomplete explanations that accompanied the election results in the press. By way of example, because the Magyar culture is at odds with the Slavic one, Hungary proved more staunchly anti-socialist than Czechoslovakia once the citizens were given the opportunity freely to express their sentiments. Equally incomplete as an account of the left-wing vote is the hypothesis, allegedly in contrast to Czechoslovakia, that emphasizes Hungary's lack of an endogenous working-class culture mobilized by the socialists before World War II, a culture expected to have outlasted 40 years of really existing socialism to become an asset to

272

the reborn social democratic parties throughout Central Europe.[2]

As for the general thought of a 'demumification process' accompanying the transitions, the spring elections of 1990 do not easily compare to the last free(-ish) elections of the respective countries so as to suggest half a century of continuity among the institutions of civil society. True, many parties, especially in Hungary, proudly claimed status as 'historical parties' and a number of party officials came from renowned political families.('Election Special'[1990], *Daily News* of the MTI; *The Hungarian Observer*, Vol. 3, No. 4, 1990.) However, generic hypotheses, such as voters casting their ballots on the basis of what the historical parties had represented during the pluralist regimes, such as voters abiding by family traditions and voting for the parties of their grandparents' choice, run into technical difficulties. First, the most successful parties in Hungary and Czechoslovakia were new on the scene. Second, the demographic turnover among the electorate ruled out the joy of party and voter reunion except in a very few cases (cf., Appendix Table A).

Personal memory of the previous democratic regime was limited to citizens of seventy years or older, but everyone shared the experience of the 1989 revolution. While not suggesting that history was a long black tunnel to Central European voters,[3] this experience was likely to condense the perspective of the electorate to span the immediate past and the immediate future. The anatomy of the transition, its trajectory over time, its agenda, its scenario, and its actors eventually produced - and aborted - the options that the voters were facing as they went to the polls in early 1990.

Social democracy, it will be suggested and tentatively substantiated in the ensuing analysis, was twice deprived of political space; first during the transition by the liberal opposition and subsequently in the election by the reform communists. Thus, social democracy was forced to rely on its historical rationale in mobilizing the vote; social democracy was an anachronism in relation to both the transition and the founding election.

As for time, it made a difference that the transition in Hungary was gradual, whereas that of the GDR was rapid and tense and that of Czechoslovakia rapid and velvety. Time in Hungary meant that the ruling Communist Party was not literally thrown out of office (rather, the party itself was left to throw out its most notorious Stalinists, subsequently to be found in the Kadarite MSzMP), that the electoral law was a compromise among embryotic parties and that the Hungarian electorate was presented with a preview of the wheeling and dealing of parliamentary politics (Bozóki 1990). All this goes toward explaining why the turnout in Hungary was sub-stantially lower than in the two other countries; in the run-off election the turnout dropped even further, probably because the disillusioned left-wing sympathizers did not care whether either the MDF or the SzDSz finally won the contested seat (Kolosi et al, 1990, 11). Also, the reformed communists' eagerness to be in front among the forces calling for a transition to pluralist democracy, 'the negotiated revolution', helped increase the MSzP's vote. Neither the PDS or the KSC were active parties to the transitions.

But, again, the GDR election was unique in so many aspects as to defy straightforward party systemic comparisons with the elections in Hungary and Czechoslovakia.[4] Nonetheless, the PDS, MSzP, and KSC probably mobilized similar constituencies across the three countries: the old *nomenklatura*, elderly people in expendable positions afraid of losing their jobs and pension bonuses, and sections of the working class employed in the obsolete smoke-stack industry. This is an interpretation which is substantiated by checking the trajectory of the transitions against the regional variance of the reformed communist vote. That of the KSC, in contrast to those of the PDS and MSzP, is evenly spread over the entire state, transcending not only the nations of Bohemia, Moravia and Slovakia, but also local contexts: it is as if the KSC's constituency was made up of people in a state of shock, unable to reflect over any other rationale of their party choice but that of wishing time had ceased to exist.

This is where the similarities end. It was to the exclusive advantage of the PDS to appeal to the electorate as the only alternative to those who wished to uphold the very existence of the state. Finally, the PDS was the choice of those who cynically toyed with the idea of living in the best of *two* worlds. To the East Berlin intelligentsia, the artists and writers, continuing to live on government allowances and having the pleasures of the market society just a few stops away along the S-Bahn was an attractive proposition. Accompanying the conflict over the German reunification process, there was also the cleavage between old and new formats of politics. The citizen initiatives that spearheaded the revolution, later to be referred to as the 'November Heroes', were reluctantly transforming themselves into parties. The Alliance '90, Greens and Independent Woman League confronted, and were badly beaten by, what was basically a party system adopted from the Federal Republic. Within this 'imported' segment, the CDU/DSU and the SPD fought one another in a campaign that looked like a West German election by proxy.

Unlike the GDR and to a certain extent also Hungary, Czechoslovakia never produced mature internal confrontations within its party system before election day. Czechoslovakia was marked by cordially subdued interchanges between the victorious forces behind the transitions. It therefore only made sense that of all the forum parties, the Civic Forum came out as the strongest. Again, time was essential to this success as it was widely understood that the CF was too unorthodox an umbrella organization to maintain internal cohesion for very long (Garton Ash 1990a).[5] The CF was a movement and as such much like the Hungarian SzDSz cum FIDESz and MDF under the same hat, comparable in terms of electoral strength, ideological worldview and the socio-economic profile of their constituencies. With the partial exception of the MDF, whose competitive position vis-à-vis the Free Democrats made it tilt to the right, the four parties represent the urban, liberal, and rationalist interests and have been spared the burden of having to accommodate clear-cut sectarian groups like the Hungarian peasantry and the Slovak nationalists.

Of course, there was more to the picture than time alone that made the social democratic parties play a modest role in the Hungarian and Czechoslovak transitions and the first few months to follow. Had it been merely a matter of time, with no social or political obstacles along the road to election day, the Socialist International was there to offer their recently liberated brethren a helping hand: the party coffers of the SPD and SPÖ in Bonn and Vienna were only hours away from Budapest and Prague. Indeed, these two parties, together with the French Socialist Party, were the principal financial contributors to the election campaigns of the MSzDP and CSD, whereas other members of the SI provided support in the form of office equipment, etc. About 100 volunteers from abroad assisted the MSzDP during the final days of the Hungarian campaign.[6]

Why was it that social democracy, as an organized party or represented by its provisional leadership, was pushed into the background during the transitions in Hungary and Czechoslovakia? Why were the MSzDP and CSD later unable to make use of, instead being hurt by, the initial advantages of being historical parties, of having access to the resources of the SI, and of the alleged 'social democratic' sentiments among the citizens?

Transitions as such, that short period of perhaps two months, do not disfavour social democracy in general since the Mediterranean transitions of the mid seventies saw social democracy take a very active part in the process and eventually ushered in PASOK, the PSOE, and the PS as 'State-carrying' parties.

This comparison of the East and South European transitions points to a perfect causality between transition from right and left-wing authoritarian regimes and the strength of political tendencies in the subsequent elections. But was there really any reason to suspect guilt by association, 'no more socialist experiments', in the cases of Hungary and Czechoslovakia? The chasm between social democracy and existing socialism was as wide as that between, say, New Democracy and the regime of the Greek colonels. The comparison is not entirely fair, however. New Democracy, unlike social democracy, profited from well-founded fears among the electorate that too radical a break with the dethroned regime would provoke a violent bid for power by those just ousted from their positions. People in Central Europe did not consider really existing socialism a potential boomerang and therefore felt no restraints in voting for a definite change: social democracy was not going to be a soft 'intermediate stop' along the way to pluralist democracy. On the contrary, the voters felt a certain psychological pleasure in taking *two* steps away from the old regime. The thoroughness of the Czechoslovak transition is also underscored by the comparative contrast to Spain, where King Juan Carlos blocked a partisan assault on the State whereas the Civic Forum was able to send its leader to the Hradcany, from where he radiated both statesmanship and partisanship in a mix inseparable to the electorate.

Hungarian and Czechoslovak social democrats were not barred, or did not feel it proper to exclude themselves, from the opposition emerging from the underground during the crucial month of the transitions. However, being a historical party probably imposed restraints on social democratic officials joining the national and local opposition leaderships. Individual initiatives had to await formal or tacit confirmation by the party hierarchy. Otherwise these initiatives later risked being looked upon as factionalization or, worse still, attempts to further one's own private cause. As for the latter aspect, there is reason to believe that the social democratic party was overly suspicious when admitting activists to its ranks, afraid of becoming the option for communists, not to mention secret service agents, abandoning their wrecks. Whatever the case, the young and industrious social democratic cadres found themselves in a frustrating situation: was the party still alive formally or was it in the process of being re-established (cf. Kolosi et al 1990, 24)? Where was the leadership, in exile or en route to Budapest and Prague? (The CSD had been member of the SI's exile group SUCEE.) What power was still entrusted, formally or by hearsay, to the old local leadership, those chairmen of the party branches and union leaders who had been allowed to stay around for a few years after WW II before Stalinism cracked down on the civilian labour movement? And if they were all gone, did the party waste time in trying to find their offspring?

A historical party expects its cadres and sympathizers to look back when seeking guidelines to the future. In addition, a historical party expects its emerging national leaderships also to look sideways, both for ideological leads and financial aid, in this case from the SPD and SPÖ and the Socialist International. However, the SI limited itself to extending moral and personal support only; it did not furnish convertible assets. But, because of its heavy load of present, former or aspiring prime ministers concerned with inter-*governmental* relations, the SI was known to have taken a pragmatic-gradualist view of the prospects for democracy behind the Iron Curtain. The record states that there were few, if any, personal links between the SI and East European regime critics who served years of prison sentences for opposition during the now defunct order and emerged as bona fide leaders of the transition.

Of course, moral support to its fellow social democrats in the east was instantly provided upon the transitions. However, the policy of the SI is bewildering on one account. The SI never rejected out-of-hand the approaches for cooperation (and ultimately membership) made by the reform-communist parties. (SI Minutes, Cairo, May 1990, 13). Bettino Craxi of the Italian PSI represented this policy of openness at the SI's Council meeting in Geneva in November 1989: 'He emphasised the need for political dialogue with all possible partners, including both reformed communists and those who had been the victims of the communist system. The SI should be very active and very open at this time'. (SI Minutes, 6) SI President Willy Brandt later confirmed Craxi's view: 'And truly reformed ex-communist parties certainly should not be excluded either'. *Socialist Affairs*, no. 1, 1990, 5) It was the initiative of the Hungarian communists to tear down the border between East and West that partly explains this undogmatic stance of the SI, of which other and less repentant communist parties were later to take advantage. But as far as MSzDP party leader Dr. Anna Petrasovits was concerned, 'The communist party was discredited in the eyes of the Hungarian people, no matter how much credit it might have in the Western world, and could not further anything that might be rightly called social democracy in their country' (SI Minutes, Geneva, p. 6).

What Petrasovits tried to make the Western members of the SI realize, in a humbleness that befits a delegate of a party whose membership is pending, was that Central European social democracy badly needed to be *dissociated* from the old regime in order to pre-empt the argument that was eventually levelled at the Czechoslovak party in the election campaign and which was liable to turn history into a burden rather than an asset: 'social democracy is the father of communism'. It is from the perspective of the Central European electorate that the SI's policy should be assessed: the voters were asking themselves how it was possible that the MSzDP and CSD fiercely attacked the old communists at home but fraternized with them in a foreign setting? Alas, there is no better word for this than 'guilt by association'.

Transitions from left-wing one-party regimes to liberal democracy have their own sociological mechanisms which reduce the likelihood of elevating social democrats to the top position among the powers-to-be. The new victorious coalition consists of the heroic critics of the old regime who earned their laurels in prison, in exile or as highly esteemed professionals doing unskilled labour. Few of these people, with their family backgrounds and/or professional careers typically implanted in the liberal bourgeoisie, have a natural affinity to an old working-class movement. (While exiles living off their own word stay around, those representing a *movement* eventually fade away.) As soon as this avant-garde of the opposition, together with the students, have succeeded in wresting a minimum of legality from a wavering regime, the forces of transition are joined by people who feel that their capacity as experienced public figures is in demand. This second wave of the powers-to-be is recruited from the churches, universities, theaters and the liberal arts, institutions and networks that were never natural social democratic habitats. And in the last wave of the transition, after the euphoria of victory has petered out, reality calls for the administration of the provisional government, a task that is too overwhelming to allow for anything but a token dismissals of the most notorious Stalinists among the ministries and government agencies. In the 'dialectical' ideological climate of this administrative reshuffling one is not advised to profess social democratic leanings if interested in being considered for the vacant positions. Indeed, in this context it made a lot of sense to take two steps away from the crumbling regime.

'Politics, like the arts, arises as they confront the public' (Ehnmark 1986, 100). Social democracy in Hungary and Czechoslovakia had no face among the public. Neither did they have the anonymous yet useful servants in the corridors of the ministries, agencies, and local governments, resource persons with (or within the reach of) access to power and patronage to be distributed under the new incoming regime. The party had missed the boat, except in the GDR where circumstances were exceptional.

But once the care-taker governments had agreed upon the laws for the upcoming elections, the struggle for the peoples' vote was fair for all. What kind of structural barriers confronted the social democratic parties? What did the parties do that was counterproductive to success at the polls?

Making sense of the social democratic vote

What does the political ecology of the social democratic vote say about the balance between the 'demumified' and contemporary support of the party and about the party's position in the competitive party setting? These are apposite questions as they bear on the viability of social democracy in Hungary and Czechoslovakia. Whatever the causes were behind the failure of 1990, the record speaks for itself: a grand old party in need of the vote of the young has to acknowledge that elections are won at the expense of other parties.

Figure 1 displays the spatial distribution of the social democractic vote in the GDR, Hungary, and Czechoslovakia. Prodding these maps for answers to questions about the ratio between the 'demumified' and 'contemporary' vote of the party violates all rules of ecological inference. Only survey data can finally rule on this issue, an issue that primarily concerns the cases of the MSzDP and CSD since the total vote of the SPD by far exceeded that which was stored in the party's 'historical reservoire' of constituents. Besides, the SPD's electoral geography of 1990, strongholds in the centre and the north and weak areas in the south, marks a break with the pattern of the Weimar years (Urwin & Aarebrot 1981, 251).

The geographies of the social democratic vote in Hungary and in Czechoslovakia differ markedly: while the MSzDP is evenly weak, the CSD is unevenly weak across the land (probably not a spurious correlation due to the greater number of regions reported for Czechoslovakia). In fact, the spatial variance in the vote of the MSzDP is lower than that of any of the other Hungarian parties running a national ticket. This may be interpreted as a confirmation of the 'demumification hypothesis': across the nation, the MSzDP alone mobilized the survivors of the old cadres and their families and closest friends. Indeed, in an opinion poll of 22 March 1990 (three days before the election), the MSzDP was the choice of 4 per cent among voters 18-39 years old, 2 per cent among those 40-59, and 10 per cent among voters 59 years old or older (Hungarian Public Opinion Research Institute, MKI).

Is this pattern equally valid for the CSD, whose conspicious strongholds were heavily industrialized northern Bohemia and eastern Slovakia separated by a wide belt of terra incognita? Since the geographical distribution of the social democratic vote in the 1946 election more or less overlaps with that of 1990 there is reason further to pursue the 'demumification hypothesis'.

Figure 1: The regional distribution of the social democratic vote in central European elections, 1990. Percentages.

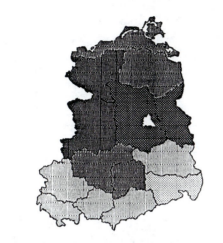

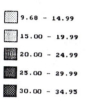

9.68 - 14.99

15.00 - 19.99

20.00 - 24.99

25.00 - 29.99

30.00 - 34.95

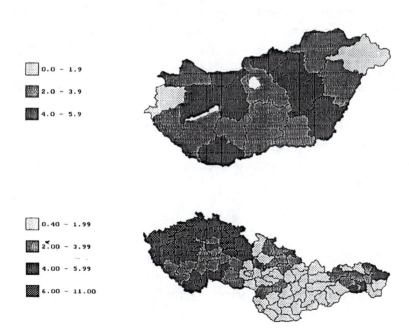

0.0 - 1.9

2.0 - 3.9

4.0 - 5.9

0.40 - 1.99

2.00 - 3.99

4.00 - 5.99

6.00 - 11.00

Table 2 reports the political ecology of the social democratic vote and is meant to identify the competitive context of the party. For obvious reasons, comparison across nations is difficult. Only one type of party, the Christian Democrats, confronted social democracy everywhere to indicate a relationship of antagonism. Country-wise, the coefficients for the SPD confirm what was to be expected: a strong negative correlation with the CDU vote (-.79) and a strong positive correlation with the PDS vote (.60), the latter suggesting that the German left-wing parties fought each other for the vote of one common constituency. The coefficients for the MSzDP are generally so weak that they do not say anything about in which contexts the party was facing unsurpassable political barriers and where it competed on an 'equal footing'. In contrast, the CSD seems to have been in a race in which every party, except the Christian Democrats and the very minor extraordinary parties, was fighting for one and the same vote as the social democrats. Note, however, the weak coefficient between the vote of the CSD and KSC (.23). This is remarkable in so far as in European electoral history the ecological correlation between the vote of communist and social democractic parties is almost invariably one of the strongest, reflecting the fact that both parties mobilize their support in the working-class environment. Thus, judging by the geographical patterns of support, there is reason to suspect that it was the CSD rather than the KSC that retained an appeal in the working-class community.

In so far as the vote of the CSD does convey an impression of having been influenced by socio-structural as well as political determinants, whereas that of the MSzDP is almost aloof from society at large, and of being positively founded upon a constituency of senior citizens, social democracy in Czechoslovakia appears to be a more viable project.

***

Did social democracy do as well as it deserved or is its leadership excused by the circumstances surrounding the elections, circumstances that once again proved that bootstrap-pulling out of the structural context is impossible?

Table 2:
The political ecology of the social democratic vote in
Central European elections, 1990. Pearson coeff.

	Ref.Comm.	Lib.	Forum	Greens	Agr.	Chr.Dem.	C-Right
SPD	.60	-.37	.51	.59	-.01	-.69	-.79
MSzDP	.06	-.09* .23**	-.12	-	.06	-.29	-
CSD	.23		.76	.71	.30	-.56	-

*SzDSz; **FIDESz. N of Regions: GDR: 15; HUN: 19; CS: 114.
Source: NSD, Bergen

History deprived social democracy of political space during the transition and history was partly responsible for the electoral debacle. Of all the parties running for office perhaps none was as uncertain about its rationale as the social democratic parties in Hungary and Czechoslovakia. The forum parties pictured themselves as the custodians of the revolution; the reformed communists consoled themselves knowing that even Martin Luther had once been a Catholic. Even the Beer Drinkers' Union felt confident about its mission.

It may well be that, in the long run - with or without the active help of a social democratic *party* - some kind of 'social democracy' is both unavoidable and agreeable to the Central Europeans. However, in order to approximate such a society, the command economy has to be replaced by a market economy. The question is how fast and at what price. The GDR election signalled something to the social democratic leaderships in Budapest and Prague: ordinary people felt they were drowning in ice-cold water and while life ashore in the market society may not consist entirely of pleasures - unemployment and rising prices for food and rent - the CDU/DSU (with the backing of Chancellor Kohl) was willing to come to the immediate rescue whereas the SPD wasted a split second brooding over *how* to rescue the drowning poor. For the West European record was there to be seen by the East Germans, Hungarians, and Czechoslovaks: it was 'capitalism with a human face', widely superior to any concept of 'socialism with a human face'.

Squeezed in between these options, the social democratic election campaigns bore the mark of schizophrenia: history as well as the party's opponents kept asking the social democratic leadership as well as the potential constituents if, when, and how the socialist legacy of the party would come alive. If socialism was altogether purged from the party's manifesto or postponed indefinitely, it made more sense to vote for the forum; if socialism was about introducing a market economy without replacing the old nomenklatura (and their pitiful clients tormenting ordinary people by making them fill in forms and stand in lines) it made more sense to vote for the reformed communists; and if socialism was needed in the near future to check the well-known side-effects of a capitalist shock-therapy, it made sense to vote for the social democratic party in the near future, only not just now.

While the SPD could ignore history by leaning on its name-sake and *its* adversary across the border, the MSzDP and CSD had to reconcile their historical identity with the challenge of the approaching elections: manifestos had to be drafted, posters printed, nominees put on the ballot papers, campaign workers had to be recruited and briefed on the message of the party.

Occupying a spacious office in the CSD's original headquarters reclaimed from the Lenin Museum, party leader Dr. Jiri Horak had returned to Prague after forty years of exile in the U.S. teaching political science.[7] Convinced that the election was going to be a television event, the party leadership was nevertheless concerned about the party apparatus, organizing it according to the blueprints of the Austrian SPÖ with its own night schools, travel agency and publishing house. The CSD, older even than the SPÖ, was going to reinstitute the red *Lager* that went back to the days of their common Habsburg origin. As for ideological inspiration, however, the CSD drew on the model of the Spanish PSOE, fully aware that the Czechoslovak electorate associated social democracy with Sweden while being immediately attracted to the West German level of private consumption.

Two months before election day the party leadership was relatively satisfied with the process of rebuilding the party in northern Bohemia, but expressed discomfort over the difficulties of recruiting local cadres, especially in Slovakia.

Politics remains an unpleasant business. Scarce resources have to be allocated, good and evil must be pin-pointed, and friend and foe identified. The CSD was willing to accommodate the interests of women, youth, workers, and the retired. Whatever guided the party leadership in selecting these groups as prime targets of its campaign - demographic breakdowns from polling institutes, pure empathy or a carefully considered political theory - there was one category implicitly excluded from the potential social democratic constituency: male non-manuals between 30 and 60, i.e., that group out of which resource persons have been recruited in all known European societies.

The election manifestos of the MSzDP and CSD were vague and non-committal and did not differ much from those of any other social democratic party in the West, except in one important aspect. These Central European parties had no real adversary, save for the old communist parties. But they were the pariah of the election and nobody expected them to be included in the next government. The MSzDP and CSD announced that they were perfectly willing to enter any coalition with the forum parties and other parties not discredited by the past. Unlike the SPD, the MSzDP and CSD had no chance of attacking the political centre by way of stigmatizing its openly declared ally on the right (cf. the DSU, reactionary papists in the eyes of the SPD). It may well be that the Hungarian and Czechoslovak electorates were not mentally prepared to accept a social democratic campaign against the custodians of the revolution, but the MSzDP and CSD could have attacked the centre by proxy, implying a future coalition in which the Smallholders' Party, the Christian Democrats and other sectarian parties would control the means to blackmail the centre. Incidentally, it was the Civic Forum itself that broke the cease-fire of the election campaign by suddenly, in the final week of the campaign, striking out against the Christian Democrats, whose figures in the polls had been rising at the expense of the CF.

Time and space, holding substance at bay, structured the vote. With few substantial differences separating the *new* parties from each other - save for the idiosyncracies that some of them were cultivating - the majority of the citizens of Hungary and Czechoslovakia were never provided with straightforward and definite cues to party choice such as class appeal and national and religious commitments. Not only was time essential to the transition process - the first ones now will later be first - time was also part of the election campaign: how long would the memory of past evils excuse the flaws of the victorious, when was history going to catch up with those who tried to escape it? While the forum parties got away with the future, the Christian Democrats got away with eternity. To the reformed communists time had ceased to exist, whereas history drew social democracy back to its infancy.

Fin-de-siècle social democracy

The euphoria of the 1989 revolution will not last forever in Central Europe. The academics will soon be returning to their universities, the priests to their churches, and the actors to their stages. And those entrusted with elected offices and cabinet portfolios will have to face, indeed *encourage*, a society of exchange and inequalities - and there will be a new election in the not too distant future, an election in which Moscow and the domestic communists will no longer serve as voo-doo dolls. The popular expectations of 1990 will then be checked against the reality of the day and many will be disappointed in their meeting with the well-known 'Christmas Eve theorem': faced with a choice between higher pay or safe jobs also the Central European picks both.

These are safe predictions about a region that has just taught us the futility of political forecasting. Everything else is in the air, such as whether there will be any freezing of the Central European party systems or an endless process of party splits and mergers (e.g., social democracy and the greens) and no voter alignments at all so as to suggest that political parties in and of themselves are obsolete structures throughout the Occident. At present, the citizens of Central Europe are simply enjoying themselves as free-floaters above party boundaries, as was shown in the returns in the local elections in Hungary in October, 1990, when eight out of ten nominees and elected candidates ran as 'Independents'.

In common parlance, the founding elections saw a low level of civic culture, since the 'non-centre-forum vote' was divided among the outcasts, segments, sects or otherwise entrapped in historical cages out of which a Central European *citoyen* will eventually have to be released.

To what extent is Central European social democracy to be dismissed as merely a pathetic attempt at copying a successful project in *Western* Europe, only to become part of the general crisis of European social democracy? Is social democracy in Central Europe just as anachronistic a project as the formation of agrarian parties would be in today's Western Europe, or does Central Europe - or Hungary more than Czechoslovakia, or vice versa - offer unique possibilities for a successful social democracy once it recovers after having been through a necessary reevaluation of its policy and leadership? History does not repeat itself, or:

> Among the Social Democrats their electoral set-back caused a party crisis. Officials began criticising the leaders and attributing the poor results to uncritical and undignified collaboration with the Communists [Civic Forum] ...The Social Democratic leaders were hard put to it to curb this unrest. They reacted to the election figures by redefining their political position, marking themselves off from the Communists [Civic Forum] on the left [right] and from the National Socialists, [Communists], in particular, on the right [left], and stressing their freedom of action and unwillingness to compromise their own interests for the sake of the 'left' ['right'], in other words of the Communists [Civic Forum] (Kaplan 1989, 151-2).

Indeed, the trauma of the immediate post-war years returned to haunt social democracy as it began reorganizing itself and subsequently appeared before the electorate. The CSD was reminded of its less than glorious past as a collaborator and tried to compensate for that in an election campaign in which anti-communism was a prominent theme in the party's rhetoric. Also the MSzDP was evidently embarrased by its ancestry, as the party got carried away and called the reform communists a 'fascist' party, whereas a faction advocating understanding with the old regime broke away to form an 'independent' social democratic party. With the benefit of hindsight, the leaderships of the CSD and MSzDP have been held accountable for the electoral debacles. However, even a Vaclav Havel - who also made a few tactical mistakes in course of the election campaign, errors later excusable in the light of victory - would have failed to elevate social democracy to prominence.

***

Political parties in Europe are confronted with a less predictable world today due to the erosion of the traditional cleavage structure that upholds both the numerical and corporate channels of democracy. Scholars, in an Aristotelian-Occamian zeal not to leave anything unaccounted for, have been busy trying to fill this void with 'post-something'. Alas, the only uniform trend in the political sociology of *fin-de-siecle* Europe is the weakening of class conflicts. More Europeans than ever before sell their labour for a living, yet the working class is obsolete as a coordinated and powerful force in the political system.

Organized labour is replaced by ad hoc militantism and the occasional mobilization of consumers against rising prices, cut-backs of public provisions, etc. Concurrently, the institutions responsible for the mental upbringing of the working class to maintain its own politico-cultural *Lager*, the microcosm that accounts for the difference between *Klasse an sich* and *Klasse für sich*, have withered away in competition with the liberal leisure industry. In effect, European social democracy is threatened by a shrinking core constituency. Middle-aged industrial workers now constitute less than 20 per cent of the economically active population. Second, the social democratic parties are growing increasingly ambivalent in their relations to the trade-unions. The international character of capital, new management philosophy, and fringe benefits to employees act as a challenge to the unions and their membership is on the decline.

Another uniform trend in European politics, east and west alike, is the *institutional* decline of the nation-state (not to be confused with nationalist mass sentiments), whose structures provided West European social democracy with the means of implementing its welfare programmes, programmes subsequently becoming ends in themselves for the party.

Although social democracy has seen better days, its prospects are only as bleak as its opposition and ultimately the party itself can manage to make them. The saliency of the conflicts that have maintained the social democratic constituency has lost in intensity, yet the old issues, and their institutionalized framework, are still alive and kicking. Work, pay, dividends, taxes, and public spending still dominate the political agenda and the fora in which decision-makers meet to distribute scarce resources, including a healthy environment, as unfairly as ever.

While West European social democracy is accustomed to the political agenda, entrenched in the fora and domesticized in the corridors that reward their ins and punish their outs (e.g., government subsidies to parties) there is little to comfort Central European social democracy. With only the embryos of an institutionalized cleavage-structure and no experience of *Sozialpartnerschaft* as a means of redistributing wealth, Central European social democracy is likely to be confronted with problems unfamiliar to a labour movement. As a party with a traditionalist, historical identity, internal frustration is certain to accompany its dealing with awkward issues such as the demands of the Magyars of Transylvania and Slovak demands for extended self-rule. And what will social democracy do about foreign investments if they threaten to reduce Central Europe to a colony of the G7?

The best Central European social democracy can hope for is that the issues involving work, pay, dividends, taxes and public spending should take on overwhelming proportions and that they are not allowed to be linked to protection of the environment, ethnicity, nationalism and religion: *Erst kommt das Fressen, dann kommt die Moral.*

In the midst of transforming precisely those institutions and processes that determine who is to eat more than others, and with what legitimate right, Central Europe is liable to face a vacuum leaving room for the old conflict between 'Us' and 'Them' to reappear above party divisions, a proto-populist cleavage unfamiliar to a social democractic party.

The new elite draw a disproportionate part of their legitimacy from their personal records as members of the different 'classes' of '56, '68, and '89. However, individuals tend to succumb to the institutions they serve: 'How you see things depends on where you sit', as Lech

Walesa also admits (Garton Ash, 1990b). Moreover, in these old institutions the new elite occupies the elected and administrative positions whereas power over production is slipping into the hands of the 'red barons' and the 'green barons'. Lacking executive man-power, Hungary and Czechoslovakia will have few options but to retain the old nomenklatura as managers or even owners of the companies and farms they commanded under the communist regime, as indeed anticipated in the MSzDP's manifesto for the election: [official party translation] 'We cannot accept that the same persons will be able to do the work of modernisation, who caused the present disaster. The country has however few well trained, experienced persons for this change, because up till now information wasn't available only for members of the past regime. We esteem that 4-5 years are needed for this gradual transformation, and that talentful and correct representatives of the past must be involved into this procedure'. This is asking for trouble come next election as the voters will be asking for a record of change, not least one that satisfies the base populist wish to watch heads roll. Worse, the anti-political language of the class of '89, emphasizing truth, unity and other moral dichotomies and shunning internal contradictions within the new regime, may soon sound indistinguishable from that of the old regime: 'United Forward to New and Higher Goals', only this time paying homage to the Nation and Market.

Not really belonging to 'Them' is the middle-class *Gründer,* the entrepreneur whose reinvestment of profits is supposed to contribute to national prosperity and ultimately - to follow Weber - democracy. It is hard *not* to picture a growing frustration among Central European small businessmen in the years to come as they will be confronted with a bureacratic tradition of red-tape and arrogance (perhaps represented by the very same faces as before the transition). A Poujadist reaction of protest may be the best we can hope for as that would prove the existence of a collectivist and constructive entrepreneur culture. The alternative is exit and it is less comfort-ing: what Central Europe needs least of all is a middle-class in-dulging in so-called conspicuous consumption. However, there is a third configuration between these extremes: the petty entrepreneur may fancy a dual existence. Holding on to his safe job with the government, he will only tend part-time to his back-yard business with the limited ambition of merely adding a gilt edge to his family's overall standard of living. 'By the mid 1980's about two thirds of Hungarian income earners gained incomes from the second economy, though most of them depended mainly from their wages and salaries, a growing proportion of them live a genuinely dual existence between market and redistribution' (Kolosi et al 1990, 6). Dual existence means that the necessary personnel turnover in the public services and administration, with its desirable consequences for civic mentality, is arrested and that the much needed domestic 'big bang' in the market is thwarted by entrepreneurial modesty in investments and risk-taking. As a consequence, international investors may be left with opportunities that soon will become a source of conflict and trigger off nationalist accusations about 'Them' selling off the family silver.

Ordinary people in Central Europe rightfully doubt that there has been a thorough changing-of-the-guards at the top of society. A turncoat nomenklatura and a spendthrift middle-class will have much to say in determining the political outlook of 'Us'. Exactly who belong to 'Us' is not known, but every single society in European history has its less fortunate citizens. Equally true, each European nation has its own more or less exclusive mode of responding to the discontent and aspirations of its less fortunate; while Hungary and Czechoslovakia share many of the causes behind the present difficulties, the two countries will part ways in dealing with them (Szelenyi, 1988).

Nonetheless, it is from among the less fortunate half of the population that social democracy is to mobilize its constituency, in stiff competition with reform communists who are eagerly trespassing into the political space where West European social democracy is located: '...there is indeed a large social-democratic constituency...in Hungary, which was unrepresented during the last elections' (Kolosi et al 1990, 20-1). What is to emanate from this pair-wise struggle between, on the one hand, the MSzDP and MSzP and, on the other, the CSD and KSC? First, what ideological means will be employed?

In a *disenchanted* world, political gospels seem to have exhausted their attractions. 'Scientific socialism' is dead and with it the residues of political millenarism in European history. Be that as it may, for the moment at least, it looks as though the European political scene has substituted millenarism for its extreme opposite. Scarcity, exchange and inequality are rarely analyzed and discussed publicly in normative *cum* structural terms within the framework of each country's political economy. The predominant *Zeitgeist*, the market ideology, makes any debate restricted to the national scene appear parochial, and with 'scientifically' founded rational-choice theorems replacing ideologically tainted structuralist theories in academia, the normative is often reduced to the private also in the public debate.

Now, the humanist and Catholic moral emphasizing personal responsibility before structural determinism, as conveyed in the reflections of Havel, Maszowiecki and others, is perhaps music to the ear of the man in the street as well, as he learned one thing from living under millenarism for half a century: 'resistance to stupidities' (Garton Ash, 1990b). In other words, the less fortunate citizens in Central Europe will refuse to let themselves be carried away to the polls on a new flying carpet bound for *Schlaraffenland*.

But, how many of 'Us' does it take and how far may inequality go before the resistance to stupidities breaks among the less fortunate - and before the eternal world saviour emerges from the dark cellar? Inequality is a perennial issue in European political culture and to believe that historicist (non-Popperian) social engineering has reached an impasse is to believe that history itself has come to an end. Moreover, holding (stupid) visions in contempt as a rationale for citizens going to the polls serves as a self-fulfilling prophecy that legitimizes motives which comply with the individualist incentives put forward in rational-choice theories on voting behaviour, i.e., immediate, tangible and selective rewards.

With these ambivalent feelings about the return of the Central European *citoyen*, the old truth that one man equals one vote is not all that trivial. Tribalism, an accurate albeit less pleasant word for rational-choice at the expense of concern for society at large, may open for neo-clientelism (one man = 10,000 votes) or political entrepreneurism (100 men = 10,000 votes). By way of example, how will social democracy and the reform communists respond if, at the next election, the local president and local trade-union leader of a Siemens AG subsidiary come out jointly to endorse the candidacy of those who promise to exempt from taxes whatever fringe benefits employees in foreign-owned companies draw?

Company-based clientelism intertwined with local government boss-rule (read: mechanisms that provide immediate, concrete and selective rewards to the voters) instead of national class conflicts as a source of party preference is not to be ruled out. What used to be common wisdom yesterday - that the less fortunate, unlike the capitalists, have a fatherland whose institutions may be forged to ease the plight of the toiling masses - need not be true in tomorrow's Central Europe.

It all comes down to this: prospects are bleak; social democracy or the reform communists (or, for that matter, any other party) will be swept back to prominence on rhetoric alone. Realism, or the loss of political innocence, among the less fortunate also precludes the forming of a nationally organized labour movement engaged in coordinating long-term efforts to *introduce* legislation for the benefit of the less fortunate as a collective unity (ad hoc protests against the *taking away* welfare provisions are more likely to occur and such actions in themselves breed further labour fragmentation). Finally, realism in combination with institutional flux in the state opens up for unconventional roles for the party organizations.

Central Europe will evolve its own configurations. For the moment, there is a deeply felt aversion among the people about readmitting any form of party politics into the work places. However, in the long run sentiments alone are not enough to rule out the Balkan-American way of mobilizing the vote of the less fortunate: machine politics. The old clan leader and boss knew how both to endorse the pompous platform of the national ticket and to de-mystify it for the grass-roots level. Such political instrumentalism may be too hard for Central European social democracy to digest - to the old communists this political landscape has been its home ground for the last twenty years.

There is a harsh irony to be considered here. To the new cadres of the MSzDP and CSD, true and uncompromised socialism still exists and is worth the effort.[8] In contrast, the party apparatuses of the MSzP and KSC are about to recover from their grief over the lost cause. Like other converts, the communist officials will be over-energetic to please their new world. Only this world is not new! As the new governments are unwilling to expel more than a symbolic handful from public office, the post-communist network will be left intact to be served by the petty civil servant.

293

In addition to the earlier 'Siemens example,' consider this scenario for the countryside. As Hungary and Czechoslovakia enter the process of privatizing farming, crafts, small trades and service outlets, the paper work will be handled by a local government in which rank-and-file reform communists ('the old-boys network') maintain a position of strength. Soon enough the word will be out that some measures and some persons work more smoothly than others in forwarding the necessary licences. This is not to suggest that corruption and kick-backs will be rampant. It is merely another round of patronage, of friends helping friends or comrades trying to make up for past wrongs, transactions in which politics grease the wheels and cogs. When, after WW II, Czechoslovak communists distributed land taken away from the Sudeten Germans to the land hungry farm labourers, the party subsequently got paid through the ballot box (Slama & Kaplan 1986, 58f). This time, however, some of the people filing for licenses to start a small business will handle their own case in their capacity as civil servants! At least, it is a theoretical possibility unless Hungary and Czechoslovakia put an effective end to dreams of 'dual existence' (civil servant cum backyard entrepreneur).

History says that Hungary is susceptible to the Balkan-American political tradition whereas Czechoslovakia leans toward the *citoyen* culture. At first glance, this is substantiated by the Hungarian run-off election in April and local elections in October, 1990. With no socialist patronage to distribute, turnout fell below 50 per cent in April. It dropped alarmingly low in October with the landslide victory of the 'Independents'. Needless to say, to the political analyst that very label is desinformation in that it only provokes images of politicians who, in more senses than one, are *more* dependent than party nominees. Extrapolation would thus suggest that whenever a MSzDP and a MSzP candidate face each other in a run-off election, the latter, likely to be a very able person, will win. For it is a matter of record that ever since the late '60s, the Hungarian Communist Party has been known to give precedence to professional talent over faith in doctrine when appointing candidates to public office. The policy of the KSC was rather the other way around after the Prague Spring of '68.

What theoretical arguments can be presented for the proposition that social democracy in Hungary will be beaten by the reform communists, whereas in Czechoslovakia the CSD will stand a better chance when challenging the KSC?

Societal density, or the extent and penetration of kinships, networks and microcosms, is said to be at odds with Rousseau's society, as *Gemeinschaft* is to *Gesellschaft* in Tönnies's world. There is an artificial conflict in this thinking. The two formats may easily coexist; in fact, big government fuels the formation of sects to make civil society even more dense. Few of these civil structures, save for families and other close kinships, contain elements and mechanisms that per se preclude them from working relationships with public institutions inhabited by the old communist nomenklatura. And since there are 'no hard feelings' on the part of the Hungarian old communists, the civil servants will operate under the motto of a concept borrowed from the restaurant industry: 'serve all, love all'.

Whether this love will then be reciprocated in a way that also boosts the vote of the MSzP (and KSC) depends on what kind of individual mentality is typical for Hungary and Czechoslovakia as people relate to the public sphere: are they (and will they go on) thinking primarily in terms of functions or do they consider persons first when trying to get something done by the public sector? If the latter is true, the credit for getting something done devolves upon the civil servant and his associates rather than on the institution. And in addition to feeling grateful to the civil servant and his associates, this type of intercourse with government also rewards the client in so far as he acquires something to be offered to his friends: contacts - in exchange for other contacts, and so forth.

Czechoslovakia, unlike Hungary, was allowed to cultivate an egalitarian citizenship culture between the two world wars. Did this dissimilarity reemerge intact in 1989 or did the years of really existing socialism do irreparable damage to Czechoslovakia while transforming Hungarian society in a direction that makes it more apt than Czechoslovakia to reopen a project on citizenship culture?

Differences in the nature of the communist regime must be accounted for. Was the KSC already before 1970 as alien to and isolated from the Czechoslovak society as is commonly held? If so, the KSC - unless it performs a miracle of metamorphosis with its recently (October, 1990) adopted policy of confrontation with the 'bourgeois' opposition - is bound to cease to exist. However, this does not necessarily mean that Czechoslovakia itself will return untarnished. The long years when Czechoslovaks lead a life away from the public spheres may have transformed the republic's original culture into one of proto-clientelism. There is certainly no reason to believe that the Czechs and Slovaks will terminate their networks and microcosms built on friendship (corruptive by definition) just to satisfy historically founded expectations about Czechoslovakia's political culture. And, true enough, this fear about the lasting imprint of forty years of Communist rule in the country is evident from the outcome of the local elections of November 1990, in which the KSC made a spectacular comeback, polling second after the Civic Forum in many municipalities. In contrast, was Kadar's policy of co-existence with the Hungarian society successful also in the sense that, relying on an increasingly elaborate civil network, ordinary people learnt how to tell the good communists (professionals) from the evil communists (apparatchiks)? Or was the 1956 Revolution a trauma that will stigmatize the reform communists indefinitely, irrespective of the fact that the Kadarite MSzMP was phased out from the MSzP?

However, the psychological mechanisms that enable people to remember and to forget are elusive unlike the institutional mechanisms; even Proust failed in his *A la Recherche du Temps Perdu*.

These comparative highlights of the predicaments and possibilities confronting the Central European left-wing in the 1990s permit a few tentative conclusions about the future options of the social democratic parties.

Conclusions

Unanimously rejecting the past in favour of the future, any future, the Central European electorates rejected social democracy in the process. Social democracy's historical affinity to socialism, however watered down over the years, was a burden to the party since socialism, in the eyes of the electorates, was drained of visionary meaning after having been used to legitimize the extravagant life of the nomenklatura at the expense of the nation at large. Perhaps the MSzDP and the CSD went too far in dissociating themselves from the negative connotations of socialism. The records were there to be seen, however, and while the CSD suffered from the legacy of 1948, the MSzDP was afflicted by factionalization concerning what to do with those responsible for 1956 and beyond.

The parties in Western Europe that served as a model of inspiration for the CSD and MSzDP, and indeed helped their poor brethren to finance much of their founding election campaign, were of little help in precisely this respect. The Socialist International was not willing to do what the CSD and MSzDP were asking for: to slam the door in the face of the reform communists.

Equally important was the harmful impact that history exerted on social democracy through the party's inherent sociology. Transitions from left-wing monolithic regimes to pluralist democracy do not easily harmonize with the class character and disciplined hierarchy of social democratic parties. Circumstances did not leave much political space for the social democratic parties. The German SPD, however, escaped its history, even more heavy in terms of ideological affinity and sociological character than that of the MSzDP and CSD, by running against a pariah party in its own country and a right-wing party in another country.

Juxtaposing the constituencies that the MSzDP and CSD were hoping for and the 'demumified' one that they got underscores the historical contradictions that trapped the party. The organization model that guided the national leaderships in reestablishing the party went back to the time of the reign of Emperor Franz Joseph (1848-1916); ultimately, the design of the organization reflects the ideological worldview of the architect. Also the local cadres drew on the historical legacy of the labour movement in trying to find their identity and rationale. But, and this is where it went wrong, the local cadres were advised to mobilize, without mentioning the embarrasing word and naming names, the vote of categories that looked as though they were copied from demographic breakdowns of American television viewers.

As for the options of Central European social democracy, there are eight observations that may be derived from the above discussion:

1. Hungary and Czechoslovakia will not evolve the societal cleavages and their institutionalized mechanisms that used to have a bearing on European social democracy's historical rationale in the

297

electoral arena.

2. Hungary and Czechoslovakia will not be given the opportunity of *expanding* the public sector in order to redistribute wealth within the format of a relatively autonomous nation-state.

3. The fragmentation of the working class into segments differentiated by its strategic position in the prosperous world economy, the retarding national smoke-stack economy, and the local entrepreneurial-clientelistic economy will render an orchestrated mobilization of the working class extremely difficult.

4. The forming of a middle class, let alone one whose surplus is used in the accumulative spirit of Protestantism instead of being conspicuously consumed in public or modestly consumed in private, will take years.

In other words, the first four claims basically amount to a warning against expecting Central European social democracy to draw on the structural cleavages that have provided the foundations of social democracy in Western Europe.

5. The struggle between the social democrats and the old communists for the vote of the less fortunate 'Us' is likely to be won by a reformed communist party in control of a well-organized secularized apparatus firmly planted inside a state that cannot afford to do away with its old institutions and manpower. The crux is whether people - and the party itself - will soon forget the party's ancestry.

6. There is only a rudimentary and anachronistic social democratic party apparatus which may be dismantled in its infancy to prevent the party from being besieged by historical bigotry.

7. The inevitable conflicts within the incumbent government in the face of its monumental tasks ahead - no European country has ever before been required to encourage inequalities upon transition to democracy.

8. The omnibus character of the incumbent centre-forum parties, a coalition prone to compensate its inherent contradictions in a language of self-destructive dichotomies, and the immature compartmentalization of the founding opposition, due to be restructured in the next election, are characteristic features of today's central European polities.

The CSD and MSzDP stand equally defeated at the polls. Assuming that they are equally gifted at recruiting potential talents for a new attempt at the polls, the two parties will challenge a context that holds some promises for the CSD while painting a less optimistic future for the MSzDP. In sum, then, the arguments are as follows:

	Czechoslovakia	Hungary
Modern Politico- Cultural Heritage:	Egalitarian- Citizenship	Hierarchical- Clientelist
Communist Regime:	Totalitarian	Post- totalitarian
Transition:	Velvet Revolution (Regime toppled by latent force)	Negotiated Revolution (Regime voluntarily resigning)
Old Comm. Party Self-Perception:	Stigmatized & Self-pity	'Born Again' Social Democrat
Dominant New Regime:	Secular- Liberal	Christian- Nationalist

------------ Predisposing for: ------------

Dominant 'Left- wing' Party:	CSD	MSzP

Appendix Table A. Parliamentary elections in Hungary and Czechoslovakia in 1945 and 1946 respectively. Percentages.

Party	Hungary	Czechoslovakia
Communist Party	17.0	38.7
Socialist Party		18.3
Social Democrats	17.4	12.1
Slovak Social Democratic Party		3.1
Radical Party	.1	
Smallholders' Party	57.0	
National Peasants' P.	6.9	
Christian Party		15.6
Citizen Democrats	1.6	
Slovak Democratic Party		14.1
Slovak Freedom Party		3.7

Sources: Rothschild 1989, 99; Bradley 1981, 18.

Notes

1. To the MSzP's vote should be added that of the Kadarite MSzMP, the ASZ (a party of agricultural technicians strongly opposed to the privatization of the rural economy advocated by the FKgP), and that of the HVK, a coalition of local honoratiores.

2. As opposed to the Stalinist working-class culture *imposed* on Eastern Europe after WW II.

3. For a discussion on Hungarian politico-cultural continuity, see Kolosi et al (1990).

4. While the case of the GDR is extremely useful in comparing the founding elections of Central Europe, the GDR will - for obvious reasons - cease to be a case in future comparative discussions on the viability of Central European social democracy.

5. In October, 1990, the Civic Forum constituted itself as a political party. Electing Finance Minister Dr. Vaclav Klaus as its first party leader, the Forum's profile became centre-right. Only a week before that, the KSC held its first post-transition congress at which it signalled that the time for national consensus was over. The two events together may open up space in the middle that can be occupied by the CSD.

6. Cf. the generous financial support provided by the SPD to the Mediterranean socialist parties (Maxwell 1986, 130).

7. This section on the electoral campaign planning of the CSD is based on an interview with party leader Dr Jiri Horak in Prague on 30 March 1990. The reflections on the results of the MSzDP by a fatigued vice-chairman, Mr. G. Fischer, are also recorded, as are other impressions of the German and Hungarian elections that I collected on site.

8. Otherwise it would not have much sense to join the social democratic parties since both patronage and the pure civic-minded incentives were more adequately satisfied by joining the centre-form parties. Incidentally, there is reason to believe that the MSzDP and CSD lost some of their 'best cadres'to the SzDSz and CF respectively, viz., those who prefer to use the political centre as a platform for an eventual attack on the social democratic leadership the instant the centre itself started to show signs of disintegration.

Bibliography

Aardal, B. and Valen, H. (1989), *Velgere, partier og politisk avstand*, Statistisk Sentralbyrå, Oslo.

Albrow, M. (1970), *Bureaucracy*, Macmillan, London.

Alestalo, M. (1989), 'Den offentliga sektorns tillväxt', in *Norden förr och nu*, Nordisk statistisk sekretariat, København, Tab.5.

Andersen, J.G. (1986), 'Electoral Trends in Denmark in the 1980's', *Scandinavian Political Studies*, Vol. 9, no. 2.

Andersen, J.G. (1989), 'Social klasse og parti', in Elklit, J & Tonsgaard, O. (eds.), *To folketingsvalg*, Politica, Århus.

Anderson, P. (1974), *Lineages of the Absolutist State*, Verso, London.

Anderson, P. (1988), 'Socialdemokratiet på 80-tallet', *Vardøger* 18,

Andersson, Å. (1988), *Universitet. Regioners framtid*, Regionplane-kontoret, Stockholm.

Arfé, G. (1977), *Storia del socialismo italiano 1892-1926*, Einaudi, Torino.

Ashford, D. E. (1988), *Ordaining Power: Discovering the State Through Policy Studies*, Working paper, Conference on Comparative Policy Studies, University of Pittsburgh, May 1988.

Bell, D. (1960), *The End of Ideology*, Harvard University Press, Cambridge, Massachusetts.

Bentzon, K.H. (1972), *Politiseringen af de danske kommunalvalg 1909-1966*, Institut for statskundskab, Aarhus universitet, Århus.

Berg, T. (1987), *'Storhetstid (1945-1965)'*, *Arbeiderbevegelsens historie i Norge*, bind 5, Tiden, Oslo.

Berger, S. D., ed. (1983), *Organizing interests in Western Europe*, Cambridge Univ. Press, Cambridge.

Bergh, T. (1987), 'Storhetstid (1945-1965)', *Arbeiderbevegelsens historie i Norge*, bind 5, Tiden, Oslo.

Berglund, S. et al. (1987), 'Alternative methods of regionalization', *International Political Science Review*. no 4.

Berglund, S. and Risbjerg-Tomsen, S. (eds.) (1990), *Modern political ecological analysis*. Åbo Academy Press, Åbo.

303

Bertolt, O., Christiansen, E. og Hansen, P. (1954), *En bygning vi rejser. Den politiske arbejderbevægelse i Danmark, Bd. I & II*, Forlaget Fremad, København.

Bilstad, K.A (1986), *Konfliktstruktur og partiavstand*, Institutt for sammenliknende politikk, Universitetet i Bergen, Bergen.

Bjørklund, T. (1982), *Mot strømmen. Kampen mot EF 1961 - 1972*, Universitetsforlaget, Oslo.

Bjørklund, T. (1989), *Regionale variasjoner valgatferden 1945-1985. Stötte til eller brudd med Rokkans modeller?* Unpublished essay, Institutt for Samfunnsforskning, Oslo.

Blau, P. and Meyer, M. (1971), *Bureaucracy in Modern Society*, Random House, New York.

Blidberg, K. (1984), *Splittrad gemenskap. Kontakter och samarbete inom nordisk socialdemokratisk arbetarrörelse 1931-1945*, Almqvist & Wiksell International, Stockholm.

Blinkhorn, M. (1984), *Mussolini and Fascist Italy*, Methuen, London.

Blomberg, G., Petersson, O. and Westholm, A. (1989), *Medborgarundersökningen. Råtabeller*. Regeringskansliets offsetcentral, Stockholm.

Bocca, G. (1982), *Storia d'Italia. Dal fascismo ad oggi*, Milano.

Borre, O. (1987), 'Some Results from the Danish 1987 Election', *Scandinavian Political Studies*, Vol. 10, no. 4.

Bozóki, A. (1990), 'Post-Communist Transition: Political Tendencies in Hungary,' *East European Politics and Societies*, Vol. 4, no. 2.

Bradley, J.F.N. (1981), *Politics in Czechoslovakia, 1945-1971*, U.P. of America, Washington, D.C.

Brenan, G. (1967), *The Spanish Labyrinth*, Cambridge University Press.

Brox, O. (1988), *Ta vare på Norge. Norge under høyrebølgen.* Gyldendal, Oslo.

Bruneau, T.C. (1986), *Politics in Contemporary Portugal. Parties and the Consolidation of Democracy*, Lynne Rienner Publishers, Boulder, Colorado.

Bryld, C. (1976), *Det danske socialdemokrati og revisionismen. Bd. I & II*, GMT, Köbenhavn.

Bull, Edvard Sr. (1922), *Arbeiderbevegelsens stilling i de tre nordiske land 1914-1920*, Det norske Arbeiderpartis forlag, Kristiania.

Bull, E. Sr. (1928), 'Den første norske arbeiderregjering', *Samtiden*.

Bull, E. (1947), *Arbejderklassen i norsk historie*, Tiden, Oslo.

Bull, E. (1959), 'Kriseforliket mellom bondepartiet og det norske arbeiderparti i 1935', *Historisk Tidsskrift*, Vol. 39, nr. 2, 1959, 121 139.

Castle, F.G. (1978), *The Social Democratic Image og Society. A study of the achievements and origins of Scandinavian Social Democracy in comparative perspective*, Routledge and Kegan Paul, London.

Cawson, A. (1986), *Corporatism and Political Theory*, Basil Blackwell, Oxford.

Clark, M. (1984), *Modern Italy 1871-1982*, Longman, New York, *L'Espresso* 18.3.1990, *L'Espresso* 1.7.1990.

Clogg, R. (1987), *Parties and Elections in Greece. The Search for Legitimacy*, C. Hurst & Company, London.

Dahl, R. and Tufte, E. (1973), *Size and Democracy*, Stanford University Press, Stanford.

Damgaard, E. (1977), *Folketinget under forandring*, Samfundsvidenskabeligt Forlag, København.

Danielsen, R. (1978), 'Nye kilder til regjeringskrisen i januar 1928', *Historisk tidsskrift* 1:78, pp. 93-102.

de Tocqueville, A. (1988), *Democracy in America*, Harper & Row, New York.

Det norske Arbeiderparti (1915), *Protokoll over forhandlingerne paa det 22. landsmøte i Trondhjem*, Arbeidernes Aktietrykkeri, Kristiania.

Diaz, E. (1979), 'Marxismo y no marxismo: Las señas de identidad del Partido Socialista Obrero Español', *Sistema*, no. 29-30, 1979, 211-232.

Douglas, M. (1982), 'Cultural Bias', in M. Douglas (ed.): *In the Active Voice*, Routledge and Kegan, London.

Douglas, M. (1987), *How Institutions Think*, Routledge & Kegan Paul, London.

Duverger, M. (1978), *Political Parties*, Methuen, London.

Duverger, M. (1980), *Les Orangers du Lac Balaton*, Seuil, Paris.

Dybdahl, V. (1969), *Partier og Erhverv. Studier i partiorganisation og byerhvervenes politiske aktiviteter 1880-1913*, Vol. 1 and 2, Universitetsforlaget i Aarhus.

Edenman, R. (1946), *Socialdemokratiska riksdagsgruppen 1903-1920*, Statsvetenskapliga föreningen i Uppsala, Almqvist & Wiksells, Uppsala.

Ehnmark, A. (1986), *Maktens hemligheter. En essä om Machiavelli*, Norstedts, Stockholm.

Eliassen, K. and Ågotnes, J.E. (1987), *Stortingsrepresentanter og statsråder 1945-1985*. Kodebok med dokumentasjon og eksemplar på informasjon, NSD Rapporter nr 71, Bergen.

Elklit, J. (1990), *Faldet i medlemstal i danske politiske partier - reflektioner over mulige årsager*, Institut for Statskundskab, Aarhus universitet, Århus.

Elklit, J. and Tonsgaard, O. (1984): *Valg og Vælgeradfærd. Studier i dansk politik*. Politica, Århus.

Elklit, J. and Tonsgaard, O. (red.) (1989), To folketingsvalg. Vælgerholdninger og vælgeradfærd i 1987 og 1988.

Elster, J. (1987), 'On the possibility of Rational Politics', *Archives Européennes de Sociologie*, XXVIII.

Elster, J. (1990), *The Cement of Society,* Cambridge UP, Cambridge.

Elvander, N. (1980), *Skandinavisk arbetarrörelse*, Liber Förlag, Stockholm.

Epland, J. (1987), 'Høyreparti og velferdsstatsekspansjon', (University of Bergen, mimeographed thesis).

Esping-Andersen, G. (1985), *Politics Against Markets. The Social Democratic Road to Power*, Princeton University Press, Princeton, New Jersey.

Farneti, P. (1985), *The Italian Party System 1945-1980*, Frances Printer, London.

Galenson, W. (1952), 'Scandinavia', in *Comparative Labor Movements*, Galenson W. (ed.), Prentice Hall, New York.

Gallagher, T. & A.M. Williams, (eds.), (1989), *Southern European Socialism. Parties, Elections and the Challenge of Government*, Manchester University Press, Manchester.

Galli, G. (1978), *Storia della D.C.*, Laterza, Roma.

Galli, G. (1983), *I partiti politici in Italia 1861-1983*, Utet, Torino.

Garton Ash, T. (1990a), *We the People*, Granta Books, Cambridge.

Garton Ash, T. (1990b), 'Eastern Europe: Après Le Deluge, Nous', *The New York Review of Books,* Aug. 16.

Gellner, E. (1977), *Patrons and Clients in Mediterranean Societies,* Duckworth, London.

Gidlund, J.E and Gidlund, G. (1989), Storstadens partier och valdeltagande 1948-88. Underlagsrapport från Storstadsutredningen, SOU 1989:68.

Gillespie, R. (1989), *The Spanish Socialist Party. A History of Factionalism,* Clarendon Press, Oxford.

Giner, S. (1984), 'Southern European Socialism in Transition', *West European Politics,* Vol. 7, 1984, no.2.

Glimell, H. and Lindgren, M. (1988), *Framtid i arbetssamhället,* Institutet för framtidsstudier, Stockholm.

Goldsmith, M. and Baldersheim, H. (1990), 'Kommuner i omstilling - et internasjonalt perspektiv', in Baldersheim, H. (ed.), *Ledelse og innovasjon i kommunene,* Tano, Oslo.

Grass, G. (1990), 'After the fall', interview in the *New Statesman Society* (22 June 1990).

Gröning, L. (1988), *Vägen til makten. SAPs organisation och dess betydelse för den politiska verksamheten 1900-1933,* Studia Historica Upsaliensia 149, Almqvist & Wiksell International, Stockholm.

Gustafsson, A. (1984), *Kommunal självstyrelse,* Liber, Malmö.

Hamilton, M.B. (1989), *Democratic Socialism in Britain and Sweden,* Macmillan, Basingstoke, Hampshire.

Hammond, J.L. (1984), 'The Portuguese Revolution: Two Models of Socialist Transition', *The Insurgent Sociologist,* Vol.12, no. 1-2, Winter-Spring 1984, 83-100.

Harder, E. (1982), *Dansk kommunalforvaltning I.* Juristforbundets Forlag, København.

Heclo, H. & Madsen, H. (1987), *Policy and Politics in Sweden: Principled Pragmatism,* Temple University Press, Philadelphia.

Heidar, K. (1974), *Institusjonalisering i Det norske Arbeiderparti 1887-1940,* Unpublished thesis, Institutt for samfunnsforskning, Universitetet i Oslo.

Heidar, K (1980), *The Deradicalisation of Working Class Parties: Study of Three Labour Party Branches in Norway,* London School of Economics and Political Sience, London.

Helenius, R. (1969), *The Profile of Party Ideologies*, Scandinavian University Books, Helsinki.

Hernes, G. (1974), 'Om ulikhetenes reproduksjon', in *I forskningens lys*, NAVF 1949-1974, Oslo.

Heywood, P. (1990), *Marxism and the failure of organised Socialism in Spain, 1879-1936*, Cambridge University Press, Cambridge.

Hine, D. (1977), 'Social Democracy in Italy', in William Paterson and Alistair Thomas, (eds.), *Social democratic parties in Western Europe*, London.

Hine, D. (1980), 'The Italian Socialist Party under Craxi', in Peter Lange and Sidney Tarrow, (eds.), *Italy in Transition, Conflict and Consensus*, Frank Cass and Company Limited, Bournemouth.

Hirdman, Y. (1990), *Att lägga livet till rätta*, Carlssons, Stockholm.

Hjellum, T. (1967), *Partierne i lokalpolitikken*, Gyldendal Norsk Forlag, Oslo.

Hoikka, P. and Kiljunen, P. (1983), *Naiset kunnallisvaaliehdokkaina ja valtuutettuina, Kunnallistieteen aineryhmän julkaisusarja A 4*, Tampereen Yliopisto, Tampere.

Holmberg, S. and Gilljam, M. (1987), *Väljare och val i Sverige*, Bonniers, Stockholm.

Hufvudstadsbladet, March 13, 1937.

Huntington, S. (1968), *Political Order in Changing Societies*, Yale Universtiy Press, New Haven.

Jääskeläinen, M., 'Demokratian kriisi', in *Valtioneuvoston historia 1917-1966 I*, Helsinki, 471-558.

Kaplan, K. (1989), 'Czechoslovakia's February 1948',' in N. Stone & E. Strouhal (eds.), *Czechoslovakia: Cross-roads and Crises, 1918-88*, McMillan, Basingstoke.

Karvonen, L. (1988a), *From White to Blue-and-Black. Finnish Fascism in the Inter-War Era*, Societas Scientarum Fennica, Helsinki.

Karvonen, L. (1988b), 'Rödmyllan i komparativt perspektiv: en forskningspropå', *Politiikka*, Vol. XXX, 1988:3, 204-214.

Karvonen, L. (1991), 'A Nation of Workers and Peasants. Ideology and compromise in the interwar years', in Karvonen, L. and Sundberg, J. (eds.), *Social Democracy in Transition*, Gower, Aldershot.

Karvonen, L. and Lindström, U. (1988), *Red-Green Crisis Agree-*

ments, Paper, IPSA World Congress, Washington, D.C.

Karvonen, L. with Rappe, A. (1990), *Social Structure and Campaign Style: Finland 1954-1987*. Paper presented at the ECPR joint Sessions of Workshops in Bochum.

Kettunen, P. (1986), *Poliittinen liike ja sosiaalinen kollektiivisuus. Tutkimus sosialidemokratiasta ja ammattiyhdistysliikkeestä Suomessa 1918-1930*, Societas Historica Finlandiae, Helsinki.

Kjeldstadli, K. (1978), 'Arbeider, bonde våre haere...' Arbeiderpartiet og böndene 1930-1939', *Tidsskrift för arbeiderbevegelsens historie* 1978:2.

Kjellander, C-G. (1990), *Slumpen utser nästa regering*, Dagens Nyheter, September 23, 1990.

Kolosi, T., Szelenyi, I., Szelenyi, S. & Western, B. (1990), 'The making of political fields in post-communist transition', paper presented at the ASA 1990 Annual Convention, Washington, D.C., 1990.

Korhauser, W. (1960), *The Politics of Mass Society*, Routledge and Kegan Paul, London.

Korpi, W. (1983), *The Democratic Class Struggle*, Routledge & Kegan Paul, London.

Kristensen, O.P. (1980), 'Deltagelse i partipolitiske aktiviteter', in Damgaard, E. (ed.), *Folkets veje i dansk politik*, Schulz, København.

Kristensen, O.P. (1987), *Væksten i den offentlige sektor*, Jurist- og Økonomforbundets Forlag, København.

Kuhnle, S. og P. Selle (1990), 'Autonomi eller underordning: Frivillige organisasjoner og de offentlige', in S. Kuhnle and P. Selle (eds.), *Frivillig organisert velferd - alternativ til offentlig?* Alma Mater, Bergen.

Kuhnle, S. og Solheim, L. (1985), *Velferdsstaten - vekst og omstilling*, Tanum, Oslo.

Kuusanmäki, J. (1987), 'Den kommunala demokratins utveckling och kommunalförvaltningens organisation 1875-1917', in Gardberg, C.J. et al., *Stadsväsendets historia i Finland*, Finlands Stadsförbund, Helsingfors.

Lafferty, W.M. (1971), *Economic Development and the Response of Labor in Scandinavia. A Multi-Level Analysis*, Universitetsforlaget, Oslo.

309

Lafferty, W.M. (1974), *Industrialization, Community Structure, and Socialism. An Ecological Analysis of Norway, 1875-1924*, Universitetsforlaget, Oslo.

Lane, J.E. (1987), 'Introduction: The Concept of Bureaucracy', in Lane, J.E. (ed.), *Bureaucracy and Public Choice*, Sage, London.

Larsen, H. (1990), 'Ordføreren - handlekraft eller samlende symbol?', in Baldersheim, H. (ed.), *Ledelse og innovasjon i kommunene*, Tano, Oslo.

Larsen, S.U. and Offerdal, A. (1979), *De få vi valgte*, Universitetsforlaget, Oslo.

Lauman, E. E. & Knoke, D. (1987), *The Organisational State. Social Choice in National Policy*, The University of Wisconsin Press.

Leinonen, A. (1960), *Vuosikymmenten valinkauhassa. Muistelmia III*, Werner Söderström OY, Porvoo.

Lenin, V.I. (1972), *Vad bör göras*, Arbetarkultur, Stockholm.

Lewin, L. (1984), *Ideologi och struktur. Svensk politik under 100 år*, P.A. Norstedt & Söners förlag, Stockholm.

Lewin, L., Jansson, B. and Sörbom, D. (1972), *The Swedish Electorate 1887-1968*, Almqvist & Wiksell, Uppsala.

Lie, H. (1988), *Martin Tranmæl - et bål av vilje*, Vol. 1, Tiden norsk forlag, Oslo.

Lindman, S. (1940), *De homogena partiregeringarna i Finland 1926-1928. I. Det socialdemokratiska regeringsexperimentet 1926-1927*, Acta Academiae Aboensis, Åbo.

Lindström, U. (1985), *Fascism in Scandinavia 1920-1940*, Almqvist & Wiksell, Stockholm.

Lindström, U. (1989), 'Politik i Norden 1889 - 1989; ett socialdemokratisk århundrade'?, in *Norden förr och nu. Ett sekel i statistisk belysning*, Nordiska statistiska sekretariatet, Köpenhamn.

Lindström, U. (1991), 'From Cadres to Clients: Toward a Theory of the Electoral Coalitions of Social Democracy', in Karvonen, L. and Sundberg, J. (eds.), *Social Democracy in Transition*, Gower, Aldershot.

Lipset, S.M. (1960), *Political Man*, Doubleday & Co., Anchor Books, New York.

Lipset, S. M. (1983), 'Radicalism or Reformism: The Sources of Working-class Politics', *The American Political Science Review*,

Vol. 77, 1983, 1-18.

Listhaug, O. and Aardal, B. (1989), 'Welfare state issues in the Norwegian 1985 election: Evidence from aggregate and survey data', *Scandinavian Political Studies*, no 1.

Lorenz, E. (1972), *Arbeiderbevegelsens historie 1789-1930. En innföring*, Pax Forlag AS, Oslo.

Lorenz, E. (1974), *Arbeiderbevegelsens historie 1930-1973*, Pax Forlag AS, Oslo.

Lowi, T. (1969), *The End of Liberalism*, Norton, New York.

Lehmbruch, G. (1982), 'Neo-corporatism in a comparative perspective', in Lembruch, G. & Schmitter, P. C. (eds.) *Patterns of corporatist policymaking*, Sage, Beverly Hills.

Lundestad, G. (1977), 'Hovedtendenser i norsk politik 1945-65', in Bergh, T. and Pharo, H. (eds.), *Vekst og velstand. Norsk politisk historie 1945-1965*, Universitetsforlaget, Oslo.

Lundquist, L. (1982), *The Party and the Masses,* Almqvist & Wiksell International, Stockholm.

Luoma, V. (1967), 'Työmarkkinajärjestöt ja työtaistelut 1919-1939', in E. Jutikkala et al, (eds.), *Itsenäisen Suomen taloushistoriaa 1919-1950*, Werner Söderström OY, Porvoo.

Madsen, H.J. (1984), *Social Democracy in Postwar Scandinavia: Macroeconomic Management, Electoral Support and the Fading Legacy of Prosperity*, Unpublished theses, Harvard University, Cambridge, Massachusetts.

Mannheim, K. (1936), *Ideology and Utopia*, Harcourt Brace, New York.

Maravall, J. M. (1976), 'Eurocomunismo y socialismo en España: la sociología de una competición política', *Sistema*, nr. 28.

Maravall, J.M. (1985), 'The Socialist Alternative: The Policies and Electorate of the PSOE', in H.R. Penniman & E.M. Mujal-León, (eds.), *Spain at the Polls 1977, 1979, and 1982*, Duke University Press, Durham, N.C.

March, J. & Olsen, J. P. (1984), 'The New Institutionalism. Organizational Factors in Political Life', in *American Political Science Review*, 70.

Martinussen, W. (1973), *Fjerndemokratiet. Sosial ulikhet, politiske ressurser og politisk medvirkning i Norge*, Gyldendal Norsk Forlag, Oslo.

Massari, O. (1989), 'Changes in the PSI leadership: the national executive committee and its membership (1976-1987)', *European Journal of Political Research* 17, 1989.

Mavrogordatos, G. Th. (1983a), *Stillborn Republic. Social Coalitions and Party Strategies in Greece, 1922-1936,* University of California Press, Berkeley.

Mavrogordatos, G. Th. (1983b), *Rise of the Green Sun. The Greek Election of 1981,* Ant. N. Sakkoulas, Athens.

Maxwell, K. (1986), 'Prospects for Democratic Transition in Portugal', in G. O'Donnell, P.C. Schmitter & L. Whitehead (eds.), *Transition from Authoritarian Rule, Southern Europe,* The Johns Hopkins U.P., Baltimore.

Meyer, P. (1965), *Politiske partier,* Nyt Nordisk Forlag, København.

Micheletti, M. (1984), *The Involvement of Swedish Labour Market Organisations in the Swedish Political Process,* Working Paper, Business and Social Research Institute, Stockholm.

Michels, R. (1925), *Zur Soziologie des Parteiwesens in der modernen Demokratie,* Alfred Kröner Verlag, Leipzig.

Michels, R. (1962), *Political Parties,* The Free Press, New York.

Mill, J.S. (1910), *Representative Government,* Dent & Sons, London.

Misgeld, K., Molin, K. and Åmark, K. (1989), *Socialdemokratins samhälle. SAP och Sverige under 100 år,* Tiden, Stockholm.

Moring, T. (1990), *Political elite action.* Finska Vetenskapssocieteten, Helsingfors.

Mouzelis, N. (1988), 'Marxism or Post-Marxism', *New Left Review,* 167.

Naroll, R. (1965), 'Galton's Problem: the Logic of Cross-Cultural Analysis', *Social Research,* Vol. 32, Winter 1965:5, 428-451.

Nash, E. (1983), 'The Spanish Socialist Party since in Franco', in D.S. Bell, (ed.), *Democratic Politics in Spain: Spanish Politics after Franco,* Frances Pinter, London.

Nilsson, K.R. (1987), 'The Italian Socialist Party: An Indispensable Hostage', in Pennimann Howard, (ed.), *Italy at the Polls 1983,* Duke University Press, Durham.

Noponen, M. (1964), *Kansanedustajien sosiaalinen tausta Suomessa,* Valtiotieteellisen Yhdistyksen Julkaisusarja, Helsinki.

Nybom, T. (1988), 'Den socialdemokratiska staten - exemplet Sverige,' *Nytt Norsk Tidsskrift*, no. 1.

Offe, C. (1983), 'Competitive Party Democracy and the Keynsian Welfare State: Factors of Stability and Disorganization', *Policy Sciences* Vol. 15.

Offe, C. (1985), *Disorganized Capitalism*, Polity Press, Cambridge.

Offerdal, A. (1976), 'Rekrutteringen av et bystyre', in Kjellberg, F. (ed.), *Kommunal politikk*, Universitetsforlaget, Oslo.

Olsen, J.P. (1988), 'The Modernization of Public Administration in the Nordic Countries: Some Research Questions' *Administrative Studies*, Vol 7/88, 1, pp. 2-17.

Olsen, J.P. (1990), *Demokrati på svenska*, Carlssons, Stockholm.

Olsen, J. and Sætren, H. (1980), *Aksjoner og demokrati*, Universitetsforlaget, Oslo.

Olson, M. (1982), *The Rise and Decline of Nations*, Yale University Press, Mass, Cambridge.

Oskarson M. (1990), 'Klassröstning på reträtt', in Gilljam, M. & Holmberg, S., (eds.), *Rött, blått, grönt. En bok om 1988-års riksdagsval*, Bonniers, Stockholm.

Overrein, A. (1988), 'Sosialdemokrati mellom stat og samfunn', *Vardøger*, no. 18.

Paavonen, T. (1987), 'The Finnish Social Democratic Party since 1918', in J. Mylly and R.M. Berry, (eds.), *Political Parties in Finland. Essays in History and Politics*, University of Turku, Political History C:21, Turku.

Palme, S.U. and Lindberg, E-F. (1962), 'De första stadsfullmäktigevalen', in *Hundra år under kommunalförfattningarna 1862-1962*, Svenska Landskommunernas förbund, Svenska Landstingsförbundet och Svenska Stadsförbundet, Stockholm.

Panebianco, A. (1988), *Political Parties: Organization and Power*, Cambridge University Press, Cambridge.

Panorama, 14.10.1990.

Parsons, T. (1954), *Essays in Sociological Theory*, The Free Press, Glencoe.

Pasquino, G. (1986), 'Modernity and reforms: The PSI between Political Entrepreneurs and Gamblers', *West European Politics* no 1, Vol 9, 1986.

Pekonen, K. (1990), 'Community as a Topic in Finnish Social

Democratic Discourse', in Hänninen, S. and Palonen, K. (eds.), *Texts, Contents, Concepts*, The Finnish Political Science Association, Helsinki.

Pesonen, P. and Sänkiaho, R. (1979), *Kansalaiset ja kansanvalta*, Werner Söderström, Helsinki.

Petersson, O., Westholm A. & Blomberg, G. (1989), *Medborgarnas makt*, Carlssons, Stockholm.

Petras, J. (1984), 'The rise and decline of southern European socialism', *New Left Review* 146, July-August 1984, 37-52.

Petras, J. (1987), 'The contradictions of Greek Socialism', *New Left Review* 163, May-June 1987, 3-25.

Pettersson, T. (1988), *Bakom dubbla lås*. Institutet för framtidsstudier, Stockholm.

Pierre, J. (1986), *Partikongresser och regeringspolitik. En studie av den socialdemokratiska partikongressens beslutsfattande och inflytande 1948-1978*, Kommunfakta förlag, Lund.

Pimlott, B. (1977), 'Socialism in Portugal: Was it a Revolution?' *Government and Opposition*, Vol. 12, no. 3, Summer 1977, 332-350.

Przeworski, A. (1980), 'Social Democracy as a Historical Phenomenon', *New Left Review*, no. 122, July-August, pp. 27-58.

Prezeworski, A. (1986), *Capitalism and social democracy*. Cambridge Univ. Press, Cambridge.

Przeworski, A. and Sprague, J. (1986), *Paper Stones*, The University of Chicago Press, Chicago.

Pridham, G. (1988), *Political Parties and Coalitional Behaviour in Italy*, Routledge, London.

Ridley, F. F. (1975), *The Study of Government. Political Science and Public Administration*, Allen & Unwin, London.

Rintala, M. (1962), *Three Generations: the Extreme Right Wing in Finnish Politics*, Indiana University Press, Bloomington, Indiana.

Rokkan, S. (1970), *Citizens Elections Parties*, Universitetsforlaget, Oslo.

Rokkan, S. (1987), *Stat, Nasjon, Klasse*, Universitetsforlaget, Oslo.

Roset I.A., *Det norske Arbeiderparti og Hornsruds regjeringsdannelse i 1928*, Universitetsforlaget, Oslo.

Rothschild, J. (1989), *Return to Diversity. A Political History of East Central Europe Since World War II*, Oxford UP, Oxford.

Rothstein, B. (1985), 'The Success of the Swedish Labour Market Policy: The Organizational Connection to Policy', *European Journal of Political Research*, 13.

Rothstein, B. (1986), *Den socialdemokratiska staten*, Lund, Arkiv.

Rothstein, B. (1987a), 'Välfärdsstat, implementering och legimitet', *Statsvetenskaplig Tidskrift*, 90.

Rothstein, B. (1987b), 'Corporatism and Reformism. The Social Democratic Institutionalization of Class Conflict', *Acta Sociologica*, 30.

Rothstein, B. (1988), 'Reformer och principer', *Zenith*, no. 2.

Rothstein, B. (1988a), 'State and Capital in Sweden. The Importance of Corporatist Arrangements', *Scandinavian Political Studies*, 15.

Rothstein, B. (1988b), 'Att organisera arbetsmarknadspolitik', in *Festskrift till Gösta Rehn*, Tiden, Stockholm.

Rousseau, J.J. (1968), *The Social Contract*, Penguin Books, Harmondsworth.

Ruusala, R. (1972), 'Luottamustehtävien kasautuminen ja jäsenten tavoitevalinnat Sosialidemokraattisessa puolueessa', *Politiikan tutkimuksen laitoksen tutkimuksia*, no 27, Tampereen Yliopisto, Tampere.

'Samråd i kristid. Protokoll från den Nordiska Arbetarrörelsens Samarbetskommitté 1932-1946', *Kungl. Samfundet för utgivande av handlingar rörande Skandinaviens historia. Handlingar del 12*, 1986, Stockholm.

Sartori, G. (1976), *Parties and Party Systems. A Framework for Analysis*, Cambridge.

Schiller, B. (1967), *Storstrejken 1909. Förhistoria och orsaker*, Akademia förlaget, Gothenburg.

Schmitter, P. C. (1974), 'Still the century of corporatism?' *Review of Politics*, 36.

Selle, P. (1988), 'Bør det meste vere som det ein gong kanskje var?' *Tidsskrift for samfunnsforskning*, Vol. 29, 371-392.

Selle, P. (1990), 'Desentralisert velferd - meir velferd og meir demokratisk velferd?' in A. Rosenhayn Hovdun, S. Kuhnle and L. Stokke (eds.): *Visjoner om Velferdssamfunnet*. Alma Mater, Bergen.

Selle, P. (1991), 'The Idea of Equality and Security in Nordic Social Democracy', in Karvonen, L. and Sundberg, J. (eds.), *Social*

Democracy in Transition, Gower, Aldershot.

Selle, P. and Svåsand, L. (1987), 'Cultural policy, leisure, and voluntary organizations in Norway', *Leisure Studies,* no. 6.

Selznick, P. (1957), *Leadership in Administration,* Row, Peterson and Company, Evanston.

Selznick, P. (1966), *TVA and the Grass Roots,* Harper & Row, New York.

Serfaty, M. (1984), 'Spain's Socialists: A New Center Party?', *Current History,* Vol. 83, no. 492.

Share, D. (1985), 'Two transitions: democratisation and the evolution of the Spanish socialist left', *West European Politics,* January 1985, 82-103.

Share, D. (1988), 'Dilemmas of Social Democracy in the 1980s. The Spanish Socialist Workers Party in Comparative Perspective', *Comparative Political Studies,* Vol. 21, no. 3, October 1988.

Siisiäinen, M. (1990), *Suomalainen protesti ja yhdistykset,* Tutkijaliitto, Helsinki.

Skocpol, T. (1985), 'Bringing the State Back In' in P. Evans et.al. (eds.) *Bringing the State Back In,* Cambridge University Press, Cambridge.

Sköld, L. and Halvarson A. (1966), 'Riksdagens sociala sammansättning under hundra år', in *Samhälle och riksdag,* Almqvist & Wiksell, Stockholm.

Slama, J. & Kaplan, K. (1986), *Die Parlamentswahlen in der Tschechoslowakei 1935-1946-1948,* Oldenbourg, München.

Soikkanen, H. (1966), *Kunnallinen itsehallinto kansanvallan perusta,* Maalaiskuntien liitto, Helsinki.

Soikkanen, H. (1975), *Kohti kansanvaltaa I,* Suomen Sosialidemokraattinen Puolue, Helsinki.

Soikkanen, H. (1986), *Kohti kansanvaltaa II,* Suomen Sosialidemokraattinen Puolue, Helsinki.

Sombart, W. (1976), *Why is there no socialism in the United States?,* Macmillan, London (first published in German in 1906)

SOU 1965:54, Författningsfrågan och det kommunala sambandet, Justitiedepartementet, Stockholm.

Spotts F. and T. Wieser (1987), *Italy: A Difficult Democracy,* Cambridge University Press, Cambridge.

Spourdalakis, M. (1988), *The Rise of the Greek Socialist Party,*

Routledge, London and New York.

Stinchcombe, A.L. (1979), 'On Norwegian Social Democracy: An Introduction for Non-Norwegians', Industriøkonomisk institutt, Bergen.

Stjernquist, N. (1966), 'Sweden: Stability or Deadlock?', in R.A. Dahl, (ed.), *Political Opposition in Western Democracies*, Yale University Press, New Haven.

Ståhlberg, K. and Djupsund, G, (1983), 'Finländsk kommunalförvaltning under förändring', in Ståhlberg, K., *Självstyrd eller dräng*, Meddelanden från Stiftelsens för Åbo Akademi Forskningsinstitut nr 89, Åbo.

Sundberg, J. (1987), 'Exploring the Basis of Declining Party Membership in Denmark: A Scandinavian Comparison', *Scandinavian Political Studies*, Vol. 10.

Sundberg, J. (1989a), *Lokala partiorganisationer i kommunala och nationella val*, Finska Vetenskaps-Societeten, Helsingfors.

Sundberg, J. (1989b), 'Premisser för politiskt massmedlemskap: partierna i Danmark i en nordisk jämförelse', *Politica* Vol. 21.

Sundberg, J. (1989c), 'Politiseringen av kommunalvalen i Norden', *Statsvetenskaplig Tidskrift*, no 1.

Sundberg, J. (1990), *Frikommun - en fri kommun?*, Svenska social- och kommunalhögskolan vid Helsingfors universitet, Meddelanden 19, Helsingfors.

Suomi, J. (1971), 'A.K. Cajanderin 'punamultahallituksen' syntyvaiheet', *Historiallinen aikakauskirja* 1971, 111-127.

Svensson, P. (1974), 'Support for the Danish Social Democratic Party 1924-39 -Growth and Response', *Scandinavian Political Studies*, Vol. 9, 1974, 127-146.

Szelenyi, I. (1988), *Socialist Entrepreneurs. Embourgeoisement in Rural Hungary*, Polity Press, Oxford.

Tanner, V. (1966), *Kahden maailmansodan välissä*, Tammi, Helsinki.

Tezanos, J. F. (1979), 'El espacio político y sociológico del socialismo español', *Sistema*, no. 32.

Therborn, G. (1978), *What does the Ruling Class Do When it Rules?* New Left Books, London.

Therborn, G. (1986), *Why are Some People More Unemployed than Others?* Verso, London.

Therborn, G. (1987), 'Does Corporatism Matter?' in *Journal of Public Policy*, 9.

Thomsen, S.R. (1984), 'Kommunale valg: Landspolitisering eller lokalpolitisering'? in Elklit, J. and Tonsgaard, O. (eds.), *Valg og vaelgeradfaerd*, Forlaget Politica, Århus.

Thomsen, S.R. (1987), *Danish Elections 1920-79*, Politica, Århus.

Tingsten, H. (1937), *Political Behaviour*, King, London.

Tingsten, H. (1941), *Den svenska socialdemokratins idéutveckling*, I och II, Tiden, Stockholm.

Tingsten, H. (1963), *Demokratiens problem*, AldusBonniers, Stockholm.

Tingsten, H. (1967), *Den svenska socialdemokratins idéutveckling*, Aldus, Stockholm, Vol. 2.

Todal Jenssen, A. (1988), 'Fra arbeiderparti til lønnstagerparti', *Vardøger*, no. 18.

Togeby, L. (1968), *Var de så röde? Tekster og dokumenter til belysning af Socialdemokratiets gennembrudsår*, Fremad, Köbenhavn.

Togeby, L. (1974), *Revisionismens betydning for Socialdemokratiets idéudvikling fra 1890erne til 1930erne*, Institut for Statskundskab, Aarhus.

Togeby, L. (1990), *Årsager til og konsekvenser af det faldende partimedlemsskab i Danmark i 1970'erne og 1980'erne*, Paper presented at the Nordic Political Science Congress in Reykjavik 15-19, August.

Torgersen, U. (1969), *Landsmøtet i norsk partistruktur 1884-1940*, Universitetsforlaget, Oslo.

Touraine, A. (1986), *The Voice and the Eye. An analysis of social movements*, Cambridge University Press, Cambridge.

Urwin, D. & Aarebrot, F. (1981), 'The socio-geographic correlates of left voting in Weimar Germany, 1924-1932', in P. Torsvik (ed.), *Mobilization, Center-Periphery Structures, and Nation-Building*, Universitetsforlaget, Bergen; Norstedts, Stockholm.

Valen, H., Aardal, B. & Vogt, G. (1990), *Endring og kontinuitet. Stortingsvalget 1989*, Central Bureau of Statistics of Norway, Oslo.

Valen, H. and Katz, D. (1964), *Political Parties in Norway*, Universitetsforlaget, Oslo.

Valen, H. and Martinussen, W. (1977), 'Electoral Trends and

318

Foreign Politics in Norway: The 1973 Storting Election and the EEC Issue', in Cerny, K. (ed.), *Scandinavia at the Polls*, American Enterprise Institute for Public Policy Research, Washington, D.C.

Viitala, H.M. (1988), *Vasemmistolainen työväenliike Suomessa. Osa 1*, Kommunistilehden julkaisusarja, Pori.

Wallin, G., Bäck, H. and Tabor, M. (1981), *Kommunalpolitikerna*, Del 1, Kommundepartementet, Stockholm.

Westergård Andersen, H. (1976), *Dansk politik i går og i dag. Fra 30'ernes økonomiske krise til 70'ernes velstandskrise*, Fremad, København.

Wörlund, I. (1990), *Kampen om det ideologiska rummet*, Statsvetenskapliga institutionen, Umeå universitet,

Åmark, K. (1988), 'Sammanhållning och intressepolitik. Socialdemokratin och fackföreningsrörelsen i samarbete och på skilda vägar', in K. Misgeld et al, (eds.), *Socialdemokratins samhälle*, Tiden, Stockholm.

Other documents

Denmark: Unpublished party data made up by Abejderbevægelens Bibliotek og Arkiv in Copenhagen.
Danmarks Statistik: Statistiske Meddelelser, De kommunale valg, Statistiske efterretninger.

Finland: Puoluetilastot 1899-1942 Suomen Sosialidemokraattinen Puolue (SDP).
SDP, Vuosikertomukset 1945-1987.
Official Statistics of Finland, Municipal Elections 1964-1988.

Norway: Arbeiderpartiets kommunepolitikk, Det Norske Arbeiderpartiets Forlag, Oslo 1931.
Det norske Arbeiderparti Beretning 1913-1987.
Norwegian Social Science Data Services (NSD), Municipal elections

statistics processings, and processings on the recruitment pattern of Norwegian MPs.

Sweden: Socialdemokraterna, Verksamheten 1987.
Central Bureau of Statistics, Municipal Elections 1919-1985.
Statisitcal Yearbook of Sweden.

CONTRIBUTORS

Einar Berntzen, Department of Comparative Politics, University of Bergen, Norway.

Ann-Cathrine Jungar, Department of Political Science, Åbo Academy, Finland.

Lauri Karvonen, Department of Political Science, Åbo Academy, Finland.

Ulf Lindström, Department of Comparative Politics, University of Bergen, Norway.

Bo Rothstein, Department of Government, Uppsala University, Sweden.

Jostein Ryssevik, Norwegian Social Science Data Services (NSD), Bergen, Norway.

Per Selle, Norwegian Research Centre in Organization and Management, Bergen, Norway.

Jan Sundberg, Swedish School of Social Work and Local Administration, University of Helsinki, Finland.

Ingemar Wörlund, Department of Political Science, University of Umeå, Sweden.

Learning Resources
Centre